BLACK WOMEN UNDER STATE

BLACK WOMEN UNDER STATE

Surveillance, Poverty, & the Violence
of Social Assistance

IDIL ABDILLAHI

ARP Books I Winnipeg

Copyright © 2022 Idil Abdillahi

ARP Books (Arbeiter Ring Publishing)
205-70 Arthur Street
Winnipeg, Manitoba
Treaty 1 Territory and Historic Métis Nation Homeland
Canada R3B 1G7
arpbooks.org

Front cover artwork and design by Irene Bindi.
Interior layout by Relish New Brand Experience.
Printed and bound in Canada by Imprimerie Gauvin.

ARP Books acknowledges the generous support of the Manitoba Arts Council and the
Canada Council for the Arts for our publishing program. We acknowledge the financial
support of the Government of Canada and the Province of Manitoba through the
Book Publishing Tax Credit and the Book Publisher Marketing Assistance Program of
Manitoba Culture, Heritage, and Tourism.

LIBRARY AND ARCHIVES CANADA CATALOGUING IN PUBLICATION

Title: Black women under state : surveillance, poverty, and the violence of social
    assistance / Idil Abdillahi.
Names: Abdillahi, Idil, author.
Description: Includes bibliographical references and index.
Identifiers: Canadiana (print) 20220420904 | Canadiana (ebook) 20220420963 |
    ISBN 9781927886588 (softcover) | ISBN 9781927886595 (ebook)
Subjects: LCSH: Women, Black—Ontario—Toronto—Social conditions—Case
    studies. | LCSH: Welfare recipients—Ontario—Toronto—Case studies. | LCSH:
    Welfare recipients—Ontario—Toronto—Social conditions—Case studies. | LCSH:
    Public welfare—Ontario. | LCSH: Women, Black—Civil rights—Ontario. | LCSH:
    Welfare recipients—Civil rights—Ontario. | LCSH: Privacy, Right of—Ontario. |
    LCGFT: Case studies.
Classification: LCC HV110.T6 A23 2022 | DDC 361.6082/09713541—dc23

*"Actions are according to intentions,
and everyone will get what they intended."*
—PROPHET MUHAMMAD (PEACE BE UPON HIM)

Contents

THE STUDIED BLACK WOMAN

As I think about how to enter into this text, I want to first say that I embark upon it with a will not only to put forth a series of findings on the realities of some Black women's lives in Toronto, and to relay how those lives are steered, limited, and repulsed by the deliberate machinations of the state, but to propose alongside and in reflection of that narrative, a thread that interrogates this research and my own role in a system that is currently deeply embarked upon a greedy consumption of Black life. This is more than mere self-implication. Black women are always, in one way or another, subject to this ever-transforming consumption, which spans everything from the perpetual feedback loop of media/culture discourse, to the performance of the state and its legal framework in generating fair and ethical practices, to, in what is a very close context for me, the equally consumptive tendencies of the academy.

This work has taken on many stages and iterations, and through the process of writing the lives and experiences of my interlocutors into this text and linking those experiences to political, historical, and other elemental formations, I have revisited the social roots of my impulse to pursue this area of inquiry—I'll not always call it study—because one thing that has emerged as a fundamental distinction for me, is that academic study in particular, which we already know to be an extraction, is not the same as the spread of social information, the amplification of a lived Black women's reality. Academic study is not social storytelling, it is not support, and my priorities will always lie in these latter things.

This book evolves from my dissertation work that looks at the lives of twenty Black women accessing social assistance in Toronto. Like many PhD students and academics who work with data sets and intimate narratives of people's lives over long periods of time, one of the most important things to state from the outset, is that I found myself through the process of writing that dissertation, engaging in different listening interpretations, leading me to update and recode differently all that I had coded at various moments in my personal and academic life. So, when it came time to create this text, I was writing in a mirrored state, looking back on previous refractions and reflections.

I was also writing during a time when I, like so many others, was under scrutiny. A time when, like the women in these pages, I was being surveilled. When my own believability, my own ethics, my own decision-making, and my own livability were in question. Not just in question, mind you, but in question against the state, and in relationship to power. Those relationships were mitigated and con-toured by issues of gender, Blackness, antiBlackness, Muslimness, disability, misfitedness; essentially all notions of my being out of order or rank: out of line. In this kind of moment where I was (and still am) writing, and in trying to bring forward the stories of the women in this book, I was living a life alongside them—revisiting, retelling, returning to proximities we shared—and also experiencing a very different moment from what I experienced when originally embarking upon my research as a graduate stu-dent. Not that I was more believed as a graduate student than in the other contexts of my life; and looking back to my childhood and the experiences of other Black girls my age, I understand that there truly has never been a time when we have been afforded that believability. Even as a child, there is no particular moment I can reflectively mark where this inherent regard—believability, deserv-ingness, and trustedness—was afforded by the culture around me. What made this moment of reviewing my research different then, is that the parallels of Black women's livability have continuities that remain the same because of Blackness and its associated gendered logics. All of this was upon me, despite being a professor, or a graduate student, or any given role that we are given to play.

Black women have always been in this unique position in relationship to Black men, white women, white men, the state, and the broader other. It's a relationship that has been described in the academic literature and spoken about at length by many Black feminists, and Black women, and Black queer scholars. These are distinctions and particularities that have been described as they play out from a wide range of contexts, from the plantation to parliament and beyond. They've been taken up within legal discourses that have sought to divide Black women's identity and/or speak to just one portion of it or another, resulting in the atomizing of Black women not only in our bodies but in the realms of policy, theory, and practice. This sequestering of us across disciplines, around social and political life, is culminating in what I also see and interpret as part of the rapid death of Black people; in many of the cases closest to me in my own personal context, of Black women.

The continuities continue, and when I say this it's not in surprise; their iterations are identical but executed at different speeds, with different kinds of automation and different job titles. The outcome in many cases is still the same. For example, Black women are on the front lines of the pandemic, they are running households and being directly impacted. How that has played out and how these narratives have been taken up by the media and public discourse matters. Who is forgotten in these narratives? Black scholars have pointed emphatically to the ways we are obliged to think about this; what lives at the intersection in every meaning of that word? In concept or space, who owns the property at that intersection? Who is managing that precinct, and under whose authority? We've long known these are the kinds of questions to ask. This is the kind of inflection we should be insisting upon. And yet we still see the same narratives retold. An increasing number of Black women in the prison system, the same issues with child welfare. Making the necessary links is a way of reiterating the urgency of taking seriously what we already know, and continuing, as the *very experts* in carceral "structure and consequences," to emphasize that Black women's knowledge is positioned uniquely.[1] "Black people," in the words of Rinaldo Walcott, are

> in a unique position to see what others might not be able to. Whether anyone listens, is, of course, an entirely different question: the logic of white supremacy still governs and determines what counts as legitimate knowledge of the ruling order, and therefore Black peoples' abolitionist dreams are often deemed impossible.[2]

And so now as I write, increasingly within a world that insists on its happenings ever more urgently, it is also much more urgent for me to actually mark these moments and make these parallels—and not make them in a way that is cheap. I'm not shouting that my life is like those of my interlocutors; obviously it isn't, not now. But the thread and threat of Black women's unbelievability vibrates steadily throughout all of our lives, and this resonance lands differently on different people.

How did I come to this subject? Black women on social assistance, on welfare, in Toronto. The answer is obvious: I came to it because I have had experiences of living in poverty and being on social assistance; I understand what it means to be on limited income; I know what it is to be parented or cared for by people who are on limited income and live in these environments, these surveilled containments; I know how these surveilled containments are transactional spaces; and I know what these experiences are because not only have I observed them in lives around me, but they have been felt and lived within me. And now, in very practical terms, I continue to be one of the people whose daily work involves filling in the many gaps of what the state refuses to provide. In practical terms, I am directly involved in dispensing support to those who need it, though no longer as a state actor. Because later in my life, making a decision to work within—and in many ways on the operational

1   Rinaldo Walcott, *On Property* (Windsor: Biblioasis, 2021), 32.
2   Ibid.

reverse—of the non-profit industrial complex as a practitioner in the role of social-worker, these containments of manufactured care reminded me of their own limitations—limitations that weren't new to me because I had lived through those services, so inflected with violence. When you've lived through them you know their limitations, but still, you enter into them. Not easily. Uneasily. As workers some of us know there's some contribution we can make. I'm not saying that some people who work within government and establishment systems cannot make change. But I am saying that the structural and systemic barriers are fundamental, foundational. They not only make it difficult to make that contribution to change, but they are structurally bolstered to sustain terrible conditions, because they are practicably built to sustain all manner of inequities.

To ignore that, to not name that, and to continue to produce a false and naïve hope around these systems through reform is disingenuous. I think about that because I know what it feels like to be disillusioned from working within these systems. I also know the disillusion of teaching students; the dilution through education of the real conditions of the world shores up a system that wants to keep things, and us, in place. I want us to change that. When teaching in academia, we must contend with this and continually bring up veils, continually push through exposures. I don't want to teach students to aspire to enter a system with a naïve hope that it can be worked with. Nor do I want them to think that any one of us is big enough to do any of this work alone. I want instead to teach them to work alongside and think alongside people who also realize that the work we have to do is to undo. To undo all of it.

My intention isn't to tell people how terrible being on welfare is; we all know this. I am not the first scholar to speak about social conditions and I won't be the last. The intention of this book is to illustrate that none of this system of social service is about our *well fare*. We are not meant to fare well. Rather, the very systems and people that we are instructed to believe are there to do some of the most mundane tasks: supplement our income; be our landlord; connect us to services—are actually imbued with, and have the power of, policing. Policing's machinations of control, its essential exercise of domination, has many branches and tendrils beyond its institutional boundaries; its reach is vast and interlinked through systems. What I want people to think about, the question I want them to ask themselves, is why are we so committed to thinking differently about what these systems are offering if in fact we cannot follow that commitment through to making the assertion that "care," in a social services sense is carceral, or that poverty is criminalized, or that Black women are criminalized and terrorized?

This book makes direct policy-practice connections between social services, in this case welfare, and the powers of police and policing via the state, and how that ends up having specific impacts on Black women's lives. The reason why this is important is because naming these parallels is one thing, but making the direct links between relationships to systems and carceral responses alongside negative sociopolitical outcomes for Black women effectively demands that we directly hold *all* of these systems accountable. It implicates certain kinds of professions—social work certainly being one of them—and other roles and disciplines that suggest, imply, and purport care.

This book also creates an opportunity to demonstrate what happens when we dig a little deeper, when we do the work of being cross-disciplinary, and when we recognize the arbitrariness of disciplinary boundaries. For example, coming to this work from a background as a practitioner—the subsequent move to doing research and working in the academy, to understand social services from policy and law perspectives—is necessary in order to be able to understand, among other things, how these systems are already being studied and understood. How do systems, and our systems of interpreting systems, interlock, overlap, and feed into each other? It serves no one to remain at a single vantage point, and so no fruit would have been borne by remaining in place, by approaching this subject from solely a social work lens, or solely a policy lens. We need an integrated knowledge that comes from understanding Black people and understanding Black people in so-called Canada from many vantages. And that can mean entering many forums, both within and outside of the academy, and state and social roles.

Thinking through Black Canadian studies as a canon, using it as a map, both to understand it as a discipline and to understand Black life in Canada, also topographized two sets of questions for me. One is a question of how to intertwine and undo method, as I was taught to understand it from a social-science perspective; to ask questions about the need for method in the way that I'd learned it. I hope this book can to some degree demonstrate, through the messy way that I've come to quilt this text together, that no method is fixed. I embrace the idea of being a bricoleur; and engaging in bricolage here is my method as a misfitted person. So my methods are misfitted, and thus thankfully and hopefully, not on the academy's frequency.

But let's be real. For one thing, there's not much that is not on the academy's frequency, and those of us who are in it know that by virtue of being in it. We also know that there's a particular way that Black people are not afforded the protection of secrecy within the academy in the way that it exists for white academics. And yet there is simultaneously an inverse pressure towards secrecy that is enforced within circles of Black studies, the idea that some Black knowledge can and must be kept, protected, and guarded. This, I would argue is a reproduction of carceral logics that extends into intellectual property. As Black women, we are sharers of knowledge. What should I be sharing? Part of what I am doing is weighing out what should be said and not said, to know the weight of words. I learned that weighing as a young Black woman. But I'm also doing the work of exposure and interruption, and that takes a certain kind of sustained commitment and a certain kind of Black woman's self-assuredness that understands values and is inherently rooted in knowing the differences between deployment, disruption, disclosure, disrespect, and discernment. If I'm telling these stories, I'm doing it for a reason that may lie beyond the academy's conception.

I know how to conduct, comport, and govern myself in social and professional spheres because my life has been that of a Black woman who has had to live in them. To have come to this country as a Black woman refugee has taught me one kind of discernment, but has also brought to my attention the necessity of a commitment to disrupting this system. So, I am committed as well to disrupting the idea of secrecy. The secrecies of the academy benefit only white supremacy. It is Black women who are always the people who are at risk and the ones who are left behind.

I am committed to trusting my intuitive knowledge and upbringing, and I know the myriad ways that secrecy can be dangerous. As Édouard Glissant and Betsy Wing point out, in policy, opaque things have severe impacts.[3] In material contexts, opaque systems have incarcerating impacts, detrimental impacts. It is work to expose just as it is work to conceal. Some Black academics are trying to be erotically evasive with the academy instead of embracing the outright understanding that this evasiveness is the refusal of an exposure, and therefore the refusal of a life. Some of the "secret knowledge" is everyday knowledge—it has utility, it has purpose, and keeping information away ultimately reproduces knowledge logics that are white supremacist.

As to method, employing critical race theory and Black feminist thought were clear choices as my primary theoretical lenses. My work sought to examine the issue of welfare surveillance from Black women's perspectives and to consider the implications of taking their perspectives seriously. I wanted to know what Toronto Black women's subjective experiences of surveillance were while on the Ontario Works social assistance program, what effects these experiences had on them, and how an understanding of Black women's realities informs both theoretical discourse and policy regarding surveillance in the program. This is a social policy context that has tended to not consider subject voices. So, my phenomenological study used qualitative interviews consisting of open-ended questions conducted with a group of twenty interlocutors. The common themes that emerged in those interviews were originally identified and analyzed with the aim of filling the gap in social-policy literature, which has typically disregarded the subjective experiences of Black women or has treated us as mere add-ons to other topics. I distinguished these themes as: surveillance, poverty, violence, and

3   Édouard Glissant and Betsy Wing, *Poetics of Relation* (Ann Arbor: University of Michigan Press, 1997).

morality. It is important to remember however, that in the context of the experience of Black people, and Black women in particular, these themes are interconnected and linked to larger social and public policy discourses. With that in mind, I am striving to do something more here than fill the above-described policy literature gap, by attempting to transmit some of that lived Black experience to a broader audience, while describing some realities of Black women's lives.

A fact pointed out by Dionne Brand in the mid-90s that is still largely true today, is that a "dearth of literature has contributed to the invisibility of Black women's struggles, not only in social sciences but also within the feminist project."[4] My work here strives to be part of a corrective to this by foregrounding the experiences of Black women in their unique interactions with the Ontario Works (OW) system. Definitions and conceptualizations of Blackness are multiple and varied and indeed, as Rinaldo Walcott states, "writing Blackness is difficult work."[5] Thus, I draw on a simple definition of Blackness to lay the foundation for this discussion. For the purposes of this project, *Black* refers to individuals of African descent. Black/Blackness is both diverse and unique. There is no essential "Black experience" or identity, but rather, numerous subjectivities and occupied spaces that are at times collective, yet always distinctly marked by each person's individual standpoint, reflections of history,

---

4   Dionne Brand, *Bread Out of Stone: Recollections, Sex, Recognitions, Race, Dreaming, Politics* (Toronto: Coach House Books, 1994), 270.

5   Rinaldo Walcott, *Black Like Who?* (London, ON: Insomniac Press, 2003), 25. On conceptions of Blackness see Patricia Hill Collins, *Black Feminist Thought: Knowledge, Consciousness, and the Politics of Empowerment* (Milton Park, Abingdon: Taylor & Francis Group, 2002); W.E.B. Du Bois, *The Souls of Black Folk: Essays and Sketches* (Chicago: A.C. McClurg & Co., 1903); Franz Fanon, *Toward the African Revolution: Political Essays* (New York: Grove, 1967); Henry Louis Gates and Cornel West, *The Future of the Race 1st ed.* (New York: A.A. Knopf, 1996); bell hooks, *Yearning: Race, Gender, and Cultural Politics* (Toronto: Between the Lines, 1990); Jared Sexton, *Amalgamation Schemes: Antiblackness and the Critique of Multiracialism* (Minneapolis: University of Minnesota Press, 2008); Rinaldo Walcott, *Black Like Who? Writing, Black, Canada* (Toronto: Insomniac Press, 1997); Rinaldo Walcott & Idil Abdillahi, *BlackLife: Post-BLM and the Struggle for Freedom* (Winnipeg: ARP Books, 2019); Robin W. Winks, *The Blacks in Canada: A History 2nd ed.* (Montreal: McGill-Queens University Press, 1997).

and narrative. In order to deepen and complicate this conception of Blackness, I've employed other theoretical frameworks that further interrogate notions of Blackness and essentialism.

Although there have been some studies exploring the experiences of racialized or people of color and their experience of poverty, there remains no research specific to Toronto that examines the experiences of Black women in relation to OW.[6] What are Toronto Black women's subjective experiences of surveillance while in the Ontario Works program? What effects do these experiences have? And how can an understanding of these realities help to inform the theoretical discourse, and importantly, policy regarding surveillance—again, a social policy context that has tended to disregard the subjects' voices? Furthermore, how is the enactment of policy dependent on cultural presumptions and conceptions that have been built up around Black women? And how can making these links contribute to conversations outside of the academy as well? My belief is that these questions, though asked microcosmically in the Toronto context with a small group of Black women, nonetheless represent a multifaceted inquiry, and that investigating and pursuing them exposes a portrait of the mechanics of wide-reaching and interconnected structures of violence. As I've attempted to ground and engage this work through the integration of critical research and critical feminist research, my use of critical race theory (CRT), which Dolores Delgado Bernal describes as an "epistemology [that] can acknowledge [B]lack people as holders and legitimate sources of knowledge where Eurocentric epistemologies consistently fail" is

---

6   See, for example, Pamela Herd, "Do Functional Health Inequalities Decrease in Old Age? Educational Status and Functional Decline Among the 1931-1941 Birth Cohort," *Research on Aging* 28, no. 3 (2006): 375–392; Punam Khosla and the Community Social Planning Council of Toronto, "If Low Income Women of Colour Counted in Toronto: Final Report of the Action-Research Project Breaking Isolation, Getting Involved," *Community Social Planning Council of Toronto* (2003), http://www.oaith.ca/assets/files/Publications/ Low_Income_Women_of_Colour.pdf; Francis Lankin and Munir Sheikh, "Brighter Prospects: Transforming Social Assistance in Ontario," (Government of Ontario, 2012), 177; Social Assistance Review Advisory Council, Gail Nyberg et al., *Report of the Social Assistance Review Advisory Council*, (2010), 33.

no doubt important.[7] And while CRT provides an entry point into an analysis of race more broadly, controversy regarding the inclusion of Black women's voices in its articulation compels me to also draw from the rich history of Black feminist thought, centering specifically on the intersectional experiences of Black women; in the words of Patricia Hill Collins, "by taking the core themes of a Black women's standpoint and infusing them with new meaning, Black feminist thought can stimulate a new consciousness that utilizes Black women's every day, taken-for-granted knowledge."[8] Putting these theoretical frameworks to practical use within the reflections of real voices, I pull in and I centralize perspectives of intersectionality and antiBlack racism in relation to understanding Black women's experiences with social assistance.

One thing we have to acknowledge in this reading and writing, as we are navigating state entities like social assistance that are ostensibly created to serve citizenry, is that the notion of citizenship in itself is a position that Black women do not have in reality in so-called Canada. The framework of citizenship assumes a singular humanity for all, and a state relationship and interaction that isn't predicated on gendered antiBlackness. So, what we see in the reference to discourses of state power and poverty, is that Blackness is still left outside of, or made contingent to these discourses, when it should be central. This is the kind of intervention that we are trying to make in the study of Black life. In order to really be able to grapple with reality and understand Black people, we have to begin by combining all of these points of analysis into a form of work that draws this into focus. So even though all social systems aren't speaking directly about Black people, they still are, without naming it. We don't see that because when reading from a particular perspective that omits the legibility of Black people, the

7   Dolores Delgado Bernal, "Critical Race Theory, Latino Critical Theory, and Critical Raced-Gendered Epistemologies: Recognizing Students of Color as Holders and Creators of Knowledge," *Qualitative Inquiry* 8, no.1 (2002): 25.

8   Patricia Hill Collins, *Black Feminist Thought*, 32. See also Kimberlé Crenshaw, "Mapping the Margins: Intersectionality, Identity Politics, and Violence Against Women of Color," *Stanford Law Review* 43, 6 (1991): 1241–1299; bell hooks, *Yearning: Race, Gender, and Cultural Politics* (Toronto: Between the Lines, 1990).

generality of that discourse is created to contain us, is based on us, and controls us, but it is never expansive enough, regardless even of being directed to Black people.

Always in this work there is risk. This book is taking a risk. I know what I'm up against with the academy. Without belabouring a link between the lives of my interlocutors and their navigation of state systems, and my own navigations of the academy as another such system, I nonetheless embrace the fact that my experience extends my ability to connect with the women in these pages in ways that the academy is not structured to contend with or support. My hope is that the words that follow will variously trigger acknowledgment, or transmit an extension of understanding to the reader, whoever you may be. It's okay to vibe with this book, or to not vibe with it. That also works for me. You're here, you've at least read this far. I thank you, and I'm still reading too.

THE WELFARE CHEAT AND SITUATING WORK

Black women have long been depicted as archetypal "welfare cheats," a designation that positions us as suspects of fraud when accessing social assistance. Surveillance of those receiving social assistance is extensive, and often differentially applied; class, gender, race, and other factors lead to more surveillance of some groups than others, despite existing research by Canadian scholars on social assistance and surveillance, little is yet known, either in academia or the mainstream, about the specific experiences of Black women receiving social assistance. Indeed matters relating to the surveillance of social assistance recipients has a long history within Canadian, American, and global public policy scholarship.[1]

1   See Carol Baines et al., "Confronting Women's Caring: Challenges for Practice and Policy," *Affilia* 7, 1 (1992): 21–44; Janine Brodie, ed. *Critical Conecpts* (Toronto: Prentice Hall) 2002; Patrick Burman, *Poverty's Bonds: Power and Agency in the Social Relations of Welfare* (Toronto: Thompson Educational Publishing, 1996); Lea Caragata, "Neoconservative Realities: The Social and Economic Marginalization of Canadian Women," *International Sociology* 18, 3 (2003): 559–580; Bruce Carruthers, *City of Capital: Politics and Markets in the English Financial Revolution* (Princeton: Princeton University Press, 1999); Andrew Cherlin, et al., "Operating within the Rules: Welfare Recipients' Experiences with Sanctions and Case Closings," *Social Service Review* 76, (2002): 387–405; Dorothy Chunn and Shelly Gavigan, "Welfare Law, Welfare Fraud, and the Moral Regulation of the 'Never Deserving' Poor," *Social & Legal Studies* 13, 2 (2004): 219-243; James Midgley, *Social Welfare in Global Context* (Thousand Oaks: Sage Publications, 1997); Patricia Daenzer, "Social welfare in global context, James Midgley, London, Sage, 1997," *Scandinavian Journal*

Analyses focused on people living in poverty and on mothers, particularly "sole-support mothers," have been especially salient, and I wanted to expand on these intertwined issues by focusing specifically on the experiences of Black women in Toronto with surveillance while receiving social assistance—the Ontario version of which is Ontario Works (used interchangeably herein with OW).[2]

One way to begin is by looking at shifts in social policy to date. Ian Morrison once advised that "careful scrutiny" of people on social assistance is required if we are "concerned about the future of social policy [in] Ontario."[3] His caution referred to the 1997 replacement of Ontario's Social Assistance Reform Act (SARA), the

of Social Welfare 7, 1 (1998): 65-67; Paul Dornan and John Hudson, "Welfare Governance in the Surveillance Society: A Positive-Realistic Cybercriticalist View," Social Policy & Administration 37, 5 (2003): 468-482; Nancy Fraser and Linda Gordon, "A Genealogy of Dependency: Tracing a Keyword of the U.S. Welfare State," Signs 19, 2 (1994): 309-336; Martin Gilens, Why Americans Hate Welfare: Race, Media, and the Politics of Antipoverty Policy, (Chicago: University of Chicago Press, 1999); Allison Harell et al., "Public opinion, prejudice and the racialization of welfare in Canada," Ethnic and Racial Studies 37, 14 (2014): 2580-2597; Ernie Lightman et al., "Welfare to What? After Workfare in Toronto," International Social Security Review 58, 4 (2005): 95-106; Margaret Hillyard Little and Ian Morrison, "'The Pecker Detectors are Back': Regulation of the Family Form in Ontario Welfare Policy," Journal of Canadian Studies 34, 2 (1999): 110-136; Margaret Hillyard Little, No Car, No Radio, No Liquor Permit: The Moral Regulation of Single Mothers in Ontario, 1920-1997 (Oxford: Oxford University Press, 1998); David Lyon, Surveillance as Social Sorting: Privacy, Risk and Automated Discrimination (London and New York: Routledge, 2003); Krystle Maki, "Neoliberal Deviants and Surveillance: Welfare Recipients Under the Watchful Eye of Ontario Works," Surveillance & Society 9,1/2 (2011): 47-63; Dianne Martin, "Passing the Buck: Prosecution of Welfare Fraud; Preservation of Stereotypes," The Windsor Yearbook of Access to Justice 12 (1992): 52; Ken Moffatt, Postmodern Social Work: Reflective Practice and Education, (New York: Columbia University Press, 2019); Ian Morrison, "Ontario Works: A Preliminary Assessment," Journal of Law and Social Policy 13 (1998): 1-46; Shoshana Pollack, "Labelling Clients 'Risky': Social Work and the Neo-liberal Welfare State," The British Journal of Social Work 40, 4 (2010): 1263-1278; Loïc Wacquant, "Deadly Symbiosis: When Ghetto and Prison Meet and Mesh," Punishment & Society 3, 1 (2001): 95-133.

2   Erica Lawson, "Single Mothers, Absentee Fathers, and Gun Violence in Toronto: A Contextual Interpretation," Women's Studies 41, 7 (2012): 805-28; Erica Lawson, "The Gendered Working Lives of Seven Jamaican Women in Canada: A Story About 'Here' and 'There' in a Transnational Economy," NWSA Journal 25, 1 (2013): 138; Patricia Hamilton, "'Now That I Know What You're About': Black Feminist Reflections on Power in the Research Relationship." Qualitative Research: QR 20, 5 (2020): 519-33.

3   Ian Morrison, "Ontario Works: A Preliminary Assessment," Journal of Law and Social Policy 13 (1998): 2.

General Welfare Act (GWA), and the Family Benefit Act (FBA), with the Ontario Works Act (OWA) and the Ontario Disability Support Program.[4] These policy reforms occurred within a context of broader national shifts in Canadian social policy that included the introduction of the Canada Health and Social Transfer (CHST) in 1996. The CHST substituted the Canada Assistance Plan (CAP), which had been in place since 1966. The change from the CAP to the CHST marked both practical changes and theoretical shifts in the ways that citizens sought and accessed public funds. Researchers identify these shifts as part of a transition from welfare liberalism to neoliberalism that led to hierarchal or two-tiered citizenship, and which ultimately contributed to the move away from Canada's previous "social citizenship vision."[5]

The most vulnerable groups in Canadian society were gravely impacted by these shifts, including those individuals unable to seek support from family, friends, or community networks. The new social assistance system was primarily concerned with and informed by a market-driven approach to "entitlement [and] benefits directly related [to an individual's] capacity to sell their labour power in the marketplace."[6] In other words, whether a seeker was deemed worthy of support came to hinge even more heavily on their ability to demonstrate, or rather prove themselves, as functional tools of market labour. These concerns however are not far removed from the original intention of social assistance programs that also leaned heavily on moral judgements. Historic Poor Laws served as a mechanism to punish, discipline, and attempt to restore "good moral values" in individuals otherwise deemed to have character deficiencies. English Poor Laws were embedded in colonial practices and protestant theology, which assumed that laziness, moral depravation, and poor judgement resulted in poverty.[7] Thus historically, in the

4   Ibid.
5   Ibid, 46. Also see Dorothy E. Chunn and Shelley Gavigan, "Welfare Law, Welfare Fraud and the Moral Regulation of the 'Never Deserving' Poor."
6   Ernie Lightman and Graham Riches, "From Modest Rights to Commodification in Canada's Welfare State," *European Journal of Social Work* 3, 2 (2000): 180.
7   Christopher Pierson and Francis G. Castles, eds., *The Welfare State: A Reader* (Malden, Mass.: Polity Press with Blackwell Publishers Ltd., 2000).

implementation of workhouses, we begin to see the early formation of moral/social regulation, surveillance, and the underlining "work for welfare" model upon which current systems are built. The goal of workhouses was to discipline, instill "good" work ethics, and encourage moral servitude in the poor. Today, while the declared intent of Ontario Works is to provide short-term residual financial assistance as a basic right, the program has been overshadowed by strict means/needs testing and eligibility criteria that entail significant barriers and difficulties for most people who try to access it.[8]

In addition to the difficulties of gaining access to OW, the ongoing scrutiny and policing of OW recipients are significant and pose significant problems for recipients. The surveillance that is part of this ongoing scrutiny is aggressive; as David Lyon describes, surveillance entails "the collection and processing of personal data, whether identifiable or not, for the purposes of influencing or managing those whose data have been garnered."[9] Some of the earliest legislated and normalized strategies of surveillance in Ontario deployed under the Harris government were within "[t]he 'anti-fraud' program [which] included a provincial welfare 'hotline' to report alleged welfare cheats, increased information demands from recipients, more intensive eligibility investigations and increased information sharing with other provincial ministries, agencies and other movements."[10]

While all individuals on OW are subject to surveillance, as Punam Khosla pointed out in the early 2000s, "differences within equity-seeking groups are becoming more pronounced."[11] These

8   Amber Gazso, "Balancing Expectations for Employability and Family Responsibilities While on Social Assistance: Low-Income Mothers' Experiences in Three Canadian Provinces," *Family Relations* 56, 5 (2007): 454–466; Julia S. O'Connor, (Julia Sila), Ann Shola Orloff, and Sheila Shaver, *States, Markets, Families: Gender, Liberalism, and Social Policy in Australia, Canada, Great Britain, and the United States* (Cambridge: Cambridge University Press, 1999); Jill Weigt, "Compromises to Carework: The Social Organization of Mothers' Experiences in the Low-Wage Labor Market after Welfare Reform," *Social Problems* 53, 3 (2006): 332–51.

9   David Lyon, *Surveillance Society: Monitoring Everyday Life* (Maidenhead, Berkshire: Open University Press, 2001), 2.

10 Ian Morrison, "Ontario Works: A Preliminary Assessment," 5.

11 Punam Khosla and Community Social Planning Council of Toronto, "If Low Income Women of Colour Counted in Toronto," 19.

increased, and increasing, differences in the scale and nature of the surveillance of these groups, specifically of Black women, would suggest that their experiences of surveillance, regulation, and monitoring while receiving OW are different precisely due to their race.[12]

Current and historical literature supports my view that Black women who are recipients of OW are at greater risk of surveillance, based on two factors: the racist constructions of Blackness; and the ways race, gender, and class intersect, such that Black women are represented and understood as the archetypal "welfare cheats." When combined, these factors directly impact the approach taken to Black women receiving public assistance; in other words, the way Black women are approached and treated in such a context rests upon these constructions and intersections, which culminate in and are correlated with increased experiences of surveillance.[13]

It is well established that oppression based on race, gender, and class, compounded, results in poor Black women having experiences of suffering and punishment that render them at once invisible and hyper-visible.[14] The hyper-visibility is negatively oriented;

12 See Julilly Kohler-Hausmann, "The Crime of Survival," 332.
13 See John Alexander, "Ending the liberal hegemony: Republican freedom and Amartya Sen's theory of capabilities," *Contemporary Political Theory* 9, 1 (2010); Dorothy E. Chunn and Shelley A. M. Gavigan, "Welfare Law, Welfare Fraud, and the Moral Regulation of the 'Never Deserving' Poor." *Social & Legal Studies* 13, no. 2 (2004): 219-243; Patricia Hill Collins, and Sirma Bilge, *Intersectionality* (Cambridge: Polity Press, 2016); Angela Davis. 1980. "Child Care or Workfare?" *New Politics Quarterly* Winter: 19-22; Angela Y. Davis, *Abolition Democracy: Beyond Empire, Prisons, and Torture* (Seven Stories Press, 2005); Angela Y. Davis, *Are Prisons Obsolete?* (New York: Seven Stories Press, 2003); Angela Y. Davis, *Women, Race, & Class* (New York: Random House, 1981); Andrea J. Ritchie, and Delores Jones-Brown, "Policing Race, Gender, and Sex: A Review of Law Enforcement Policies," *Women & Criminal Justice* 27, 1 (2017): 21-50.
14 See Sedef Arat-Koç, "Invisibilized, Individualized, and Culturalized: Paradoxical Invisibility and Hyper-Visibility of Gender in Policy Making and Policy Discourse in Neoliberal Canada," *Canadian Woman Studies* 29, 3 (2012): 6; Beverly Bain, "Uncovering Conceptual Practices: Bringing into 'Lived Consciousness' Feminists' Activities on the Toronto Police Sexual Assault Audit and the Follow-up Sexual Assault Audit Steering Committee," *Canadian Woman Studies* 28, 1 (2009): 15; Himani Bannerji, "The Paradox of Diversity," *Women's Studies International Forum* 23, 5 (2000): 537-60; Dionne Brand, *Land to Light On* (Toronto: McClelland & Stewart, 1997); Bristow et al., *We're Rooted Here and They Can't Pull Us Up: Essays in African Canadian Women's History* (Toronto: University of Toronto Press, 1994;

criminality and hyper-sexualization, amorality, and deceitfulness are all foci. The invisibility is socially and politically constructed; as Black women we are erased as visible participants in social, political, and cultural narratives, in part so that we may be disallowed from

Agnes Calliste, and George Dei. "Note from the Editor." *Race, Sex & Class* 2, 1 (1994): 4-6; Lea Caragata, "Neoconservative Realities: The Social and Economic Marginalization of Canadian Women." *International Sociology* 18, 3 (2003): 559-80. Errlee Carruthers, "Prosecuting Women for Welfare Fraud in Ontario: Implication for Equality," *Journal of Law and Social Policy* 11, 10 (1995); Collins, Patricia Hill. "Gender, Black Feminism, and Black Political Economy." *The Annals of the American Academy of Political and Social Science* 568, 1 (2000): 41-53; Gillian Creese, and Daiva Stasiulis, "Intersections of Gender, Race, Class, and Sexuality," *Studies in Political Economy* 51 (1996): 5-14; Kimberle Crenshaw, "Mapping the Margins: Intersectionality, Identity Politics, and Violence Against Women of Color," *Stanford Law Review* 43, 6 (1991): 1241-99; Patricia M. Daenzer, "Social Welfare in Global Context. James Midgley. London, Sage, 1997" *Scandinavian Journal of Social Welfare* 7, 1 (1998): 65-67; Jane Doe, Amanda Dale, and Beverly Bain et al., "A New Chapter in Feminist Organizing: The Sexual Assault Audit Steering Committee," *Canadian Woman Studies* 28, 1 (2009): 6; Paul Dornan and John Hudson, "Welfare Governance in the Surveillance Society: A Positive-Realistic Cybercriticalist View," *Social Policy & Administration* 37, 5 (2003): 468-82; Enakshi Dua and Angela Robertson, *Scratching the Surface: Canadian, Anti-Racist, Feminist Thought* (Toronto: Women's Press, 1999); Martin Gilens, *Why Americans Hate Welfare: Race, Media, and the Politics of Antipoverty Policy* (Chicago: University of Chicago Press, 1999); Allison Harell, Stuart Soroka, and Kiera Ladner, "Public Opinion, Prejudice and the Racialization of Welfare in Canada," *Ethnic and Racial Studies* 37, 14 (2014); Julilly Kohler-Hausmann, "'The Crime of Survival': Fraud Prosecutions, Community Surveillance, and the Original 'Welfare Queen,'" *Journal of Social History* 41, 2 (2007): 329-54; Erica Lawson, "Single Mothers, Absentee Fathers, and Gun Violence in Toronto: A Contextual Interpretation," *Women's Studies* 41, 7 (2012): 805-28; Erica Lawson,. "The Gendered Working Lives of Seven Jamaican Women in Canada: A Story About 'Here' and 'There' in a Transnational Economy," *Feminist Formations* 25, 1 (2013): 138-56; Erica Lawson, "Bereaved Black Mothers and Maternal Activism in the Racial State," *Feminist Studies* 44, (2018): 713-35; Althea Prince, *Being Black: Essays* (Toronto: Insomniac Press, 2001); Sherene Razack, Melinda Smith, and Sunera Thobani, editors, *Race, Space, and the Law: Unmapping a White Settler Society* (Toronto: Between the Lines, 2002); Makeda Silvera, *Silenced: Makeda Silvera Talks with Working Class West Indian Women About Their Lives and Struggles as Domestic Workers in Canada* (Toronto: Williams-Wallace, 1984); Sunera Thobani, "White Wars: Western Feminisms and the War on Terror," *Feminist Theory* 8, 2 (2007): 169-85; Loïc Wacquant, "Deadly Symbiosis"; RinaldoWalcott, *Black Like Who?*; Rinaldo Walcott and Idil Abdillahi, *BlackLife*; Jill Weigt, "Compromises to Carework: The Social Organization of Mothers' Experiences in the Low-Wage Labor Market after Welfare Reform," *Social Problems (Berkeley)* 53, 3 (2006): 332-51.

influencing such structures. This dichotomy is of course connected: our presumed criminality is also what presumes to warrant such erasure. And ultimately these perceptions also result in our deaths: literal deaths, as well as political and social deaths. We die because of this dually constructed invisibility and hyper-visibility. Forced upon us, and flowing along an unbroken historical trajectory, these deaths are very easily forgotten by culture and state. Today, within these same contexts, I would argue, Black women are only remembered as adjacent-to, and not as our own distinct beings with our own distinct impacts.

These compounding factors governing oppression make the experience of Black women distinctive. Audre Lorde outlines the nuance of difference when she says, the oppression of women, "knows no ethnic or racial boundaries, true, but that does not mean it is identical within these differences.... To deal with one without even alluding to the other is to distort our commonality as well as our difference."[15] To centralize then, Black women's experiences itself requires a centralization that delineates rather than groups by expanse. While many scholars and researchers in Canada and the United States have acknowledged that the experiences of Black women are vastly different from those of other women, those experiences as defined and articulated *by* Black women are still largely sidelined and missing both from the scholarship and from community-based responses to poverty, social assistance, surveillance, and antiBlack racism.[16] By looking to this group, I see something much more than a gap constituting regional omission in historical research; this is instead a site of discussion, of the social and political trajectories of Black women's lives—all of our lives.

The Black woman as archetypal welfare cheat is a cultural product, and neoliberalism and white supremacy continue with both

15   Audre Lorde, *Sister Outsider: Essays and Speeches* (Trumansberg, NY: Crossing Press, 1984), 70.
16   Punam Khosla and Community Social Planning Council of Toronto, "If Low Income Women of Colour Counted in Toronto"; Julilly Kohler-Hausmann, "'The Crime of Survival'"; Audre Lorde, *Sister Outsider*; Dianne Martin, "Passing the Buck"; Mariana Valverde, ed. *Studies in Moral Regulation* (Toronto: Centre of Criminology, University of Toronto, 1994).

vehemence and inertia to generate and facilitate such archetypes amidst a damaging, evolving discourse within many social services, including OW. Attention must be given to what Loïc Wacquant describes as "the social service bureaucracies [that] take an active part, [and which] possess the informational and human means to exercise a close surveillance of 'problem populations' [referred to as] social panopticism."[17] In a civic environment that, according to the City of Toronto's website, purports to uphold ideas of equity, this writing serves to reveal and describe the barriers to adequate or improved quality of service, of livable life, within the City's antiBlack, neoliberal context.

What we need here is a twofold counter-discourse. First, one of voice; this is a discussion that strives to amplify the voices of Black women in Toronto who have been disproportionately impacted by surveillance under OW but whose narratives have never been directly engaged using theories and frameworks that are informed by a critical analysis of race and gender. Second, one of critical engagement; this is a counter-discursive policy narrative to mainstream policy studies discourses, which continue to either not name the experiences of Black women at all, or to speak to the experiences of Black women and Black people as an additional category outside of citizenry. I wish to counter the pervasive lens that views and projects Black women as outside of a "citizen"-centered social and political position, a view that has been historically shaped, and is to this day influenced, by colonial, (new)diasporic, and state relationships. To counter these colonial antiBlack trends, then, we must delineate spaces in and around which Black women can build critical consciousness, organize, and engage in resistance work.

It is in this spirit that, in turning to the experiences of Black women surveilled on the Ontario Works program in the Greater Toronto Area (GTA), I rely and expand upon existing literature that centres Black women, in process and theory, at the intersections of race, poverty, surveillance, and social services. Many such studies have emerged from the United States and focus on US subjects, but very few focused Canadian regional studies currently exist.

17   Wacquant, "Deadly Symbiosis," 407.

As such, much of the research that is relied upon to discuss and frame the experiences of Black women within the Canadian context is derived largely from the United States, and more specifically from Black feminist literature, law, policy, and language within the United States that speaks to and outlines the realities of the Black "welfare queen." As I'll discuss at more length, the experiences of Black women are undeniably interconnected and global. That said, there is an urgent need to articulate the unique features of Black women's lives and experiences in their particular geopolitical and social locations globally, and this is certainly much needed within the so-called Canadian context. I share here the experiences and narratives of Black women, which are in many respects both similar to and divergent from those in the United States and elsewhere across the globe, while working through an understanding that the particularities determined by the so-called Canadian and GTA context are exactly what, through analysis, make room for a penetrable and understandable narrative more broadly. The process of documenting the experiences of Black women *here*—spatially, in Toronto—is also an effort to intervene and create space for BlackLife as it plays out with in the national context, not as a derivative of the experience of Black American women, but rather as intertwined with, and in addition to, and in many respects refracted through the broader coloniality of those experiences within what is, for better or worse, our practical nationhood in "Canada."[18]

In my reflection on the studied Black woman—and a commitment to remain true to Rinaldo Walcott's regional assertion, "something happens here," and further build on the complications of (un)belonging, Black humanity, and the "taken-for-granted[ness] of Blackness"—I attempt to bridge and enter numerous potential pathways within Black Canadian studies scholarship.[19] My hope is that this text contributes to an evolving understanding, one that encompasses areas of scholarship that focus on the experiences of the

18   The term "BlackLife" as it appears here, emerged first in *BlackLife: Post-BLM and the Struggle for Freedom* (Winnipeg, ARP Books, 2019) co-authored by myself and Rinaldo Walcott, and is meant to emphasize the fact that "living Black makes BlackLife inextricable from the mark of its flesh, both historically and in our current time."

19   Rinaldo Walcott, *Black Like Who?*, 14.

surveilled in general, as well as specifically on Black people's, and Black women's surveillance. I hope that this focus on the experiences of Black women in so-called Canada, on women who continue to be absented, refused, and redacted from the national archive and un/under-theorized or made unintelligible in the academy, is able to circulate not only within, but beyond, by reaching consciously outside of that academy as well.[20]

I am inspired by Saidiya Hartman, who restores, recollects, and recreates the narrative of Black women from historical archives, particularly those deemed "wayward," and expresses Black girls' and women's disenfranchisements from state, gender, and Blackness.[21] Piecing together the moments and movements of restrictedness of Black girls and women, Hartman uses the (un)returned gaze of girls and women in old photographs as a refusal of antiBlack (un)livability. Her method involves writing into and outside of the literal and figurative frame, to narrate what was removed and resisted in the historical archive.

This is in a sense, also my approach. The lives of the women who participated in this study can never be reduced to mere data, even when that data encompasses words in a qualitative research project with a phenomenological design. There are things still unsaid and perhaps unsayable. There are things said in between saying, which is where we come back to weighing. Something profound is lost—not only lost but discarded—in *reducing* these women's experiences to objects of analysis in this structural way, and it is important to recognize that there are personal and social facts and realities that have not been preserved, nor recorded. In my interpretation and analysis, and my sharing something of these Black women's vast realities, my aim is nevertheless to, as much as possible, hear what was not always fully expressed, to write onto and into the unwritten, and thereby reveal some truth of life while exposing the banishment of Blackness.

20   See Christina Sharpe, *In the Wake: On Blackness and Being* (Durham, NC: Duke University Press, 2016).

21   Saidiya Hartman, *Wayward Lives, Beautiful Experiments: Intimate Histories of Riotous Black Girls, Troublesome Women, and Queer Radicals* (New York: W. W. Norton & Company, 2019).

I approached this work from multiple complex and contradictory positions. At the time of my fieldwork, I was a working-class, precariously employed graduate student, attempting to complete my doctoral work within a system that often felt strange and alienating. I had struggled to find and use my voice within the ostensibly white, antiBlack, liberal, anti-Indigenous, neoliberal, academic industrial complex—a context in which I often lost my activist, Black Canadian feminist, Muslim, and African voice. I do not attribute this loss of voice merely to individual people—such a critique would be simplistic and irresponsible. Rather, I attribute it to a colonial and colonizing university environment that actively engages in and enforces the erasure of already marginalized people (as much as it now feigns the reverse); and more specifically, the erasure of Black Canadians and our histories, experiences, knowledges, and livabilities. This rendering silent, of "voicelessness," began in my early university coursework, which functioned as what I deemed, and still deem to be an implicit training ground to whitewash, dismiss, and redact or Black-out my experiences.[22] When I spoke about race, antiBlackness, and antiracism, I was disciplined and punished. Eventually, recognizing that system as a detriment to both personal and scholarly, or rather, intellectual, health, I made a choice to resist the oppressive conditions in which I was situated, where in so much of BlackLife, as Christina Sharpe puts it, "social and political work is redacted, made invisible to the present and future, subtended by plantation logics, detached optics, and brutal architectures."[23]

Thus, deciding to conduct my research from a critical race and Black feminist standpoint was a conscious act of resistance, and an attempt to reclaim my authentic voice. My commitments are firmly grounded within communities that have supported, and serve to benefit from, the several forms of education, and abuse, I have received while in academia. For this reason, it is imperative that I do not return to my community as a "stranger bearing

22   Christina Sharpe, "Black Studies: In the Wake," *The Black Scholar* 44, 2 (2014): 59-69.
23   Christina Sharpe, *In the Wake*, 114.

a message," but that instead, I act as a betrayer of white suprema-cist knowledges, that I speak in languages and within realties that are grounded in material experience, and not those hidden within databases, books, and research studies that are inaccessible to the people who are the "objects" or "subjects" of academic study.[24] My critiques must also account for my privileges, derived from my cur-rent location in academia. While I do not often fit squarely into normative institutional confines as a "knower" and a young Black Muslim woman, I also do not fit neatly into the communities with which I conducted research, regardless of our shared identities as Black women, some shared geographic and spatial realities, and our shared experiences with OW. To presume that Blackness grants me access, or connects me, to a universal shared "sisterhood" or "Black womanhood" would be to minimize the struggle and complexity of non-essentialized Blackness and being.

In situating myself in this research and writing, I must implicate myself in the conditions in which I conducted and benefited from it. The idea that there might be "a space that is not one of social control—but one of social innocence" is troublingly naïve, and my insider/outsider identity requires examination.[25] I approach this research as a former social worker who has spent the past twenty years working in Toronto. This means that while I sought to explore the complexity of the experiences of surveillance of Black women, I do so as someone who has not just been subject to, but has engaged in such surveillance, directly and indirectly; it is important to understand that being Black and a woman did not prevent me from playing a role in carrying out the neoliberal agenda. As Ken Moffatt et al. state, "any person can be randomly placed in a pos-ition within the great machine, and the efficiency and effectiveness of the exercise of power will not be compromised."[26] While I have been placed in the position—as a clinician, "social worker," practi-tioner, and community worker—to surveil marginalized people, I

---

24   Kirstie Ball et al., *Routledge Handbook of Surveillance Studies* (Hoboken: Taylor & Francis Group, 2012), 458.
25   Amy Rossiter, "Innocence lost and suspicion found: Do we education for or against social work?" *Critical Social Work* 2, 1 (2001): 7.
26   Ken Moffatt et al., "Advancing citizenship: A study of social planning," *Community Development Journal* 34, 4 (1999): 312.

have also made serious efforts over the years to engage in resistance work and to support and challenge individuals, groups, and systems that have impacts on issues of marginalization, antiBlackness, (cis)sexism, capitalism, ableism, racism, and other power vectors. I recognize my state-sanctioned prerogative to trespass, and that "trespasses are the harm brought to others by our participation in the governing ways of envisioning and making the world."[27] Thus, while I believe that it is important to expose, analyze, and understand the subjectivities that give rise to racist hyper-surveillance and the antiBlack attitudes and actions of many caseworkers in their individual interactions, the experiences of OW recipients, as well as the presentation of their narratives and firsthand descriptions of their experiences, are more powerful and relevant narratives to bring forward. Because "[t]respassers are not the active hands-on instruments of wronging, but the 'responsible', well-behaved predictable subjects of social order who reinforce and extend its pattern of rule," it is important for me to bring into light and to keep within that light Black women's voices and perspectives with active primacy.[28]

My commitment to this research is predicated on my commitment to Black freedoms, praxis, resistance, activism, and community organizing. All of these commitments are informed directly by an approach that holds relationship-building as significant to the research process. This kind of Black feminist approach, according to Nancy Naples,

> broadens the ground upon which individual[s] will share deeply felt experiences. Rather than attempt to keep a distanced stance in an effort to achieve more "objective" analyses, feminist researcher[s] acknowledge that power is infused in social relations including in relationships between researchers and "informants."[29]

27   Melissa Orlie as discussed in Amy Rossiter, "Innocence Lost and Suspicion Found: Do We Educate for or Against Social Work?" *Critical Social Work* 2, 1 (2001): 7.
28   Ibid.
29   Nancy Naples, *Feminism and Method: Ethnography, Discourse Analysis, and Activist Research* (New York and London: Routledge, 2003), 63.

My goal therefore, was not to produce positivistic research disconnected from concrete individual realities. While quantification and numeration are often valuable, they are not responsible or rigorous choices, neither theoretically nor methodologically, for the type of investigation I'm interested in. The collection of data cannot and should not be seen as a measure for Black freedom, "emancipation," or liberation; this notion is a positivist trope that has grave consequences for BlackLife and Black enumerated bodies.[30] I hope here to build on the works of Black women thinkers who have, in the words of Patricia Hill Collins, "laid a vital analytical foundation for a distinctive standpoint on self, community and society."[31] In other words, I want to bring all of the ideas and reflections that academic tools can bring, in order to serve back to the lives and perspectives of Black women, rather than to serve back to the academy.

My interlocutors were eighteen years of age or older, either had been on or were currently on Ontario Works, all identified as Black and as women, and all lived in Toronto. I circulated a call to low-income and women-centred service providers across the GTA. These service providers included shelters, transitional housing, drop-ins, employment training programs, daycare centres, community centres, food banks, and race-specific spaces. Additionally, the call for interviewees was sent to the City of Toronto Community and Social Services Information email and bulletin. A consent form was reviewed with potential interlocutors before commencing the interviews. Upon completion of our conversations, all of the women chose to have their contributions remain in the research.

It was an imperative for me that the women felt comfortable to share information about themselves, and that they were comfortable to share the information that they felt was relevant. So they were

---

30   See Rinaldo Walcott, *The Long Emancipation: Moving Toward Black Freedom* (Durham NC: Duke University Press, 2021); Rinaldo Walcott and Idil Abdillahi, *BlackLife*; Rinaldo Walcott, *On Property: Policing, Prisons, and the Call for Abolition* (Windsor, ON: Biblioasis, 2021).

31   Patricia Hill Collins, "Gender, Black Feminism, and Black Political Economy," *The Annals of the American Academy of Political and Social Science* 568, 1 (2000): 3.

asked to share demographic information that they deemed necessary and within their realm of comfort. My aim was to give my inter-locutors the opportunity to truly guide the research in meaningful ways. What these women felt was more than simply of relevance, it was, and is, of central significance. This also meant that interviews often extended well beyond a planned one-and-a-half hours. Out of the twenty original interviews, seventeen conversations lasted, on average, three hours.

Upon gathering and transcribing all of this material, I shared and reviewed each transcript with each woman who had participated in an interview. Interlocutors were therefore able to tell me whether the transcripts adhered well, not simply with their impression of the interview itself, but with the experiences discussed within it—the experiences they wished to convey. These actions also underly the interlocutors' ability to review data through collaborative pro-cess. In the context of the experiences of Black women, whose believability I have already outlined as being always under question, this collaborative step's enhancement of credibility becomes all the more important. A frequent focus in the type of research context I undertook is the concept of transferability, which is concerned with the "fittingness of study findings to other settings, popula-tions, and contexts," and it's a concept that I would like to trouble; I was focused on ensuring that the essences of the experiences of the women I spoke with were captured correctly, by which I mean to say, accurately in their eyes, across themes of importance to them.[32] Any "transferability" would and should in this context be a reversal; instead of formulating a broad applicability in approach-ing the "subject" in an essentialized manner, any applicability to other contexts would not be pre-formulated but would necessarily flow from the kind of genuine engagement I have described, due to the existing threads of experience that unite Black women. When we embrace the experiences of the most marginalized, rejected, ignored, and abused, we suddenly have gifts of information that illuminate and respond to the realities of everyone. The truth is that

32   Winston Jackson and Noreen Verberg, *Methods: Doing Social Research*, 4th ed. (Toronto: Pearson Prentice Hall, 2007), 179.

these particular stories, while telling us more about the brutaliz-ation of Black women on OW, can and do reflect the experiences of other women, and how those realities are embodied on Black women becomes instructive to all of us through both similarity and difference.

WHERE SURVEILLANCE TAKES AND LEAVES US

I can't presume to know who you the reader might be, so it is important to outline the social historical context of social assistance for Black women specifically, to take time to point to the broad construction and some generally accepted understandings of such programs, and by extension some of the foundational context and concepts that surround them, in addition to tracing key perspectives in the work that has been done toward breaking and undoing such constructions. Scholars of social policy, surveillance, critical race, and feminist theory have clearly identified mechanisms, techniques, and processes of surveillance.[1] Many of these same scholars, however, fail to delineate the historical trajectory of the relationship between Black people and the experience of surveillance—a relationship that results from the complex interactions between the state and Black communities. The creation of the Canadian welfare state following World War II was founded upon Keynesian economics:

1   See Krystle Maki, "Neoliberal Deviants and Surveillance: Welfare Recipients Under the Watchful Eye of Ontario Works," *Surveillance & Society* 9, 1/2 (2011): 47-63; Ken Moffatt et al., "Advancing citizenship: A study of social planning," *Community Development Journal* 34, 4 (1999): 308-317; Ian Morrison, "Ontario Works: A Preliminary Assessment," *Journal of Law and Social Policy* 13 (1998): 1-46.

specifically the idea that the well-being of all citizens is attainable through national policies that include the entire populace. In other words, the state accepts, in word, responsibility for the provisions of comprehensive and universal welfare for its citizens.[2] As of 2019, most cases in OW serve single adults without children. Single adults also rely the most on social assistance, given they are not supported by other social systems, such as child and family welfare. However, lone parents and their families/dependents account for the largest group of recipients—44% as of 2019.[3] A July 2022 Maytree Social Assistance Summary also notes that "On average, there were just under 241,000 families or individuals receiving Ontario Works in 2019-20, there were about 619,000 cases (families and single adults) in Ontario's social assistance programs during 2019-20."[4]

In the 2012 "Brighter Prospects: Transforming Social Assistance in Ontario" report, there were "477,339 people or 264,834 cases" receiving social assistance in 2012.[5] The term "case" is used in this context to refer to the number of families accessing the support. Forty-seven percent of this total province-wide number of recipients of OW live in the Greater Toronto Area.[6] More than half, "54 percent of primary applicants are women," and among sole-support recipients, ninety-three percent are female-led households.[7] Social assistance in Ontario is made of two main components: Ontario Works (OW), also referred to as social assistance; and the Ontario Disability Support Program (ODSP). Each program sets out specific eligibility guidelines fashioned by state regulations to ostensibly respond to the needs of individuals seeking to access it. In order to qualify for OW, a person must be sixteen

2   See James J. Rice and Michael J. Prince, *Changing Politics of Canadian Social Policy*, 2nd ed. (Toronto: University of Toronto Press, 2000).

3   Ontario Ministry of Children, Community and Social Services, "Social Assistance in Ontario: Trends Report—Ontario Works" https://www.mcss. gov.on.ca/en/mcss/open/sa/trends/ow_trends.aspx.

4   Maytree: Poverty, Rights, Change. "Social Assistance Summaries: Ontario." https://maytree.com/social-assistance-summaries/ontario/

5   Francis Lankin and Munir A. Sheikh, *Brighter Prospects: Transforming Social Assistance in Ontario* (Government of Ontario, 2012), 128.

6   Ibid.

7   Ibid.

years or older (eighteen in Toronto unless "special circumstances" apply, for example abuse or absence of home support), must reside in Ontario, and must express financial need.[8] In the case of an individual applicant, their income, assets (which cannot exceed program limits), and housing costs are calculated to determine first, whether they qualify for income support, and second, how much income support they will receive.[9] When families apply collectively for OW, the primary applicant and all other members of the family are assessed, and the income calculation is made according to that assessment. Beyond the income replacement recipients receive, they have additional entitlements including minimal drug and dental coverage, eyeglass benefit, diabetic supplies, and moving and eviction costs; in many cases, access to these resources is at OW's discretion. Even though there are situations where policy would suggest eligibility, it is not guaranteed.

Several researchers have noted that the shift from general welfare to Ontario Works involved an important shift in the means of verifying eligibility: the "difference between the power to demand information necessary to determine eligibility (the former rule) and the new power to prescribe what is acceptable verification."[10] Again, the verification of "entitlement to benefits [is] directly related to [one's] capacity to sell [one's] labour power in the marketplace," and thus individuals become labour commodified as their social supports are limited and eroded.[11] Programs focus on workfare or welfare-to-work and compulsory participation programs that prioritize the "work-first" model.[12] These work-first programs, which essentially

8   Province of Ontario, "Eligibility for Ontario Works financia assistance," 2022. https://www.ontario.ca/page/eligibility-ontario-works-financial-assistance. City of Toronto, "Assistance Through Ontario Works," 2022. https://www.toronto.ca/community-people/employment-social-support/support-for-people-in-financial-need/assistance-through-ontario-works/.
9   Ibid.
10   Ian Morrison, "Ontario Works: A Preliminary Assessment," 30.
11   Ernie Lightman and Graham Riches, "From Modest Rights to Commodification in Canada's Welfare State," *European Journal of Social Work* 3, 2 (2000): 180.
12   See Ernie Lightman, et al., "Cycling Off and On Welfare in Canada," *Journal of Social Policy* 39, 4 (2010): 523-542; Ernie Lightman, et al., "Welfare to What? After Workfare in Toronto," *International Social Security Review* 58, 4 (2005):

encourage swift labour market (re)entry, are in fact ineffective; they are predominantly used by individuals entering OW with limited education, training, or skills, and these are precisely the people who do not enter the labour market easily.[13] Researchers have also noted that return-to-work programs serve as a temporary solution that subjects some of the most vulnerable people in Canadian society to precarious, risky, non-standard work.[14] There's been a substantial shift in the described aims of these programs away from the development of an expansive national anti-poverty response or the development of better, sustainable skills training, job coaching, or job development for recipients of social assistance.

Furthermore, while the report of the Social Assistance Review Advisory Council implied that the goal of income-replacement programs was to assist people during a time of economic hardship, it made specific reference to the experience of job discrimination as one of many factors that contribute to people's use of OW.[15] The report highlights that "some groups are particularly vulnerable to becoming the working poor, such as youth, women, recent immigrants, racialized Ontarians, and First Nations."[16] While discrimination and racism clearly exist outside of workfare programs, we can't assume that job-ready or transition-to-work programs, whether facilitated by OW or not, are unaffected by the same discrimination that exists in the broader labour market. The move toward neoliberalism has been extremely relevant to social assistance, as expressed by researchers looking at the increased digitization of case

95–106; Leah Vosko, ed.. *Precarious Employment: Understanding Labour Market Insecurity in Canada* (Montreal: McGill-Queen's University Press, 2006).

13   See Ian Morrison, "Ontario Works: A Preliminary Assessment."

14   See Marc Frenette et al., "Rising Income Inequality in the 1990s: An Exploration of Three Data Sources," Ottawa: Business and Labour Market Analysis Division, 2004; Marc Frenette and Garnett Picot, "Life After Welfare: The Economic Well-being of Welfare Leavers in Canada During the 1990s," Statistics Canada, Analytical Studies Branch Research Paper Series, 2003; Ernie Lightman et al., "Welfare to What?"; Leah Vosko, *Precarious Employment*.

15   Gail Nyberg et al., "Recommendations for an Ontario Income Security Review, Report of The Social Assistance Review Advisory Council," 2010.

16   Ibid, 2.

work.[17] For instance, Lea Caragata explains that women continue to obtain university degrees in what is seen as gendered work, while we also see a rapid increase in the use of technologies in the workplace.[18] Meanwhile, men continue to enter fields such as "computer science and engineering—obviously important choices" she says, "to ensure one's place in high-value, high-technology workplaces."[19] So increased technology use within OW and other NGOs in the name of modernization and efficiency is wielded and weaponized against women with various impacts, one of these arguably being women's access to work, as well as our status at work—an ascendant technologization that acts instead to support the entrenchment of role restrictions, rather than an expansion of labour access.

Looking at this more broadly, with overwhelming responsibility within the home, women are often seeking alternatives to employment outside of it. It is important to keep in mind that this is often not by choice but rather due to unreasonable labour market demands and precarious work. For these reasons, often hidden from the public labour market and relegated to employment within the home, women are, by way of the new globalized marketplace, being positioned as the "new entrepreneurs."[20] The disproportionality of women's labour needs to be taken very seriously; the idea that technologization allows women to work from home doesn't take into account that when women are home there is an existing labour disparity—with the lioness's share of domestic labour still falling on women's backs. Most women are therefore consistently doing double. This is not to say that technologies don't also provide forms of access for women to work from home if they choose in some

17   See Krystle Maki, "Neoliberal Deviants and Surveillance"; Ian Morrison, "Ontario Works: A Preliminary Assessment"; Ken Moffatt, et al., "Advancing citizenship: A study of social planning," *Community Development Journal* 34, 4 (1999): 308–317; Ken Moffatt, "Social Work Practice Informed by Philosophy: The Social Thought of Edward Johns Urwick," *Canadian Social Work Review* 11 (1994): 133–49; Donna Baines, *Doing Anti-Oppressive Practice: Social Justice Social Work* (Winnipeg: Fernwood, 2011).
18   Lea Caragata, "Neoconservative Realities: The Social and Economic Marginalization of Canadian Women," *International Sociology* 18, 3 (2003): 559–580.
19   Ibid, 569.
20   Ibid, 566.

circumstances, but we need to think about the risks of unequal distribution of labour in domestic spaces, and factors such as intimate partner violence, that affect women on a vastly higher scale. What bears our consideration and concern in light of this, is the way that working from home can involve a loss of skills, safety, and access to resources required in the so-called knowledge-based economy.[21] Connecting social rights and citizenship with labour-market participation forces us to consider how Black women have and will continue to be gendered and invisibilized, placed "at risk for loss of status and presence as actors in the public realm," and kept out of the public discourse.[22]

In any discussion of invisibilization and technologization, we must also look at the fact that the highly technological and specialized kinds of work that Black women have historically done and continue to do—for instance as birth workers—are not validated, and access to these specializations, knowledge, and ways of being, are un- and under-valued. New technological formulations are therefore also going to be participating in that ongoing continuum of invisibilizing. And Black women's labour and skilled contributions are deskilled, devalued, and disregarded. These nuances must be part of our discussions as well.

In other words, it can be expected that those who face gender discrimination and racism within the labour market would also be correspondingly less likely to receive access to job placement and job-ready programs, and even more so when race, gender, and a situation of being on assistance intersect. This, in turn, would make Black women more reliant on OW, being less able to enter the workforce in a way that guarantees stability.

A national study by Marc Frenette and Garnett Picot found that while individuals on Ontario Works might in fact stop receiving assistance, this did not guarantee the acquisition of a livelihood within the labour market.[23] It was reported that the Ministry does

21   Ibid, 568.
22   Ibid, 577.
23   Marc Frenette and Garnett Picot, "Life After Welfare: The Economic Well-being of Welfare Leavers in Canada During the 1990s."

not have adequate information regarding "the number of people finding employment who attribute their success to their participation in the Ontario Works Program, by nature of work found and whether the work was full-time, part-time, or temporary."[24] It becomes apparent therefore, that leaving OW to enter the labour market does not ensure success; rather, it pushes unskilled workers into labour-market conditions that are discriminatory and unsafe. People who leave OW often move to other income-replacement programs, like Employment Insurance, or they return to OW.[25] I echo the interrogations of Ronald Kneebone and Katherine White, who critically question whether Canada has in fact made meaningful advances to (sustainably and humanely) keep individuals who are in need off of social assistance.[26]

While within the last several decades we have observed infrequent periods of low enrollment, this does not necessarily correspond with higher rates of employment and could in fact indicate that during periods in which Ontario has seen some decline in the use of OW, that the decrease might be due to reduced applications for other reasons, including the disqualification of entitlements, or the lack of adherence to [unrealistic] rules and regulations, rather than an indication of successful return-to-work or exit programs.[27] In other words, people are not necessarily leaving Ontario Works because their lives or employment status has improved as a result of the program. It is clear that individuals access OW with a variety of skills and barriers to employment, including barriers related to race and experiences of racism.[28] This is especially troubling since it has

24   See Ontario Ministry of Community and Social Services, "Ontario Works Program" annual report, 1998. https://www.auditor.on.ca/en/content/annualreports/arreports/en98/302en98.pdf, 66.
25   City of Toronto, "Assistance Through Ontario Works," 2017. https://www.toronto.ca/community-people/employment-social-support/support-for-people-in-financial-need/assistance-through-ontario-works/
26   Ronald Kneebone and Katherine White, "The Rise and Fall of Social Assistance Use in Canada, 1969-2012," *The School of Public Policy Publications* 7, 5 (2014): 7.
27   See Ian Morrison, "Ontario Works: A Preliminary Assessment."
28   Sheila Block and Grace-Edward Galabuzi, "Canada's Colour Coded Labour Market: The gap for racialized workers," Canadian Centre for Policy Alternatives and Wellesley Institute, 2011; Grace-Edward Galabuzi,

been found that people positioned in society as having minimal to no social or human capital and who are streamed into precarious work, have a higher likelihood of experiencing "more permanent exclusion," which in turn puts them at risk of further precarious employment and longer term exclusion.[29] Again, what is upheld is actually an entrenchment of social and economic suppression.

David Lyon's discussion of "surveillance sorting" points to the ways surveillance can be used to categorize its subjects into different groups, for subsequent differential forms of surveillance or governance.[30] This is especially disturbing since the Ontario Works Act, which essentializes recipients as neoliberal deviants, tends to construct recipients as suspects rather than as citizens with access to social rights, as is professed by the state.[31] It bears pointing out that the language used in the Act itself serves to produce and dictate this perspective, operating as its own embedded set of ideological directives.[32] As I will discuss later, this is a deliberate function of a biased legal framework. Jack Haas and William Shaffir have argued more specifically that the deeply entrenched nature of the interrelation between poverty and state-based services means that Black women in particular are represented as deviant citizens. Drawing on this definition, the construction of OW recipients as deviant relates structurally to the notion that "the matter of who is defined and treated as deviant is not so much determined by what people do as by the social distance between agents of control and deviating

"Re -locating mineral -dependant communities in the era of globalization, 1979-1999: A comparative study of the Zambian Copperbelt and Timmins, Ontario," (Phd diss., York University, 2006).

29   Ernie Lightman, Andrew Mitchell, and Dean Herd, "Cycling Off and On Welfare in Canada," *Journal of Social Policy, Cambridge University Press* 39, 4 (2010): 526.

30   David Lyon, *Surveillance as Social Sorting: Privacy, Risk and Automated Discrimination* (London and New York, Routledge, 2003), 192.

31   See Krystle Maki, "Neoliberal Deviants and Surveillance: Welfare Recipients Under the Watchful Eye of Ontario Works," *Surveillance & Society* 9,1/2 (2011): 47–63 on OW recipients' characterization as deviants; and Ken Moffatt, "Surveillance and Government of the Welfare Recipient," on the construction of recipients as suspects.

32   *Ontario Works Act*, 1997, SO 1997, c 25, Sch A, (79(4)). <https://canlii.ca/t/54bkl>.

persons."[33] This, along with the fact that what "constitutes deviant behaviour changes over time and across social groups" lends support to the assessment that poverty is one of the determinants that has categorized Black women as deviant.[34] In short, when policy-makers are "absolutist in their thinking [and] assume that the basic problem facing society is the individual rule breaker," they locate the problem of poverty and the impact of surveillance in Black women and other marginalized bodies themselves, rather than in the systems that give rise to the experience and material realities of antiBlackness, poverty, misogyny, as well as to the very processes of surveillance and its implementation.[35] Surveillance, as a result, effectively serves as a punishment for being poor and needing to access public funds, and acts as even severer punishment for being poor, and a Black woman, and needing such access.

Notions of deviance relate closely to historical associations with pauperism and criminality.[36] Representing the pauper and the wayward as "the criminal" served to facilitate "revenge of the sovereign against a criminal," and allowed for the creation of a societal premise that made permissible the "public spectacle" and surveillance of the poor.[37] The criminalization of the poor is socially constructed,

33   Bernard Schissel and Linda Mahood, eds., *Social Control in Canada: A Reader on the Social Construction of Deviance* (Oxford: Oxford University Press, 1996), 374. Also see Jack Haas and William Shaffir, eds., *Decency and Deviance: Studies of Deviant Behaviour* (Toronto: McClelland & Stewart, 1974.

34   Bernard Schissel and Linda Mahood, *Social Control in Canada*, 1. See also Paul Henman and Greg Marston's assessment: Paul Henman and Greg Marston, "The Social Division of Welfare Surveillance," *Journal of Social Policy* 37, 2 (2008): 187–205.

35   Paul Henman and Greg Marston, "The Social Division of Welfare Surveillance," 2.

36   See Anne O'Connell, "Deserving and Non-deserving Races: Colonial Intersections of Social Welfare History in Ontario," *Intersectionalities: A Global Journal of Social Work Analysis, Research, Polity, and Practice* 2 (2013).

37   Saidya Hartman, *Wayward Lives: Beautiful Experiments*; Ken Moffatt, "Surveillance and Government of the Welfare Recipient" in *Reading Foucault for Social Work*, edited by Chambon, Adrienne S., Allan Irving, and Laura Epstein (New York: Columbia University Press), 220. Also see Errlee Carruthers, "Prosecuting Women for Welfare Fraud in Ontario: Implication for Equality," *Journal of Law and Social Policy* 11, 10 (1995): 250; Sidel, Victor W, and Barry S Levy. "Security and Public Health." *Crime and Social Justice* 29, 3 (2002): 108–19.

with long historical precedent, and has at its roots a state-based rationale. This conception of the social perception of poverty is distilled by Dorothy Chunn and Shelley Gavigan, when they write that "to be poor [is] to be culpable, or at least vulnerable to culpability."[38] In the United States this criminalization of poverty can be seen with jarringly unimpeded linearity, in cases where welfare recipients have historically had to collect social assistance cheques from police stations.[39]

Punam Khosla submits that race, gender, and poverty are defining factors responsible for an assumption of culpability for transgression, as experienced by recipients of OW.[40] This is an important claim, since while Ken Moffatt, for instance, also asserts the ways case workers make recipients visible "through identification and individualization [by] scripting them into text," he does not account for broader social constructions of race that give rise to Black women's imposed hyper-visibility."[41] Employing a Foucauldian analysis, he misses some key considerations, such as Charles W. Mills expression that calls for and applies the "theorizing of a racial polity—in this case a white-supremacist polity—and a rethinking of the political around the axis of race."[42] While Moffatt analyzes the complexities of power, his analysis is limited by failing to differentiate between power as it is taken up in varying subjects. He does not account for the ways surveillance is most relentlessly deployed against Black people, far more than against people occupying more privileged spaces within the mainstream. I am in agreement with Chunn and Gavigan, who in critiquing welfare systems and their impacts, compellingly highlight the fact that we must move beyond traditional Foucauldian analyses and conceptualizations of regulation.

38   Dorothy Chunn and Shelley Gavigan, "Welfare Law, Welfare Fraud, and the Moral Regulation of the 'Never Deserving' Poor," *Social & Legal Studies* 13, 2 (2004): 220.

39   Julilly Kohler-Hausmann, "The Crime of Survival."

40   Punam Khosla, "If Low Income Women of Colour Counted in Toronto," 13.

41   Ken Moffatt, "Surveillance and Government of the Welfare Recipient," in *Reading Foucault for Social Work*, edited by Adrienne S. Chambon, Allan Irving, and Laura Epstein (New York: Columbia University Press, 1999), 219–246.

42   Charles W. Mills, *Blackness Visible: Essays on Philosophy and Race* (Ithaca and London: Cornell University Press, 1998), 123.

After the implementation of the Ontario Works Act in 1998, it became apparent that the Act was intended to do more than aid individuals experiencing life contingencies.[43] According to Ian Morrison:

> The heart of the Act lies in its extraordinarily sweeping regulation-making powers. One subsection alone of s.74, the principle regulation-making power, has 49 sub-paragraphs—some of which themselves contain multiple regulation-making powers. This choice of legislative vehicles has extremely important implications both for the role of "law" in relation to the future of the program and for the whole political future of social assistance policy in Ontario.[44]

Morrison goes on to describe how the OW Act's loose framework makes it so that even drastic changes to the system can be made "without notice, consultation or debate," amongst the public or the people most affected, recipients, and without submission to legislative processes.[45] He goes so far as to refer to the legislation as "a shell."[46] This unchecked "shell" then becomes the general housing where surveillance is permitted to thrive.

Despite many studies and reports that aim to address concerns regarding surveillance, there seems to be more focus on how to increase the transparency of the surveillance process itself than on addressing the actual effects of surveillance. Thus, an aim to "better communicate program rules" is put forward as the alternative to addressing broader issues of the harms of surveillance that could negatively impact recipients."[47] Morrison cautions that "miscommunications, cultural misunderstandings, language or perceptual barriers and simple bureaucratic bungling can never be entirely

---

43 Gail Nyberg et al., "Recommendations for an Ontario Income Security Review, Report of The Social Assistance Review Advisory Council," (2010), 33.
44 Ian Morrison, "Ontario Works: A Preliminary Assessment," 5.
45 Ibid, 6.
46 Ibid.
47 Francis Lankin and Munir Sheikh, "Brighter Prospects," 134.

avoided in welfare administration."[48] This ultimately means that Black people remain marginalized even in the context of a generalized better-communication approach, insofar as the specific ways that surveillance affects and is disproportionately imposed upon Black people are not ever addressed or rectified. The reality, and key missing piece, lies in the fact that Black people are never intelligible within a system that is built and predicated upon our unintelligibility.

A critical social policy response to surveillance that is rooted in the fact that Blackness is a political demarcation would explore how surveillance is actively deployed as a tool and would identify and critically analyze the uses of this tool against Black people. Errlee Carruthers contends that the imperatives regarding surveillance of individuals on OW serve a larger political project, which is to mobilize non-welfare recipients in order to pit them against those on welfare.[49] This is not the only possible interpretation nor by far the only form of weaponization. But any critical social policy response would examine processes of surveillance and analyze the ways identities are constructed through the categorization of populations in information gathering to "inequitably scrutinise citizens in the seemingly routine and mundane processes of distributing services and resources."[50] How indeed, do such programs affect social dynamics of the population in its entirety? Behaviours and attitudes toward those on social assistance are not restricted to only those who directly engage with such programs. Paul Henman and Greg Marston note that surveillance is a relational concept.[51] So while some scholars, such as Paul Dornan and John Hudson critique the use of targeted surveillance as employed under the guise of support or service provision, their critique does not consider that some groups enter the system while already hyper-surveilled due to intersecting race-, gender-, and class-based oppressions. Precisely

48   Ian Morrison, "Ontario Works: A Preliminary Assessment," 23.
49   Errlee Carruthers, "Prosecuting Women for Welfare Fraud in Ontario: Implication for Equality," *Journal of Law and Social Policy* 11, 10 (1995): 241-262.
50   Paul Henman and Greg Marston, "The Social Division of Welfare Surveillance," *Journal of Social Policy* 37, 2 (2008): 203.
51   Ibid.

due to the logics of "neoliberal rationality, the governance of social problems suggests an ability to mark and monitor marginalized populations in order to determine and formulate equations for individual "risk," with an aim to control social behaviours that might be deemed risky."[52] And as we know, one behaviour that neoliberalism considers risky is any deviation from the established gendered order.

Moralizing discourse is found in macro-level policies that are largely based upon a gendered-order concept of a stable working class made up of nuclear families, comprised of so-called male breadwinners and female homemakers.[53] That gendered order is deeply ingrained in social welfare systems in Canada, which have perceived women as either deserving or undeserving of state assistance based on their roles and status in society. Women have not been depicted as productive members of society; rather, we are depicted as recipients of state-based interventions who are in need of both moral and social regulation.[54] Still, within this analysis, gender discourse and gender relations exist in a white imaginary that fails to take up race, and the very absence of racial discourse in these discussions must itself be taken up with urgency. The idea of morality is also embedded in white supremacy and notions of whiteness. It is predicated on a concept that whiteness is moral, and Black people and other not-white people are immoral and "other." The absence of discussions of whiteness in these theoretical spaces of gender and morality presupposes and prioritizes a concept of white universality that is tied into a parallel concept of the inherent danger of Blackness. This concept of the moral exists in a deeply ingrained cultural questioning of the capacity of Black people to be logical enough to be moral and reasoned, which itself represents a dehumanization, a fundamental questioning of our humanity/humanness.[55]

52   Ibid, 194; John Gilliom, *Overseers of the Poor: Surveillance, Resistance, and the Limits of Privacy* (Chicago: University of Chicago Press, 2001).

53   James J. Rice and Michael J. Prince, *Changing Politics of Canadian Social Policy*, 2nd ed. (Toronto: University of Toronto Press, 2000), 260.

54   For example, recipients of social assistance in Ontario; see Margaret Hillyard Little, *"No Car, No Radio, No Liquor Permit."*

55   David Brion Davis, *Inhuman Bondage: The Rise and Fall of Slavery in the New World* (Oxford: Oxford University Press, 2006).

While there have been multiple proposed definitions of moral regulation, for the purposes of this text, moral regulation refers to systems, attitudes, policies, practices, and processes that impose valuations and moral or moralizing discourses, here specifically on and about Black women who use Ontario Works.[56] Explicit social orders are created by moralizing discourses, as Philip Corrigan and Derek Sayer emphasize, the "normalizing, rendering natural, taken for granted, in a word, obvious, what are in fact ontological and epistemological premises. ... Moral regulation is coextensive with state formation, and state forms are always animated and legitimated by a particular moral ethos."[57] These ontological and epistemological structures are in fact antiBlack. Given its connection with state structures, antiBlack moral regulation seems inevitable in some societal form. We need to look more closely at who certain forms of moral regulation are aimed at, how, why, and to what extent. The intensity with which these regulations are exercised is in and of itself informed by gendered antiBlackness. The behaviours and attitudes that frame laws and policies give systemic permission for individual actors to be suspicious of Black people, guard against us, and unduly exercise violence against us. These intense actions are based upon extrajudicial, policy, and response scripts that are inherent in a culture of white supremacy.

Framing moralizing discourses within the social policy debate allows us to explore the nuances of ordering practices as experienced by women, since, as Margaret Hillyard Little argues, moral regulation alone is insufficient as a lens through which to observe and understand the experiences of women.[58] Rather, Little suggests that we draw upon experiences and analyses of moral regulation to understand the nature of relationships that give rise to regulating

---

56   See Dorothy Chunn and Shelly Gavigan, "Welfare Law, Welfare Fraud, and the Moral Regulation of the 'Never Deserving' Poor," *Social & Legal Studies* 13, 2 (2004): 219-243.

57   As cited in Dorothy Chunn and Shelly Gavigan, "Welfare Law, Welfare Fraud, and the Moral Regulation of the 'Never Deserving' Poor," 4.

58   Margaret Hillyard Little, "A Litmus Test for Democracy: The Impact of Ontario Welfare Changes on Single Mothers," *Studies in Political Economy* 66 (2001): 9-36.

practices within welfare policy.[59] With increased conservative ideologies and government policy directives, the challenges inherent in substantiating one's worthiness are amplified.[60] In the case of welfare, the determination of the worthiness of recipients becomes less about immediate economic need than about provinces' authority to shape the criteria for who is deemed both in need of welfare and worthy of being a recipient of state-based support.[61] The process of determining eligibility within the welfare system thus involves moral regulation, through this very concept of worthiness. The embedded concepts of need and morality, when combined, have shaped the foundation upon which social policy operates as it relates to the ways women citizens have been represented and conceptualized, specifically as dependent by nature. In addition to this, how women have been understood and positioned by the state has had a longstanding impact on government policy related to women's issues, from the formulation of policy to the deployment of services. Thus, these foundational assumptions about women have impacted how we engage with the state as citizens. This is true to some extent for all women and gender non-conforming people, and while engaging in this research I witnessed and identified many ways that women collectively experience marginalization by way of paternalistic policy discourse. However, concepts of morality are further complicated by experiences of Blackness. As Frantz Fanon reminds us, "the Negro symbolizes the biological danger," thus illuminating Blackness bodily as an intersecting site of, and for, further interrogation.[62]

Specifically, Black women experience valuation and moralizing discourses differently due to social constructions, identities, and material realities including race, class, disability, and sexuality. Patricia Hill Collins notes that "Black women have been assaulted with a variety of negative images [including] stereotypical mammies, matriarchs, welfare recipients, and hot mommas [which]

59   Ibid.
60   Ibid.
61   Ibid.
62   Frantz Fanon, *Toward the African Revolution: Political Essays* (New York: Grove, 1967), 165.

help justify… Black women's oppression."[63] Such representations
of the Black woman's body effectively "transmit distinctive message[s] about the proper links among female sexuality [and] desired
levels of fertility for working-class and middle-class Black women."[64]

We can consider, for example, differential representations related
to single motherhood.[65] As Lea Caragata has noted, ninety percent of "sole-support" parents in Canada are women.[66] In addition,
Michael Ornstein remarks that "very high proportions of female
lone parent families…are African and Black."[67] Some recent efforts
have been made to present a counter-discourse to the stigmas surrounding single motherhood. Jennifer Ajandi, for example, refers to
single motherhood as a choice in an effort to portray single mothering as a site of resistance, agency, and strength.[68] However, while
Ajandi provides a space for some women, namely white women,
to occupy single motherhood as a liberating identity, she fails to
recognize that single motherhood is the stereotype that all Black
women have to contend with—including Black women who are
not single mothers. Ajandi's critique about single motherhood lacks
the historical vantage point that informs us that Black women enter
the discussion about single motherhood differently and often not
by choice. In particular, Black women often do not have a choice
regarding the ways their mothering is understood and constructed
in relation to social systems.[69] Cultural notions of single mother-

63   Patricia Hill Collins, "Gender, Black Feminism, and Black Political Economy,"
      The Annals of the American Academy of Political and Social Science 568, 1
      (2000): 69.
64   Ibid, 84.
65   See Patricia Hill Collins, "Gender, Black Feminism, and Black Political
      Economy" (2000), and *Black Sexual Politics: African Americans, Gender, and the
      New Racism* (New York: Routledge, 2004).
66   Lea Caragata, "Neoconservative Realities: The Social and Economic
      Marginalization of Canadian Women," *International Sociology* 18, 3 (2003):
      559–580.
67   Michael Ornstein, "Ethno-Racial Inequality in the City of Toronto: An Analysis
      of the 1996 Census," City of Toronto Access and Equity Unit, (2000), 112.
68   Jennifer Ajandi, "'Single Mothers by Choice': Disrupting Dominant Discourses
      of the Family Through Social Justice Alternatives," *International Journal of Child,
      Youth and Family Studies* 3, 4 (2011): 410-431.
69   See Patricia Hill Collins, *Black Sexual Politics: African Americans, Gender, and the
      New Racism* (New York: Routledge, 2004); Patricia Hamilton, *Black Mothers*

hood and choice relate differently to Black women than to other women. Thus, without Black feminist and critical race analyses, Ajandi's argument effectively ignores and minimizes the plight of motherhood (and even presumed motherhood) among Black women.[70] The overly simplistic move to choice-related rhetoric is damaging to the status and dignity of Black women. There is a dearth of literature that refers to Black women as having made the choice to parent alone. Given the prevalent image of the hypersexual and hyper-fertile Black woman who uses her body, specifically her womb, as a means to escape labour-market participation while concurrently contributing to an immoral and lazy future workforce by way of her children, this notion of single mothering by choice must be better informed by a Black feminist lens.

In the US context, the term "welfare" is steeped in discourses about race, specifically discourses about Black Americans. As Maura Kelly points out, "African Americans are overrepresented in the news stories about poverty and public assistance" while "research has shown that negative attitudes towards public assistance are correlated with negative attitudes towards African Americans."[71] Accordingly, Black women are held responsible for their experiences of poverty as if these women exist independent of racist capitalist structures, labour market concerns, and various forms of oppression. Black people face what Christopher Pierson terms the "double process of disadvantage" in relation to welfare state apparatuses: Black peoples' sociopolitical positioning within society makes them "more reliant upon provisions through the welfare state," which in turn puts them at greater risk of surveillance within a system that

---

and Attachment Parenting: A Black Feminist Analysis of Intensive Mothering in Britain and Canada (Bristol: Bristol University Press, 2021); Patricia Hamilton, "'Now That I Know What You're About': Black Feminist Reflections on Power in the Research Relationship," Qualitative Research 20, 5 (2020): 519–33; bell hooks, Yearning: Race, Gender, And Cultural Politics (Toronto: Between the Lines, 1990); Maura Kelly, "African Americans Are Overrepresented in the News Stories About Poverty and Public," Journal of Poverty 1, 14 (2010).

70   Patricia Hamilton, "'Now That I Know What You're About.'"
71   Maura Kelly, "African Americans are overrepresented in the news stories about poverty and public," 79/93.

already treats Black people "less favourably than members of the dominant community."[72]

There are several ways in which Black people are depicted "less favourably." As Collins explains, the images of the Black bitch "depict Black women as aggressive, loud, rude, and pushy."[73] Nancy Fraser and Linda Gordon bring forward a discourse that assumes that welfare recipients are mentally ill, referencing dependency on state assistance as a "form of personality disorder."[74] There is a strong link to be made between these two categorical targets: the Black woman assigned with aggressiveness, and the welfare recipient ascribed mental illness. The notion of welfare recipients as mentally ill compounds the negative discourse of Blackness, creating and repeating a pathologizing process that often presumes that Black women are not only aggressive and rude, but are also to be confined, controlled, and treated as problems to be corrected.[75]

I do not take lightly the correlation between illness and gendered oppressions, and I want to draw attention to a diagnosis that, in both current and historical terms, continues to be deployed against women in order to mark and control us. It is compounded by a significant body of literature that conceptualizes Black women and

72   Christopher Pierson, *Beyond the Welfare State? The New Political Economy of Welfare* (University Park, Pennsylvania: Pennsylvania State University Press, 1991), 23.

73   Patricia Hill Collins, *Black Sexual Politics: African Americans, Gender, and the New Racism*, 123.

74   Nancy Fraser and Linda Gordon, "A Genealogy of Dependency: Tracing a Keyword of the U.S.Welfare State," *Signs* 19, 2 (1994): 326.

75   See Bristow et al., *We're Rooted Here and They Can't Pull Us Up: Essays in African Canadian Women's History* (Toronto: University of Toronto Press, 1994); Angela Y. Davis, *Abolition Democracy: Beyond Empire, Prisons, and Torture* (New York: Seven Stories Press, 2005); Robyn Maynard, *Policing Black Lives: State Violence in Canada from Slavery to the Present* (Black Point NS & Winnipeg: Fernwood Publishing, 2017); Makeda Silvera, *Her Head a Village: & other stories* (Vancouver: Press Gang Publishers, 1994); Makeda Silvera, ed., *The Other Woman: Women of Colour in Contemporary Canadian Literature* (Toronto: Sister Vision Press, 1995), Makeda Silvera, *The Heart Does Not Bend* (Toronto: Vintage Canada, 2003); Althea Prince, *Being Black : Essays* (Toronto: Insomniac Press, 2001); Andrea Ritchie, *Invisible No More: Police Violence Against Black Women and Women of Color* (Boston: Beacon Press, 2017); Idil Abdillah, *Blackened Madness: Medicalization, and Black Everyday Life in Canada* (ARP Books: forthcoming, 2024).

non-white women as the prototypical welfare cheat, marked by "single motherhood—statistically on the upswing—pathological and disease-like, contaminating society, contributing to its destruction and degeneration."[76] Black women on welfare serve as the "class of prima facie suspect people ... whose activities warrant continual scrutiny."[77]

These concepts of the welfare cheat and the suspect person are complex constructs. Morrison, for instance, focuses on the social construct, saying that fraud in the context of OW is not embedded in legal or criminalizing discourses, but rather is about "moral disapproval," and that the function of this "rhetoric in conservative anti-welfare campaigns is [to] subvert claims of need not by confronting or denying them directly, but by side-stepping them," in turn helping to "construct a generalized atmosphere of oppression and fear which constitutes much of the lived experience of poverty."[78] However, while Morrison suggests that criminalization is not a central concern, Punam Kholsa trains focus onto legal and policing apparatuses, suggesting that criminalizing discourses are a reality and of absolutely central importance, particularly for the Black community, which is heavily over-policed.[79] Let's look then, at some of the criminalization and surveilled spaces within which this multi-construct of the scrutinization of the Black woman unfolds, and how this leads toward neoliberalism's false narratives of inclusion.

76   Martha Fineman as quoted in Errlee Carruthers, "Prosecuting Women for Welfare Fraud in Ontario: Implication for Equality," *Journal of Law and Social Policy* 11, 10 (1995): 250.

77   Errlee Carruthers, "Prosecuting Women for Welfare Fraud in Ontario," 244.

78   Ian Morrison, "Ontario Works: A Preliminary Assessment," 29.

79   Punam Khosla and Community Social Planning Council of Toronto. "If Low Income Women of Colour Counted in Toronto: Final report of the Action-Research Project Breaking isolation, getting involved," Community Social Planning Council of Toronto (2003).

ILLUSORY SOLIDARITY IN A SURVEILLED CITY

Between 1999 and 2000, the Toronto Police Service was increasing dispatches to highly racialized (though not solely Black) communities, including social housing communities such as Regent Park, Parkdale, Jane-Finch, Rexdale, and Glendower, under the guise of community-based policing initiatives.[1] During this same period, Ontario Works offices employed several off-duty police officers to "track down ineligible welfare recipients."[2] Though there is still a large societal contingent that may not want to accept the fact that criminalization and incarceration are deployed in inequitable ways, the evidence is clear that this is the case. Loïc Wacquant reminds us that prisons in the US function as a new home for Black people, serving as "an instrument of control and containment of a population considered as a lower caste with which one should not mix."[3] He further suggests that prisons serve as a policy response to social issues, as he references "increasingly frequent, [...] routine, use of imprisonment as an instrument for managing social

1   Punam Kholsa, "If Low Income Women of Colour Counted in Toronto," 32.
2   Julilly Kohler-Hausmann, "'The Crime of Survival': Fraud Prosecutions, Community Surveillance, and the Original 'Welfare Queen'," *Journal of Social History* 41, 2 (2007): 335.
3   Loïc Wacquant, "The Penalization of Poverty and the Rise of Neo-liberalism," *European Journal on Criminal Policy and Research* 9 (2003): 402.

insecurity," and expresses the "usefulness of the penal apparatus in the post-Keynesian era of employment of insecurity."[4]

Ken Moffatt et al. describe this policing in terms of surveillance, the technological use of panoptic devices through which "surveillance could be both continuous and constant" without interruption to the worker.[5] The caseworker, for example, can often access multiple surveillance systems and gain access to intimate details of OW recipients' lives without the recipients' awareness. Krystle Maki similarly conducts a review of several central surveillance tools used to police, discipline, sanction, and monitor poor women and families accessing OW.[6] These tools include "Consolidated Verification Procedure (CVP); Maintenance Enforcement with Computer Assistance (MECA); Service Delivery Model Technology (SDMT); Ontario Works Eligibility Criteria; Eligibility Review Officers (EROs); Audit of Recipients; and Drug Testing and Welfare Fraud Hotlines."[7] While many investments were made to monitor OW recipients, the data indicates that these monies were poorly spent. In 2006, while upwards of five thousand fraud investigations were conducted, only 0.003 percent of the cases resulted in legal sanction. Similarly, in 2001–2002, the rate of "actual instances of criminal convictions for fraud [was] exceptionally low: convictions represented roughly 0.1% of the social assistance caseload in 2001–02, notwithstanding more than 38,000 investigations being undertaken."[8]

The use of surveillance reached a notable high in the early 1990s with the introduction and proliferation of "biometric scan-voice scan, finger print, finger scan, palm scan, retina scan" technology,

4   Ibid, 404-405.
5   Ken Moffatt, et al., "Advancing citizenship: A Study of Social Planning." *Community Development Journal* 34, 4 (1999) 225.
6   Krystle Maki, "Neoliberal Deviants and Surveillance: Welfare Recipients Under the Watchful Eye of Ontario Works," *Surveillance & Society* 9, 1-2 (2011): 47–63.
7   Ibid, 47.
8   Janet Mosher and Joe Hermer 2005, "Welfare Fraud: The Constitution of Social Assistance as Crime," paper prepared for the Law Commission of Canada, as cited in Krystle Maki, "Neoliberal Deviants and Surveillance," 54.

along with the requirement of up to fifty pieces of identification per family.[9] Moffatt offers an understanding of surveillance using two interconnected frameworks: firstly, one which seeks to serve as an "instrument of normalizing judgement," and secondly, a system that seeks to monitor "financial inscription."[10] When these mechanisms are combined, caseworkers are given flagrant license to gather information about OW recipients' health, identity, and changes to their financial status.[11]

We must be mindful of definitions that assume we are all impacted by poverty and other forms of marginalization in the same way. In Ontario, "African, Black and Caribbean ethno-racial groups, including Jamaicans, Africans and Blacks [sic], and people from other Caribbean nations experience much more poverty and have family incomes considerably below the average for Toronto."[12] Further, "Ethiopians, Ghanaians [and] Somalis experience devastatingly high levels of poverty and extremely low median incomes."[13] While the broader Black/African population experiences poverty, the above examples illustrate that many groups often understood as "homogeneous" continue to be differentially impacted by poverty.

I therefore offer a challenge both to the meta-definitions and to commonplace discourses of surveillance. These discourses, which address collective experiences shared by whites/off-white and racialized people who are not Black, omit the experience of racism and instead merely discuss neoliberalism, which serves as a system of

9   Ken Moffatt, "Surveillance and Government of the Welfare Recipient," in *Reading Foucault for Social Work,* edited by Adrienne S. Chambon, Allan Irving, and Laura Epstein, 238-241 (New York: Columbia University Press, 1999), 238; Ian Morrision, "Ontario Works: A Preliminary Assessment."

10   Ken Moffatt, "Surveillance and Government of the Welfare Recipient," 241.

11   Errlee Carruthers, "Prosecuting Women for Welfare Fraud in Ontario: Implications for Equality," *Journal of Law and Social Policy* 11 (1995): 241-262; Maura Kelly, "African Americans Are Overrepresented in the News Stories About Poverty and Public"; Krystle Maki, "Neoliberal Deviants and Surveillance; Ken Moffatt, "Surveillance and Government of the Welfare Recipient"; Ian Morrison, "Ontario Works: A Preliminary Assessment"; James Patrick Mulvale, *Reimagining Social Welfare: Beyond the Keynesian Welfare State* (Aurora, Ontario: Garamond Press, 2001).

12   Michael Ornstein, "Ethno-Racial Inequality in the City of Toronto: An Analysis of the 1996 Census," (City of Toronto Access and Equity Unit, 2000), 112.

13   Ibid.

oppression that marks and disciplines OW recipients. Although it is obvious that neoliberalism functions in this fashion, such discourses effectively depoliticize and de-historicize the racist social histories that are in operation within, and that therefore inform, the OW structure. Whom does it benefit when we do not seek to understand the nuanced experiences of Black women as they relate to both social assistance and surveillance? What commonplace understandings of poverty, neoliberalism, gender, and surveillance seek to center dominant public policy discourses on neoliberalism, racelessness, and white womanhood while simultaneously concealing the experiences of others? Uzma Shakir provides the following insight:

> [T]o suppose a monolithic solidarity in a meta-definition that governs the social inclusion discourse in Canada is to create an illusion of solidarity that has no basis in lived reality and that, in fact, creates discursive harmony by deliberately masking the material conditions of inequality.[14]

This is an important point, with far-reaching implications. For example, while Anver Saloojee provides a substantive discussion on inclusion, racism, and democratic citizenship underscored by a discussion on poverty, he offers a misguided response to racism and the racialization of poverty and discrimination. He offers "an anti-oppression discourse with social inclusion as process and outcome [as] an incredibly powerful impetus to social change and political solidarity."[15] However, while some scholarship alludes to an antiracism lens falling under the wide-ranging anti-oppressive category, other research problematizes the notion of antiracism as a response to and framework for marginalization.[16] Anti-oppressive and antiracist

14   Uzma Shakir, "Dangers of a New Dogma: Inclusion Or Else...!" in *Social Inclusion: Canadian Perspectives,* edited by Ted Richmond and Anver Saloojee (Halifax, NS: Fernwood, 2005), 208.
15   Anver Saloojee. "Social Inclusion, Anti-racism and Democratic Citizenship," *Joint Centre for Excellence for Research on Immigration and Settlement,* 14 (2005), 201.
16   See, for e.g., Claire Harris, M. Nourbese Philip and Dionne Brand, *Grammar of Dissent: Poetry and Prose by Claire Harris, M. Nourbese Philip and Dionne*

perspectives are surely not interchangeable in their utility as entry points into understanding social phenomena. Providing a critical perspective that centers on the experiences of race and racialization in the social world, antiracism seeks to name race and locate power within a framework of intersection.[17] Indeed, "an anti-racism perspective specifically looks at processes of racialization that grant to those who are White the power and privilege to function in a world that mirrors their needs and aspirations."[18] A broad anti-oppression discourse serves in this context as a popular, liberal, palatable response to race and racism. Rather than offer a direct focus on racialized realities, Saloojee downplays a central tenet of anti-oppression discourse itself, which requires that we name, interrogate, and eradicate hierarchies that give rise to oppressive conditions.[19] This criticism can also be extended to the practical implementation of institutionally based initiatives, which include antiracism and anti-oppression initiatives, appointments, and offices under the umbrella of Equity, Diversity, and Inclusion (EDI).

But if EDI has taught us anything, it is that naming is not enough. EDI and antiracism initiatives are in fact negotiations *out* of the discussion of antiBlack racism, when they fall as they do within white supremacist overlapping frameworks and are set in place by ubiquitous white supremacist practices. EDI thus inevitably takes a turn to align with those mainstream structures. This

Brand (Fredericton: Goose Lane, 1994); Zenzele Isoke, "Black Ethnography, Black(Female)Aesthetics: Thinking/Writing/Saying/Sounding Black Political Life," *Theory & Event* 21, 1 (2018): 148–68; Charmaine C. Williams and April A. Collins, "Defining New Frameworks for Psychosocial Intervention," *Psychiatry (Washington, D.C.)* 62, 1 (1999): 61–78.

17   George J. Sefa Dei, *Anti-racism Education: Theory and Practice* (Winnipeg: Fernwood, 1996).

18   June Ying Yee, Axelle Janczur, Helen Wong, and CERIS, *Examining Systemic and Individual Barriers Experienced by Visible-Minority Social Workers in Mainstream Social Service Agencies: A Community Project*, 57; CERIS—The Ontario Metropolis Centre (2007), 5.

19   See Lisa Barnoff, "New Directions for Anti-oppression Practice in Feminist Social Service Agencies," (PhD diss., University of Toronto, 2002); Lisa Barnoff and Ken Moffatt, "Contradictory Tensions in Anti-Oppression Practice in Feminist Social Services," *Affilia*, 22, 1 (2007): 56–70; Lena Dominelli, "Deprofessionalizing Social Work: Anti-Oppressive Practice, Competencies and Postmodernism," *British Journal of Social Work* 26, 2 (1996):153–175.

is a failure embedded within antiracism practices that evict and evacuate Black people from the discourse that concerns us, instead placing Black people as the stand-in and representation—by which I mean *marker alone*—for diversity. The very fact that I am currently writing this critique of antiracism practices, and that other Black scholars and activists are concurrently doing the same, is evidence of the deep failures of antiracist, anti-oppression, and EDI initiatives.

It is clear from the background reviewed here that surveillance is experienced by those accessing social assistance, and in Toronto specifically this reality is in part due to the neoliberal nature of OW and the current social policy climate.[20] Women have been a focal point of analysis in social policy and welfare-based discussion for many decades.[21] These existing critiques have made significant contributions to gender and policy theorizing, creating space for alternative questions to be asked of policymakers. However, although Black women have been present within this literature to some degree, the accounts of their specific experiences have been minimal. And Toronto is also not the only context within which specific research addressing Black women's experience with social

20   Caroline Andrew, "Women and the Welfare State," *Canadian Journal of Political Science / Revue Canadienne de Science Politique* 17,4 (1984): 667–683; Lauren Applebaum, "The Influence of Perceived Deservingness on Policy Decisions Regarding Aid to the Poor," *Political Psychology* 22, 3 (2001): 419–442; Bistow, et al., *We're Rooted Here and They Can't Pull Us Up*; Baines et al., eds., *Women's Caring: Feminist Perspectives on Social Welfare 2nd ed.* (Oxford: Oxford University Press, 1998); Patrick Burman, *Poverty's Bonds: Power and Agency in the Social Relations of Welfare* (Toronto: Thompson Educational Publishing, 1996); Krystle Maki, "Neoliberal Deviants and Surveillance."
21   Mimi Abramovitz, "The Largely Untold Story of Welfare Reform and the Human Services," *Social Work* 50, 2 (2005): 175–186.; Carol Baines et al., "Confronting Women's Caring: Challenges for Practice and Policy," *Affilia* 7, 1 (1992): 21–44; Caragata, "Neoconservative Realities"; Bruce Carruthers, *City of Capital*; Margaret Hillyard Little, "A Litmus Test for Democracy: The Impact of Ontario Welfare Changes on Single Mothers," *Studies in Political Economy* 66, 1 (2001): 9–36; Margaret Hillyard Little, "Manhunts and Bingo Blabs": The Moral Regulation of Ontario Single Mothers," *The Canadian Journal of Sociology / Cahiers Canadiens de Sociologie* 19, 2 (1994); Margaret Hillyard Little & Ian Morrison, "'The Pecker Detectors are Back': Regulation of the Family Form in Ontario Welfare Policy," *Journal of Canadian Studies* 34, 2 (1999): 110–136; Margaret Hillyard Little, "Manhunts and Bingo Blabs": The Moral Regulation of Ontario Single Mothers," *The Canadian Journal of Sociology / Cahiers Canadiens de Sociologie* 19, 2 (1994).

assistance and surveillance from a Black feminist, critical race, and antiBlack-racism perspective is yet to be seen. Black women have long engaged in a difficult and complex relationship with the paternalistic state, a relationship that is marked by either imposed dependency or presumption of the same, and further marked by imposed narratives about personal irresponsibility necessitating regulation.[22] For these reasons, this text ventures upon a demythologization, providing a new perspective on surveillance in Toronto, as directly experienced by Black women, and informed by frameworks that recognize the intersectional nature of Black women's lived experiences and standpoints. These are basic understandings from which to embark.

22   Peggy Bristow, *"We're Rooted Here and They Can't Pull Us Up": Essays in African Canadian Women's History* (Toronto: University of Toronto Press, 1994); Patricia Hill Collins, "Gender, Black Feminism, and Black Political Economy," *The Annals of the American Academy of Political and Social Science* 568, 1 (2000): 41–53.

MAPPING A LEGAL REGIME OF "PUBLIC SAFETY"

While exploring the contextual landscape of Black women's experience with social assistance in Toronto we must incorporate an understanding of Ontario Works as a complicated legal regime. Concealed as a service entity/office focused on income support and replacement, its functions are often detached from the municipal and provincial legislative regulations that underline its governing practices. Given the high stakes for Black women—namely loss of freedom and loss of privacy, health, and in some cases life— clarity is important, if for no other reason than to articulate the very nature of the relationship between the benefit recipient and OW, which operates within an implicit framework of a commitment to "public safety," and assumptions of being a purveyor of the same. I use the term "public safety" intentionally, referencing popularized "violence-prevention" doctrine applied by facets of the carceral state (including policing) explicitly, in order to bring forward the context in which exchanges and relationships occur; that is, within a public intellectual framework of guarding taxpayers and the broader citizenry against the misuse of "good, hardworking taxpayers' funds," and threats to their property. Public safety, in this context, is borrowed from a legal framework—one based on *regulation*. If a service recipient is understood as "dishonest" or does not disclose information, be it by omission or ignorance, they are not simply accountable to their case worker. Rather, the worker's function is to protect the state and public monies from being "misused." Therefore, caseworkers are not simply an incidental conduit to the criminalization of benefit recipients, but they are expected to actively engage in the capture of service recipients by regularly deploying legal standards and assessments that act as a backdrop for the framing of discourses with outcomes such as accusations of fraud, dishonesty, deception, or disingenuousness.

This is important because the legal framework of fraud is used in order to investigate and officially criminalize a recipient. Section 380(1) of the Criminal Code of Canada identifies a perpetrator of fraud as:

> Everyone who, by deceit, falsehood or other fraudulent means, whether or not it is a false pretense within the meaning of this Act, defrauds the public or any person, whether ascertained or not, of any property, money or valuable security or any service.[1]

Particularly notable here is the idea of "public or any person." "Public" in the context of social assistance refers to the broader social world, hence my application of the concept of "public safety" above when questioning the idea of the public as a particular person to whom the welfare recipient is accountable. Crucially, as recipients of income replacement, benefit recipients are excluded from this "public"; they are seen as the other, the threat that the public needs to protect itself from. By the same token, they are excluded from the protection afforded this public, including protection from its most powerful representatives—the state and its agents—including service workers and police.

Ontario Works caseworkers and Eligibility Review Officers are not bestowed with a police badge or state-issued firearm, but the absence of these markers of power do not negate nor revoke their ability to wield and exact authority of similar weight. In fact, due to the very absence of these markers, we assume their presence is

---

1   *Criminal Code*, RSC 1985, c. C-46, s 380(1).

benign; I would argue it is instead equally dangerous, and that we must not be distracted from this danger, must instead see and name its concealed and unclarified power. Among many similar examples, the case of *R. v. D'Amour* (2002) is indicative of the structural intermingling of social services and police, and it illustrates how OW caseworkers have what has been accurately described as, "plainly law enforcement powers."[2] It is important to articulate these relationships, particularly in the context of my interlocutors, who are all Black women. One of the central things that the voiced realities of these Black women serve to concretize is how caseworkers' powers parallel and are consistent with the immensely invasive powers of police; they include, "powers of entry and removal of evidence from premises, demand for inspection, demands for information—supplemented by search warrant request authority for residential dwellings."[3] When thinking and (re)reading our realities in defense of BlackLife, what emerges from these connections between Ontario Works and more traditional roles of police and policing is how we are collectively victim to state-sanctioned violence to differing degrees. The stories of the twenty Black women recounted in this text serve as a necessary testimony to what is often hidden—what can easily be dismissed as an exceptionality when it happens to non-Black people, but emerges as a steady pattern here. It therefore bears pointing out that even though these narratives speak to the experience of Black women distinctly, what we have in these permissibly bold dismissals of and infractions upon our humanity, is a reflection of state roles more broadly, and on how those state powers are wielded against a refracted range of variously afflicted peoples.

These Black women's experiences demonstrate a larger climate within the social services sector that operates as a barometer demonstrating that those most marginalized are likely to experience, and have always experienced, the brunt of public persecution.

2   John Shields, 2000. R. v. D'Amour, 2002 CanLII 45015 (ON CA), <https://canlii.ca/t/1cskn>, retrieved on June 2, 2022.
3   John Shields, "R. v. D'Amour, 2002 CanLII 45015. (ON CA). Court of Appeal Ontario. August 13, 2022. https://www.canlii.org/en/on/onca/doc/2002/2002canlii45015/2002canlii45015.html.

Reckoning with public policy from a perspective that highlights its tendency to be informal and surreptitious allows for the indictment of care spaces both within and outside of the non-profit industrial complex; such spaces can then be identified and approached as the policing-driven entities that they are. These critical interpretations in defense of BlackLife make unambiguous the role and functioning of Ontario Works as one among many of the state's apparatuses of social control, concealed within the rhetoric of social care and social responsibility.

Black women's ongoing struggle and our critiques of the system are often dismissed, reductively interpreted as mere histrionic irrationality, hypersensitivity, sensationalisms, or simply untruths, but disciplined narratives reveal the commonplace impunity of the enactors of surveillance and policing practices in Black women's lives. Many of the accounts of the women I interviewed do not involve direct police interventions, but they are nevertheless dictated by the presence of similar and adjacent laws, as the conditions of income replacement interactions criminalize and eventually often incarcerate as well. This is not unintentional. It is rather due to the intrusive nature of the framework set in place for access to public funds and particularly Ontario Works, where recipients of the benefit are asked to provide forensic details of their personal and public lives. It has been repeatedly noted that case workers and their practices are crucial in the surveillance and policing of eligibility and authenticity.[4] This is only confirmed and reaffirmed by the data herein, as ninety-five percent of my interlocutors identified Ontario Works, and their relationship to Ontario Works, as a catalyzing site, creating multiple pathways to interactions with and surveillance by other state systems.

Nineteen out of the twenty interlocutors identified Blackness, and their relationship to poverty coupled with their interactions with the state, as key determinants of what other systems they

4   Todd Gabel et al., "Welfare Reform in Ontario: A Report Card," Fraser Institute Digital Publication, September, 2004; Dianne Martin, "Passing the Buck"; Kiran Mirchandani and Wendy Chan, *The Racialized Impact of Welfare Fraud Control in British Columbia and Ontario*, (Toronto: Canadian Race Relations Foundation, 2005).

may become forcefully involved with. They also expressed a lack of understanding and clarity regarding: what kind of information is disclosed; for what purpose; to what intent; and to whom it would be disclosed/made available. Interlocutor 3, for example, shared the following experience, which had multiple damaging effects:

> *When we first arrived in Toronto my girlfriend and I were both on welfare, separately. My immigration claim was approved and hers wasn't. We didn't have the same worker, but we were assigned to the same office. I had mentioned to my worker, I was feeling stress and now my employment searches were going much slower because I was worried about my girlfriend. She asked why and I told her. My worker obviously had a conversation with my girlfriend's worker and shortly after the border patrol showed up at her apartment. She asked a border patrol why they were at her door, and they told her that they were following up to ensure that her address was the same but also now required her to check in on a monthly basis, until she was deported. All of this was unnecessary. It also wasn't fair. But there's nothing you can do about it.*

Interlocutor 3's account of her and her partner's experience corresponds with the findings of David Moffette and Karl Gardner, who found in their report entitled "Often Asking, Always Telling: The Toronto Police Service and the Sanctuary City Policy Toronto Police," that Toronto Police Service made "3,278 calls to Canada Border Services Agency CBSA, [and] 83.4 percent of the calls were for status checks."[5] They identified that "the broad criterion of officer suspicion is fertile ground for the practice of racial profiling."[6] Moffette and Gardner estimate that Toronto Police Service (TPS) made approximately one hundred phone calls to the Canada

---

5   David Moffette and Karl Gardner, "Often Asking, Always Telling: The Toronto Police Service and the Sanctuary City Policy," (No One is Illegal—Toronto, 2015), 5.

6   Ibid, 6; also see Nicolas Keung, "Toronto police urged to stop immigration 'status checks'," *The Toronto Star*, November 24, 2015.

Border Services Agency (CBSA) daily, frequently resulting in no formal detention, apprehension, or arrest. Moreover, 93 percent of the calls made by TPS to the CBSA concerned people who did *not* turn out to have outstanding immigration warrants, suggesting, according to the migrant justice group No One Is Illegal, "that TPS officers racially profiled the individuals, and chose to contact CBSA without cause."[7]

The relationship between service caseworkers and benefit recipients is central to this informal system of racial profiling and criminalization, and its ambiguity can make it particularly dangerous. The nature of this relationship, therefore, needs to be demystified: caseworkers are not therapists. They are not advocates, support people, nor necessarily "social workers" registered to the Ontario College of Social Workers and Social Service Workers. Even when they are registered to the College, this effectively means nothing; it means that they can be held "accountable" by the College, that they'll get a monthly newspaper, and that they'll be asked to renew their annual fee. A caseworker is a unionized employee of the municipality and often does not have to have specific "social work training" or knowledge in order to occupy this role, since it is classified as an "administrative role." I am not suggesting that the inherently colonial practice of social work or having a social work educational background would interrupt the experiences of the Black women in this book. Rather, this distinction is made because all twenty women in this research identified that they were under the impression that caseworkers were supposed to provide some form of *care* and/or that they had some "therapeutic" training. This interpretation is not surprising; given the opaque nature of labels such as "social," "services," and "support," it makes sense that benefit recipients would be confused, and that they would extrapolate that they are interacting with trained care workers who are looking out for their interests. That is, until they realize that their interests are actually not being supported, at which point

7   As quoted by Michelle Da Silva, in "Toronto police sell out sanctuary city," *NOW Magazine*, February 11, 2016. https://nowtoronto.com/ toronto-police-sell-out-sanctuary-city.

they are still forced to navigate the complex assumptions inherent in the labels and social framing that surround caseworkers, social care, and their inevitable effects.

Another woman, Interlocutor 11, put it the following way: *"Her job is to make sure I'm not stealing their money."* I asked her who "their" is. She responded: *"The people. Like, I know don't know… the people? Like her, my worker. She's the people."* Put plainly it is the so-called good public's money and state resources that are attached to those who are deemed good citizens, that is, her caseworker or people other than herself.[8] Therefore we must understand a caseworker's disqualification of recipients as yet another measure of ensuring a carceral concept of "public safety." To counter this interpretation, we must consider how the very people who are constructed as—and who see themselves as—outside of cultural categories of "the people," or "the public," also happen to be those already overrepresented within the social care and penal systems, and how gendered antiBlack racism thus creates harsher outcomes for the women in this research and other women like them. There is a social spectrum here that is adhered to by all parties, and its cloaked nature allows its continuance, which is a violent facilitation as much as it is a facilitation of violence.

8   Interlocutor 11, in person interview with author, Toronto 2018.

THE MONITORING STATE

Like many scholars, Black and otherwise, I assert a point that should at this historical juncture, be uncontroversial: that Black people are not new to being subjects of surveillance in its many iterations.[1] Whether or not academic discourses of surveillance and surveillance technologies are accessible to Black people, the experience of surveillance for Black people is ubiquitous. Simone Browne identifies this experience as racializing surveillance.[2] Browne illustrates how BlackLife is entangled with and marked by surveillance. In fact, she asserts that "the fact of antiblackness" is the fundamental architecture on which much of western life, the modern sciences, and notions of humanity are built.[3] Thus, be it an algorithm, or an HP pencil, the archetype of the surveilled, the cargo, the castrated, and the concealed—the commodified and excluded—is Black.[4]

1   Ruha Benjamin, "Cultura Obscura: Race, Power, and "Culture Talk" in the Health Sciences," *American Journal of Law & Medicine* 43, 2-3 (2017): 225-238; Ruha Benjamin, *Race after Technology: Abolitionist Tools for the New Jim Code* (Newark: Polity Press, 2019); Safiya Umoja Noble, *Algorithms of Oppression: How Search Engines Reinforce Racism* (New York: New York University Press, 2018); Simone Browne, *Dark Matters: On the Surveillance of Blackness* (Durham, North Carolina: Duke University Press, 2015); Angela Ritchie, *Invisible No More: Police Violence Against Black Women and Women of Color* (Boston: Beacon Press, 2017).
2   Simone Browne, *Dark Matters: On the Surveillance of Blackness*, 8.
3   Ibid, 10.
4   Ruha Benjamin, *Race after Technology*; Safiya Umoja Noble, *Algorithms of Oppression*.

It is Blackness that is held in contempt. It is Blackness being convicted. It is "darkness" or Blackness that is deemed defiant and disenfranchised. It is also Blackness at stake, in all of its new and innovative neoliberal formations. The slaveship, the auction block, and the plantation continue in all of their contemporary iterations, visible in the refugee camp—today in Palestine, Eastleigh, Quebec, or at the Polish-Ukranian border—at the shelter, on the case management "load," in a prison indeterminately contained by border services (or comparably by review boards), or barricaded behind psychiatric institutions. Browne alerts surveillance scholars to the fact that "the conditions of blackness—the historical, the present, and the historical present—can help social theorists understand our contemporary conditions of surveillance."[5]

As the sanctity upon which the foundation of whiteness is built, we must also consider this foundational antiBlackness in the context of property. The variations of property and its foundations are vast in a way that cannot be addressed here, but what must be understood is its ubiquity and fluidity. Property can be the public's money, a woman's genitalia, the embodiment of your public expression as a Black person. In the context of Blackness and state relationships and the post-Atlantic slave trade, it is ultimately both the framing and the frame with which we interpret, ostracize, and keep Black people on a docket and agenda. The antiBlack access to permission to possess us is what negates and undergirds our unfreedom, and among its many forms of access is the stand-in state designate who can pop up at any point to regulate Black people. This license ties into antiBlack notions of deviance and pauperism already discussed. It is indicative of many things that bleed and interblend. If the "client"—a Black woman—is property, then the property manager is a state worker, and the owner is, de facto, the state.

All of this is principally instructive given Canada's commitment to a practice of continuously casting BlackLife "anew," (re)interpreting historicities and materialities of Black subjugation in so-called Canada, likewise anew.[6] This ongoing recasting

---

5   Simone Browne, *Dark Matters: On the Surveillance of Blackness*, 8.
6   Look to the works of Dionne Brand, Austin Clarke, Cecil Foster, and Rinaldo Walcott, as well as the specific texts: Dionne Brand & Lois De Shield, *No*

produced, and continues to produce, fabrications at each juncture of what is referred to as Canadian life. Often when the state interacts with the issue of antiBlack racism or Black people, every interaction is "new" despite a wealth of documentation (including documentation of lived experience) demonstrating that Black people in what was called Upper Canada by invading powers, have been advocating for themselves and fighting for freedom and against unfreedom since 1799 and prior.[7]

There has been a disconnection between the various instruments of surveillance—data, standardized tools, and the very discourse of assessment itself—and an understanding of their context as apparatuses envisioned and created by the same white supremacist rationales, and rationalism, that continue to reinvigorate their historical purposes and outcomes. As articulated by Ruha Benjamin, racism must be understood as "a set of technologies that generate patterns of social relations, and these become Black-boxed as natural, inevitable, [and] *automatic*."[8] What Benjamin is gesturing toward is the fact that, irrespective of any specific technological apparatus or algorithm, antiBlackness and its expression in surveillance systems is "not only a symptom or outcome, but a precondition for the fabrication of such technologies."[9] In short, there can not be technological tools created outside of an entrenched schema of racism, and more specifically antiBlack racism.

The interconnected social services systems, as described by my interlocutors, are embedded in neoliberal logics and notions of efficiency and modernization. Building interconnected systems

Burden to Carry: Narratives of Black Working Women in Ontario, 1920s–1950s (Toronto: Women's Press, 1991); Peggy Bristow, Dionne Brand, Linda Carty, Afua P. Cooper, Sylvia Hamilton, and Adrienne Shadd, *We're Rooted Here and They Can't Pull Us Up: Essays in African Canadian Women's History* (Toronto: University of Toronto Press, 1994); Sylvia Hamilton, *And I Alone Escaped To Tell You* (Kentville, NS: Gaspereau Press, 2014).

7   Robin W. Winks, *The Blacks In Canada: A History 2nd ed.* (McGill-Queens University Press, 1997), 47; also see Afua Cooper, *The Hanging of Angélique: The Untold Story of Canadian Slavery and the Burning of Old Montréal* (Toronto: Harper Collins, 2006).

8   Ruha Benjamin, *Race after Technology: Abolitionist Tools for the New Jim Code* (Oxford, England: Polity, 2019), 44-45.

9   Ibid, 44.

was the intended outcome of the Ministry of Community and Social Services' (MCSS) 1996 Modernization and Business Plan for Ontario Works.

In 1996 the MCSS began a Business Transformation Project (BTP). The stated purpose of the BTP undertaking was to develop a mechanism of welfare reform in Ontario under the Ontario Works Act. As such, in 1997 MCSS hired the Andersen Consulting group to establish and implement a new social assistance Service Delivery Model (SDM). This new model was celebrated for the "efficiencies" it would bring at the service-recipient level and was heavily endorsed by politicians and state actors as having "no impact on Toronto Social Services' year 2000 net budget" conferred by the Commissioner of Community and Neighbourhood Services Report 2000 (Toronto City Council).[10] In the context of discussing Ontario Works, it is important to recognize the intermingling of systems of surveillance and this kind of rhetoric that is imbued with notions of cost saving for municipalities and provinces at the expense of Black and other racialized people dealing with issues of privacy and surveillance.

Elsewhere I have written about how ideas and calculations about cost savings are motivated by, and concretized by and through, logics of non-humanness and antiBlack violence(s). In *BlackLife: Post BLM and the Struggle for Freedom,* Rinaldo Walcott and I proffer that:

> the existence of the nonhuman in relation to the Canadian State is for purposes of enumeration. Those whose humanity remains in question are incalculable, and to this end, the enumerating of "black" must not be conflated with the of enumerating of the human, the citizen or the social/political actor. The calculating of "black" is in reference to the body and never the Black person, the human or our humanity. Therefore, how does

10   Toronto City Council. Community and Neighbourhood Services -Community Services Grants Program Review. Report No.3 (2001). https://www.toronto.ca/legdocs/2001/agendas/council/cc010424/au3rpt/cl001.pdf.

one construct and calculate care for the nonhuman, more precisely the "black" enumerated State body? And who are those black bodies?[11]

This reality of the Black enumerated body is reflected concretely in the narratives that Black women I spoke with shared about how policy—formal or informal, scripted and unscripted—is indiscriminately leveraged to exercise control over their lives and bodies. This reality also brings into the frame the need to understand broader policy initiatives—including but not limited to Ontario Works—which, despite not naming Black people as its targets, function to keep Black people and Black women especially at the centre of state apparatuses of control and dehumanization. To this end we must recognize that for over two decades in Toronto our municipality and province were engaged in and advanced digital economies that had direct implications on platform capitalism, centralizing large private data sets and regulating information across social services, resulting in huge privacy infringements.[12] In the 1996 BTP report and related OW policy documents, privacy as it relates to service recipients is not addressed. Instead, the report, which is touted as one of the province's paramount system platforms cost-saving interventions in the last two decades, signals both the failure in policy intentions and lack of service recipient regard. Take for example MCSS and BTP policy documents that repetitively assert language around "efficiencies," "effectiveness," "validation" and systemwide "efficacy."[13] At no point in the document are there any cautions that would suggest the inherent dangers and potential liabilities for social service recipients involved in their efforts to "increase access" and create a vast network of interconnected technological systems.

In recent years, Toronto has witnessed increased dialogue about policing and surveillance, with part of the focus on the practice of

11   Rinaldo Walcott and Idil Abdillahi, *BlackLife*, 90–91.
12   Jen Katshunga, et al., *Black Women in Canada*. Behind the Numbers. http://behindthenumbers.ca/shorthand/black-women-in-canada/.
13   Toronto City Clerk. "Community and Neighbourhood Services—Community Services Grants Program Review," 2021, https://www.toronto.ca/legdocs/2001/agendas/council/cc010424/au3rpt/cl001.pdf.

THE MONITORING STATE   75

police stop-and-search, referred to as "carding" or "street-checks."[14] Police stop-and-search commonly refers to the arbitrary stopping of individuals to be questioned or searched by the police, and not because of any specific behaviour or act contrary to the Criminal Code. Rather, these stops often occur on the basis of race, with racism and racialization at their core.[15] They also occur in spaces that are disproportionately working-class communities, in what I call Blackened city-sites.[16] It is equally important to note that they are not restricted to these spaces, as racialized people are also targeted for street-checks when they leave these sites to go about their lives in the broader community as well.[17]

I make this distinction to illustrate the intersections and to explicitly highlight how "geography is a reliable proxy for race, particularly when it comes to antiBlack racism."[18] Often, police officers are lurking and pursuing "suspicious" activity or people in an effort, they claim, to "prevent" crimes before they occur. According to the Ontario Human Rights Commission's 2003 inquiry, "Paying the Price: The Human Cost of Racial Profiling," racial profiling, which underpins the practice of carding, is defined as:

> any action undertaken for reasons of safety, security or public protection that relies on stereotypes about race, colour, ethnicity, ancestry, religion, or place of origin rather than on reasonable suspicion, to single out an individual for greater scrutiny or different treatment.[19]

---

14 See Desmond Cole, *The Skin We're In: A Year of Black Resistance and Power* (Toronto: Penguin Random House, 2020); and Ontario Huma Rights Commission, "Toronto Police Service racial profiling and carding: deputation to Toronto Police Services Board" (April 8, 2014), https://www.ohrc.on.ca/en/news_centre/toronto-police-service-racial-profiling-and-carding-deputation-toronto-police-services-board.

15 Desmond Cole, *The Skin We're In*; Robyn Maynard, *Policing Black Lives: State Violence in Canada from Slavery to the Present* (Black Point NS and Winnipeg: Fernwood, 2017).

16 Idil Abdillahi, *Blackened Madness* (Winnipeg: ARP Books, forthcoming 2024).

17 Rinaldo Walcott, *On Property* (Windsor, ON: Biblioasis, 2021).

18 Ruha Benjamin, *Race After Technology*, 35.

19 According to the Ontario Human Rights Commission's 2003 inquiry *"Paying the Price: The Human Cost of Racial Profiling,"* 2003, 6.

While there have been numerous and ongoing debates about the definitions, philosophy, and practice of street-checks, the policy directives and intention of this practice were made clear by the Toronto Police Services Board when they determined that the practice included: "non-detention, non-arrest interactions between service and community members that involve the eliciting and/or recording of personal information." They continue, "This policy is not intended to prohibit or guide informal greetings or conversations," stating instead that "Community Safety Notes (CSNs) are investigative records of information that will be generated by some contacts."[20]

The Toronto Police Services Board (TPSB) and Toronto Police Service (TPS) have generated myriad justifications to inform and reinforce the practice of carding/street-checks. The two entities declared that the practice of carding/street-checks and the collection of CSNs was unrelated to race or racism and went so far as to state that:

> service members do not consider race, place of origin, age, colour, ethnic origin, gender identity or gender expression in deciding whether to initiate a contact unless one or more of these factors form part of a specific suspect, victim or witness description.[21]

Beyond the obvious ridiculousness of denying racial profiling, the pronouncement does not account for how "invisibility, with regard to Whiteness, offers whiteness immunity," in the words of Benjamin; "to be unmarked by race allows you to reap the benefits but escape responsibility for your role in an unjust system."[22] Also left unacknowledged are the ways in which the "usual suspect" is constructed in the first place by way of a wide range of disciplining tools, tactics, and philosophies.

There are significant alignments between those who are carded and the women with whom I spoke, as well as similarities in the circumstances surrounding their various interactions with official

20   Toronto Police Services Board April 24, 2014.
21   Ibid.
22   Ruha Benjamin, *Race After Technology*, 4.

and unofficial "law enforcement." The women were "visible" in specific ways and engaged by case workers in public and private spaces based on the kind of culturally assigned visibility that manifests in the markings of social undesirability—in this case poverty, womanhood, and Blackness. Likewise, those groups carded and/or surveilled—inevitably also including Black women—are similarly populations who, publicly and privately, are spatially located in what are deemed to be undesirable bodies and within undesirable boundaries.[23] Undesirable boundaries are, importantly, not limited to Blackened city-sites but can also be defined in terms of the interpretation and logics that assume that particular bodies should not exist in certain spaces.

Reflecting the informality, unscriptedness, and resulting ambiguity of the interactions of my interlocutors with Ontario Works employees, interactions in the context of carding and policing are similarly deemed casual and neutral, and yet are also indicative of levels of power exercised by the service member against or over the individual and their own agency in these interactions. The notion of initiating contact for the purposes of data collection or for investigative purposes is not ultimately neutral; to be "selected" inherently means to be targeted, and although seemingly less overt, the selections that manifest in the decisions of OW service agents are no less targeted, because they are based in the very same logics and indeed zero in on the very same targets. This is what an extended structure of enforcement looks like. Notions of tabulating, surveilling, and enumerating those deemed outside the social frames of acceptability are historical and concomitant with being "proper" and/or of being property.[24] The cultivated illusion of neutrality along with significant powers of discretion granted to the state agent is common to both the practice of street-checks and to the various OW interactions, as well as their parallel surveillance technologies.

Colonialism and patriarchy simultaneously delineate between those who must be surveilled and those who are the surveillants.

23   Of course undesirable bodies are not limited to Black people. Constructed as undesirable, dispossessed, and interpreted as not belonging or being out of place—are the bodies of disabled, queer, transgender, mad, addicted, and houseless people as well.

24   Fred Moten, *The Universal Machine*; Rinaldo Walcott, *On Property*.

Saidiya Hartman reminds us that "although assertions of free will, singularity, autonomy and consent necessarily obscure relations of power and domination, the genealogy of freedom, to the contrary, discloses the intimacy of liberty, domination, and subjection."[25] Part of what this text demonstrates is the scripted and unscripted intimacies of antiBlack patriarchal violence in daily life. This calls us to place greater attention on gender and how antiBlackness typifies white supremacist cis-masculinity to the detriment of Black women. Noted above, for instance, TPSB policy explicitly states that individuals will not be discriminated against according to race and/or gender. What remains unstudied, however, and what is often poorly represented within both Canadian academic and public discourse, is how the intersection of Blackness and gender is under-theorized, resulting in a narrow historical understanding of and limited efforts to tackle the experiences of Black women and policing in Toronto more generally. Again, Black women are relegated to a periphery, in this context not only within mainstream criminology literature but also within pseudo-progressive, feminist legal studies and antiracist socio-legal studies. As a result, these studies place Black women in proximity to violence while simultaneously imagining us as protected from its wrath. Scot Wortley and Akwasi Owusu-Bempah write:

> Although black females are less likely to be stopped and questioned by the police than black males, they are significantly more likely to report police stops than white or Chinese females. In fact, black females (9%) are more likely to report three or more police stops than white (8%) or Chinese males (6%). On average, black females report 0.7 police stops in the past two years, compared to 0.4 stops for white females and 0.2 stops for Chinese females.[26]

25 Saidiya Hartman, *Scenes of Subjection: Terror, Slavery, and Self-making in Nineteenth-century America* (New York: Oxford University Press, 1997), 123.

26 Scot Wortley and Akwasi Owusu-Bempah, "Crime and Justice: The Experiences of Black Canadians," in *Diversity, Crime and Justice in Canada*, ed. Barbara Perry (New York: Oxford University Press, 2011), 127-150.

Black women's experiences remain absented. We are an afterthought in public discourse as well as more specialized legal discussions around police violence and surveillance. We can see this even in the proclamations of the Ontario Human Rights Tribunal, which by stating that they are "deeply concerned about what remains of the practice [of carding] and its impact on the African Canadian community, particularly young Black men,"[27] thereby defines Black women and Black women's experience exclusively in relation to Black men, effectively erasing not only our autonomy, but our distinct reality as ongoing subjects of state surveillance.

It would be one thing if the lone implication for Black women were a gap in intellectual knowledge production or representation in data, but there is something more urgent to address. Blackness and gender, when absented in this way, have a direct correlation with how the city's political actors have come to understand and respond to the experience of carding and state surveillance more broadly. Carding is intrinsically linked to the "Black man/boy" in Toronto, which re-inscribes national gendered logics that absent women and gender-diverse Black people and reify the Black Canadian subject as Black man/boy, an erasure that is problematic for Black men and boys and for the Black women, girls, nonbinary, gender fluid, and agender people who are ignored in the process. It is crucial to add these lacking dimensions to the understanding of and discourse around raced, gendered, and working-class experiences of surveillance, by illuminating what the experiences of Black women and Black people who are not men can teach us. For one, the experience of being both hyper-visible and targeted on the one hand, and unseen and ignored on the other, such that one suffers the violence of the state but without that injustice being noticed or conceptualized as a problem. For another, state uses of platforms, technologies, and prescriptive-predictive surveillance that is disguised as neutral but is in fact deeply inscribed in ideologies around gender, poverty, race, and undesirability.

Rich and longitudinal descriptions depicting the interlacing of

27 Ontario Human Rights Commission, Special report: Human rights and racial profiling, 2014. https://www.ohrc.on.ca/en/book/export/html/11816.

poverty, gender, and surveillance were given by many of the Black women I spoke with:

Interlocutor 9: *I remember when the welfare workers used to come in your house, when they used to check your fridge and check out your house. I remember this even as a teenager. My mom used to make sure that everything was in order before they came. This is long before you were even thinking about doing research. Maybe even before you were born? [laughter] This also happened to me sometime in the 90s, when I was on welfare and living in [redacted] with my eldest. About the same time, my worker came to do a home check.*

Idil: *What same time?*

Interlocutor 9: *Oh, oh. I meant in the 90s ... when they come to visit you, they have a time to leave. You know, there's a certain amount of time they have to do their work or ... umm ... go back to the office or whatsoever. She was there and the police came and bam bam bam [knocks on table] on my door! And they said it was because she was supposed to be somewhere and she wasn't. All that kept running through my mind was the police know my address ... and ... they know I'm on assistance.*[28]

Interlocutor 9 automatically identifies the dangerous connection between "welfare" and policing, without needing to explain to me, another Black woman, the inherent link.

It is important to note that the worker's productivity at this time superseded the privacy of the service recipient; that prioritization is exercised in the context of safety. As a worker you are perceived to be dealing with potentially unsafe people. The employer, OW, is also surveilling the workers, of course, and this is one way that state surveillance is also a trickle-down system. Certain clues can ignite this system via implications of "unsafety," whether or not the links are founded. The state's function demands to know where poor people are and what they are doing. No matter how surveillance

28   Interlocutor 9, in person interview with author, Toronto, 2018.

is being doled out, the person who is most precarious is the person who is there alone, having done nothing to have invoked any intrusion into her life, let alone of such a scale. These systems are united without the need of any documentation or reference history. The worker can just pick up the phone and give some details—and who knows what the other worker does with that information? It also bears noting that these kinds of communications are not limited to state services but are also part of the way that many community social service organizations function as well; it is as though our only way to deal with problems is via varying levels of surveillance. Being absent, for example, often results in efforts for you to be found, and efforts to be found are societally guided by a system that invariably involves the police.

As we can see, the intermingling carceralities that encircle the lives of Black women are severe and deeply ingrained. Weaving together these routinized and intimate experiences with surveillance and surveillance technologies led me to explore the connection between the Business Transformation Project (BTP, which later became linked the Service Delivery Model or SDM) database and implications of collection of CSNs by Toronto police. The complications of being documented or even of being *noted* are nuanced. As the women describe, the physical and psychological experiences of these forms of surveillance are explicit acts of violent intrusion. This is the location where an abstract ideology of neoliberalism is animated as "public safety," where concepts of safety and public interest are deployed against specific individuals. In the case of those on social assistance, these active deployments come with the justification that they are being used in order to ensure that those who access OW are not being wasteful of the state's funds.

The hyper-visibility/invisibility of Black women is particularly disturbing when one notes that although we make up only 3.1 percent of the Canadian population, we represent 6 percent of the federal prison population.[29] One of the many reasons why this disproportionality cannot be ignored is because one does not enter a prison without having to first engage multiple other state systems.

29 Jen Katshunga et al., "Black Women in Canada," 2020.

Black women come into contact with systems more readily by virtue of being poor, and/or being a leader of the household in which child welfare is deployed against them in ways that it would not be for Black men, white/off-white people, or other racialized groups. Black women are also surveilled and policed in relation to their partners and their partners' legal involvement, even when the women themselves are not directly involved. The women who contributed to this research illustrated through their narratives an inevitability of criminalization, and ultimately illustrated their graduated incarceration process through various state systems with exactitude.

What this helps to clarify are some of the most explicit effects of neoliberal models of governmental hegemony and policing for poor Black women. The anti-poverty policy of the Harris government centred Blackness, gender, and configurations of the concept of the dangerous and dishonest Black citizen. Integrated systems of surveillance and platform capitalism were a direct result of the Harris government's work-fare system, which connected state agents across Ontario, ultimately to prevent fraud. Identical logic underpinned the deployment of welfare officers into neighbourhoods on "cheque day." The primary victims and casualties of this system were working-class people, particularly women, the gender diverse or non-conforming, and children.

The concept of "welfare fraud" illustrates the ways in which women, and Black women in particular, were targeted by welfare police officers on cheque day, through fraud-tip lines and Resource Enforcement Officers—all trained and paid by the TPS.[30] Thus, just as it is often argued that Black boys and men are unduly targeted by police services, the evidence illustrates that Black girls, women, and mothers were and are not only targeted, but subjected to multi-pronged surveillance interventions, given that their personal information is already accessible to police services. The state,

---

30   Punam Kholsa and Community Social Planning Council of Toronto, "If Low Income Women of Colour Counted in Toronto: Final Report of the Action-Research Project Breaking isolation, getting involved," Community Social Planning Council of Toronto, 2003; Simon Shields, "Welfare (Ontario Works) Legal Guide, Chapter 12—Fraud and Prosecutions" 2 (d), 2020. http://www.isthatlegal.ca/index.php?name=fraud.welfare_law_ontario.

as a result, could monitor the movements of Black women and poor people for the last five days of the month and the first five days of the next month. All of these efforts, it needs to be pointed out, were in direct correlation with "innovations" related to the modernization of services, technological or administrative.

We have witnessed conversations that are critical of the modernization of policing.[31] However, what is often absent from these critiques and conversations is a mapping of the ways in which social services have also been utilizing the concepts of "modernization," "efficiencies," and "technological advancements," for decades, and in parallel to official policing practice, in their interactions with service recipients in Toronto. According to the MCSS and Commissioner of Community and Neighbourhood Services report, the "Ministry indicated that a new technological platform, supported by new business processes, would be required to both support the fundamental changes it was making at the policy level and to modernize the service delivery system across the Province."[32] After the launch of the SDM program in January 2000 there were some critical goals and objectives outlined by the Province and municipality:

> from the Province's perspective, the SDM's major components, notably the new technology platform and modified intake and case management functions, form the basis for a new, integrated and streamlined delivery system that will be implemented across Ontario by municipalities. The Province's intention, through the SDM, is to create a more efficient, cost-effective social assistance delivery system. The SDM's stated goals are to:
> - improve access to information for both clients and caseworkers;
> - ensure faster and more accurate eligibility calculations;

31   Desmond Cole, *The Skin We're In: A Year of Black Resistance and Power* (Toronto: Penguin Random House, 2020).

32   Ministry of Community & Social Services, and Commissioner of Community and Neighbourhood Services Report, 2000, 1. https://docplayer.net/52085196-Ontario-works-service-delivery-model.html.

- increase program integrity; and
- provide better client service.[33]

How these parameters are defined and how they are weighted is another thing altogether; what do "access to information," "program integrity," and "better service" actually mean? A key area that further reinforces the "modernization" project is its adherence to neoliberal ideologies, undergirded by capitalism, that boast streamlining and swiftness as inherent goods, while not addressing the negative impacts of a "platform [that] replaces the five or more separate systems that municipalities now rely on."[34] This enforced amalgamation either disregards any consideration of the ways in which these systems unjustifiably entangle particular groups of people, or it facilitates this entanglement, all the while indiscriminately disregarding privacy in the context of poverty. Winifred Poster states that "racial proclivities and assessments are given a space within the digital infrastructure [...] making the consumer the focal point," and thus increasing the commodity of communicative capitalism.[35] The entrenchment of verification (for example, two-step intake), technology, and interrelated systems of communication (for example, third-party verification sources, including private and public banks and lenders) are all couched in the guise of "improved" services whose intent is the ease of recipients' access. Under the OWA, the Province may also prescribe the technology systems used to collect and store information and establish their own performance standards. It is within this legislative context that the SDM was developed.

The more I delved into my work and research on this subject, the more it became obvious to me that it is important not only to place the Province's technological modernization efforts in conversation

33   Ibid, 1-3.
34   City of Toronto Commissioner of Community and Neighbourhood Services, "Ontario Works Service Delivery Model" 2000, 2-3. https://docplayer. net/52085196-Ontario-works-service-delivery-model.html.
35   Winifred Poster, "Racialized Surveillance in the Digital Service Economy," in *Captivating Technology: Race, Carceral Technoscience, and Liberatory Imagination in Everyday Life*, edited by Ruha Benjamin (Durham: Duke University Press, 2019b), 137.

with the current practices of policing, but also to clearly identify and make these direct links within the effects of policy and practice. Ultimately, we must take note of the ways notions of verification are directly linked with and informed by discourses and assumptions around who "needs" to be verified and measured against both scripted and unscripted policy. The processes of eligibility and assessment are always described as rudimentary standardizations, but we must recognize how they are primarily "aimed at better protecting the integrity of the social assistance program [and] consolidat[ing] several existing verification processes."[36] In the simplest of terms, the one thing that the social assistance system serves is its own maintenance, and the concept that in its current form it serves human needs is a falsehood that we must dispel.

36   City of Toronto, "Ontario Works Service Delivery Model," 2000, 1-6.

WHAT PUBLIC?

"Poor people can't afford privacy," one of my interlocutors stated matter-of-factly; and according to the accounts of ninety-seven percent of the women who spoke with me, poor Black women in particular are not afforded privacy.[1] As Black women living in poverty, my interlocutors described and discussed privacy as a fiction. In various regards, they linked their experiences of poverty to displays of, or interactions that coincided with or symbolized, their public need. Interlocutor 7:

> *I live in a small hood. The strip-mall or plaza in my area has everything: Food Basics, Tim Hortons, the post office, Shoppers, the walk-in clinic, some little Dollar Mart thingy and the welfare office…and oh, the bank is across the street, a block away from the LCBO. Point [being], everybody in the mall knows your business. It wouldn't be so bad if everyone didn't hang out at the mall or outside the mall. The cabbies are outside the Tim's or Food Basics, the old men sit in the same place at the food court, and the young people just chill outside.*[2]

The relations of the experience of public need as forcibly undertaken in public social space, and imbued with all of its complex social logics, decreased both access to and expectation of privacy for the women. They identified their experiences and the public markings

1   Interlocutor 1, in person interview with author, Toronto, 2017.
2   Interlocutor 7, in person interview with author, Toronto, 2018.

of poverty as directly or indirectly correlated with decreased public privacy and described the nature of their spatial interactions with public/publicized poverty as an additional source of non-consensual surveillance of poor people, and more specifically of themselves as poor Black women. In a completely different suburb, nearly fifty kilometeres away from Interlocutor 7, another woman, Interlocutor 12, shared similar sentiments:

> *They wouldn't put a hospital in a food court, but they would put* [a] *food court in a hospital!? You see what I'm showing you, Idil?… All I'm saying is any and anybody going shopping doesn't need to know I'm on wellie* [welfare]. *I don't know what's in their pocket, am I right?*[3]

Both women designate here how social assistance offices,[4] a so-called public service, fail even before the moment of access. These "public services" in effect fail them before they enter the building within which they are meant to gain assistance, by failing to respect their privacy and autonomy, and setting them up at the outset for exposure and scrutiny. Here I need to be clear: these women were not ashamed of whether or not they need to access public services, but they are pointing out the thoughtlessness of things like planning. Access to social assistance is not considered something around which anyone deserves any privacy, and as systems and individuals fail to account for shared communities, privacy and access decrease as poverty increases. So again, this is not a matter of shame; what is at issue is privacy, and the expectation—based on experience—of these women, is that they face a reality in which there is no thought of their own privacy put into planning.

In considering who in society is emboldened to point out this kind of targeted inequity in planning, we can also look to the ways that these interpretations by Black women speaking to the spatial measures enforced through their access to OW within the

---

3   Interlocutor 12, in person interview with author, Toronto, 2018.
4   Throught this text I use the terms "welfare office," "social assistance office," and "OW office" interchangeably.

Toronto city space are similar to those of Black artists, poets, and intellectuals who have scaled, (un)marked, and documented the Blackened sites of Toronto—the locations central to BlackLife in the city. Nevertheless, such contributions remain ignored and outside of what many recognize as disciplines and/or "scholarly" sites attendant to these concerns. Austin Clarke, Dionne Brand, Abdi Osman, Canisia Lubrin, Amanda Paris, and M. NourbeSe Philip are a few who have created integral city-space readings of BlackLife that also result in a texturing and narrating of the antiBlack cartography of Toronto.[5] Among many other artists and intellectuals, they illuminate sites in the city that are often forgotten or understood as devoid of Blackness and Black livabilities. The combined invocation of the voices of the women in this book and those of the Black artists, intellectuals, and thinkers who live in this city allows, if taken seriously, for us to engage in sensations and readings of space outside the mainstream, and not only to gather an understanding of how these spaces are experienced by Black people, but of how in fact they are structured in order to ensure that specific kinds of strictures ensue, and endure.

Perhaps seemingly disparate, these are nonetheless the voices against officialdom. I should add that this is not to say that academics can never be voices against officialdom. After all, I am here; but we are so much more constrained, funneled, and prescribed in our words and their structuring than the artist, intellectual, and Black voice that is not tethered (in select contexts) to institutional rules and commitments. I could also add that that officialdom is not the exclusive domain of the academy; the blue checkmark is its own constraint. It is noteworthy that the critical works of Black artists and intellectuals have not traversed into and onto ostensibly whitewashed disciplines such as urban planning, which becomes primarily relevant because Toronto is a large urban metropolis. When contending with all of this we must consider the ways in which "urban" is often synonymous with Black, racialized, and

5   Also see Phoebe Wang, Canisia Lubrin, and Dionne Brand *The Unpublished City: Volume II essays* (Toronto: Bookthug. 2018).

working-class or poor communities. Therefore, centring Black livabilities should by virtue of this become a task of the urban planning profession but also a site of struggle, given that we are aware of the erasure inherent in disciplinary, often subliminal, white supremacist messaging. Specific to the field of urban planning, scholars Edward Goetz, Rashad Williams, and Anthony Damiano remark that this gap in both study and social awareness is due to "insufficient theorization of White supremacy" in the field, and their sentiments can indeed be echoed across a variety of disciplines.[6]

In critiques of the concept of urbanness and its connection to race and racism, some argue that a narrow, essentialized categorization, that focuses discourses around "racial concentration," give rise to and increase structural inequity through such focus, by downplaying the role of advantaged communities.[7] Not only is white supremacy revealed "in producing and perpetuating regional inequality, [but t]he unjust social burdens of 'dark ghettos' are mirrored by the unjust advantages conferred upon White neighborhoods of affluence."[8] In Canada, scholars such as Karina Vernon, Cheryl Teelucksingh, and Igrid Waldron have been doing formative work probing the Canadian landscape for its ongoing racist, classist antiBlackness, while underscoring the fact that these apparatuses were also exercised on Indigenous peoples across Turtle Island in a way that served, and continues to serve, as a blueprint of raced domination.[9]

A dearth of literature and research on geographic and environmental racism still exists, but the experiences of the interlocutors bring to bear several novel, necessary, and at times contradictory

6   Edward G. Goetz, Rashad A. Williams, and Anthony Damiano, "Whiteness and Urban Planning," *Journal of the American Planning Association* 86, 2 (2020): 142.

7   Ibid.

8   Ibid.

9   Karina Vernon, *The Black Prairie Archives: An Anthology* (Waterloo, Ontario: Wilfrid Laurier University Press, 2019; Cheryl Teelucksingh, "Environmental Racialization: Linking Racialization to the Environment Canada," *Local Environment* 12,6 (2007): 645–661; Ingrid Waldron, "Re-Thinking Waste: Mapping Racial Geographies of Violence on the Colonial Landscape." *Environmental Sociology* 4,1(2018): 36–53.

entry points for analysis. On the one hand, as we have seen, some of the women address the deserted, and often industrial communities to which they had to travel far to seek services. Others highlighted the impact of having the welfare office situated directly within their immediate communities—for example, inside the mall, or at storefront buildings that face main streets, and/or at the corner of busy intersections.

Interlocutors also illuminated the industrial locale and the prison-like architecture of the welfare office and other such sites, which necessitates some nuanced analysis. This kind of far-flung site goes beyond the existing narrow scope of a "not in my backyard" discourse that continues to be contentious. Taken together, these textured narratives also speak to a concept of access by exile, that may on the surface seem to contradict the overexposure and removal of privacy inherent in the ultra-visible or centralized site of access. But systems of control are varied, and contingent on numerous other factors. By placing these narratives into figurative conversation with each other, we can see a multivalenced and layered set of revocations of privacy and already limited autonomy within Black women's experiences of space and place.

I frame the term surveillance with broad intent to describe the ways Black women's humanity and personhood are marked, controlled, and ultimately policed in their interactions, not only with OW as a service but also as a policy that enforces a social and racialized spatial system. The experience of surveillance as described by the women who spoke with me often began prior to their entry into the OW office. Six of them described their spatial interactions and the public marking of their poverty prior to entrance. Interlocutor 3:

> *The welfare office faces the main street, Sheppard Avenue West. I get off the bus and everybody knows where I was going. That may not matter to other people, but I live on Sheppard West and I take that bus all the time.*[10]

---

10   Interlocutor 3, in person interview with author, Toronto, 2017.

What Interlocutor 3 reveals here is the significance of the street as not merely a locale but as a space imbued with racialized capitalist meanings, which demarcate various socio-geographical and status markings of personhood, including the relationship between the self and the spatial constitution of the social self. What appears mundane to others—exiting a bus at your designated stop—is in fact "demonstrating that *geography*, the material world, is infused with sensations and distinct ways of knowing,"[11] or minimally illuminates distinct ways of experiencing movement as raced, transportation as raced, and the mundanity of Black existence as raced, restricted, dangerous, and dispossessed.[12]

We come to conceptualize Black people as shipment.[13] The fact that the systems that house, transport, and incarcerate us do not have to recognize that we are participants in these accounts further substantiates the claims that we as Black people are considered property and non-citizen, and therefore not deserving of regard.[14] Discussing the brilliance of scholar and poet Dionne Brand, Katherine Mckittrick writes that Brand's decision,

> to disclose that geography is always human and that humanness is always geographic—blood, bones, hands, lips, wrists, this is your land, your planet, your road, your sea—suggests that her surroundings are speakable. And this speakability is not only communicated through the poet, allowing her to emphasize the alterability of space and place, to give up on land and imagine new geographic stories; in [our] work, geography holds in it the possibility to speak for itself.[15]

11   Katherine McKittrick, *Demonic Grounds* (Minneapolis: University of Minnesota Press, 2006), ix.

12   See the works of M. Jacqui Alexander, Beverly Bain, Toni Cade Bambara, Dionne Brand, Peggy Bristow, Carole Boyce Davies, Linda Carty, Afua Cooper, Enakshi Dua, Saidiya Hartman, Canisia Lubrin, M. Nourbese Philip, Angela Robertson, Adrienne Shadd, Christina Sharpe, Makeda Silvera, Julia Sudbury, and Sylvia Wynter.

13   M. Nourbese Philip, *Zong* (Middletown, Conn.: Wesleyan University Press, 2008).

14   Rinaldo Walcott, *On Property*.

15   Katherine McKittrick, *Demonic Grounds*, xiv.

The words of Interlocutor 3 speak to the geography of "the Black poor," the working-class and (un)workable, (un)categorized Black woman; the (un)seen Black woman, literal and figurative in her state-sanctioned bivouac. She is subsumed in Fanon's concept of solely the exterior in being, as if the realm of the socially recognized "personal" does not ensure the privacy of the truly personal, and as if the ways that society consumes all of her iterations, imagination, and interminability, necessitates obliviousness to the white supremist cartographies that control and create Black existence in so-called Canada.[16]

It is the bus stop—the *stop*, the *interruption*—that observably removes her from notions of productivity and meaningful citizenship, which mark her as "poor," branding her and her Blackness as destinationally destitute. Her relationship with space, with the geography of poverty, marks her as requiring state surveillance and intervention and of being below the lines of efficacy, social productivity, legitimacy, and innocence, thus permitting interventions based on this presumed Black incapacity and culpability. This all signals what a BlackLife is in the Canadian context: again, none other than gendered, raced, spaced, and demarcated as Black and as working-class, and often as dangerous.[17]

This marking of Interlocutor 3 through her destination set her apart from the general occupant and rider of the TTC (Toronto Transit Commission); for her, it translated into a removal from community, including from an already under-employed and working-class Black community. She added, *"shame isn't shame if you're smart. If people know you work, and you're doing your thing…then cool! But otherwise, welfare is heat on all levels. No one wants to go to that place* [the location of the welfare office]." The bus ride "outs" and demarcates her as poor, or poorer than most on the Sheppard

16   See Franz Fanon, *The Wretched of the Earth*, translated by Constance Farrington (Harmondsworth, England: Penguin, 1967); and Franz Fanon *Black Skin, White Masks* (London: Pluto, 2008).

17   See *Philip and Dionne Brand* (Fredericton: Goose Lane, 1994); Canisia Lubrin, *Voodoo Hypothesis: poems* (Hamilton: Buckrider Books, 2017); M. Nourbese Philip, *Blank: Essays & Interviews* (Toronto: BookThug, 2017).

bus. Therefore, poverty for Interlocutor 3 as a lived experience, is also connected to a discourse of privately/publicly shared poverty, including the shared social housing unit in which she resides, and what she describes ultimately is a public poverty that can manifest in the mere geographic locating of her status in a stop or interruption in her life, namely the publicly marked social assistance office. While this may not make sense for most, it is real, substantive, and logical, both for Interlocutor 3 and in my own experience. It is a creation of hierarchy, animated by social services and a culturally assigned shame of "need," that may or may not be invisible to the reader.

The bus ride essentially replicates the broader social world in which Interlocutor 3 lives. While she may live in social housing, and in a broader context of poverty evident to those who share the same condition, she shares a particular reality and narrative with the people that ride the Sheppard West bus. Those individuals may understand her first as a young mother, a Black woman, and someone who reads to her child on the way to daycare. While for Interlocutor 3 or for myself, these narratives are not in contradiction with her being a recipient of social services, these delineations are particularly prevalent for her as signifiers of Blackened and impoverished spaces, but also spaces of unshared citizenship primarily based on journey, race, and class.

The status marking of self occurs with a certain degree of agency but is plagued by need and the resulting system engagement that stems from that need. The will is involved, but insofar as it is to engage a system based on need, to participate only in that specific, limited, and need-based interaction; it is not engaged in order to mark the self as permanently spatially and socio-politically oriented to a geographic space that is being accessed in order to survive. In other words, survival-driven, and perforce forced, such spatial relationships do not root the self into accessed space, but instead push one's existence to be always a temporal encounter, in an unending cycle of temporal encounters. Interlocutor 20 speaks to this forced public marking:

I remember the first time I parked my car in their [Ontario Works's] *parking lot, the guy working in the booth* [lot attendant] *asked me where I was going. I told him. He gave me a different-coloured parking receipt from everyone else in line; I felt embarrassed! I didn't want to tell him where I was going because it was a public parking lot, but I had no choice.*[18]

Colour, and in this case the coloured slip, is and remains representative of difference in the social world, be it in one's private life, in public policy, in popular culture, or in a parking lot. The solicitations that demand differential interactions are underscored by Blackness/antiBlackness and its associated logics. This is what Interlocutor 20 describes above, emphasizing how exchanges mark, rank and mitigate identity within spaces and how silences and things unspoken are often colour-coded and antiBlack, imbued with meaning and dictating a dynamic of power. In the Canadian context, notions of colour or race as a dynamic of freedom and/or the right to movement for Black people is not new. Take for example the Code Noir (1685 and 1724), which "protect[ed] white [people] from forms of slave violence: theft, revolt, and escape" while limiting Black people's movement and spatial autonomy.[19]

Interlocutor 20 evokes another curious point when she says, "*I didn't want to tell him where I was going because it was a public parking lot, but I had no choice.*" What she foregrounds as urgent is the immediate grappling that had to occur—her need for privacy against her need to access service—which ultimately, for her, was where she was defined by poverty. Hence, being poor placed her in a position in which she had no privacy in the geographic space. Of course, one could argue that anyone who experiences poverty might have experienced the same tension. I certainly cannot disagree with that, but what remains notable is that Interlocutor 20 added, "*and…I was the only Black person in line.*"

18   Interlocutor 20, in person interview with author, Toronto, 2018.
19   Robin W. Winks, *The Blacks In Canada: A History 2nd ed.* (McGill-Queens University Press, 1997), 7.

As mentioned earlier, space and body, or the "vessels of human violence" are interrelated for Black people, and for Black women more acutely.[20] The Black women in this book experience geography in a way that shapes their physical and environmental experience of poverty and antiBlackness. This is within the very nature of most of our interactions and the architectures we navigate. We must challenge ideologies that dislocate Black humanity from space materially, because as we "anchor our selfhood and feet to the ground, it seemingly calibrates and normalizes where, and therefore who, we are."[21] This can also mean where we should or should not be, based on who we are. Interlocutor 17 highlighted her experience of feeling like she was removed from the rest of the world:

> *The office was in God's back! They sent me to the middle of nowhere! Why would the welfare office be in the middle of factories? Far from the TTC? There was nothing else in sight besides the factories, me, and my kids. Why wouldn't the fucking office be near people who need it? It was...like, like, I was being sent to the middle of nowhere as a punishment* [shakes head and sighs]*...maybe the office was so far away so we don't get there? I don't know...it was in God's back, trust me!*[22]

Interlocutor 13 shared similar feelings:

> *It was like they were throwing us away. The welfare office wasn't close to where we live. It was hard to get there but because it was far. I was also late for my appointments and they* [the workers] *hate that.*[23]

Various symbolic conditions make banal racism possible via "boundary-making practices supported by policy and law and how

---

20   Katherine McKittrick, "Reclaiming Difference: Caribbean Women Rewrite Postcolonialism," *Resources for Feminist Research* 31, 3/4 (2006): 146-148.
21   Katherine McKittrick, *Demonic Grounds*, xi.
22   Interlocutor 17, in person interview with author, Toronto, 2018.
23   Interlocutor 13, in person interview with author, Toronto, 2018.

the spatialization of racial and other identities inform the spatial segregation and containment of Indigenous and racialized bodies in spaces associated with poverty, crime, and waste and pollution."[24] The convergences of geographic racism, poverty, financialization, and antiBlack racism are not new discussions. However, the women in the above examples are describing the figurative shifts and boundarylessness that existing literature often speaks to but does not concretize. Their accounts provide direct synthesis by directing our understanding to how the welfare line as a physically contained and geographic space, *moved* from that space (the building) into the parking lot or to the bus stop, and became a part of intimate yet public interactions with the lot attendant and on the bus.

All of my interlocutors expressed the ways in which poverty, geography, and race collided in order to create conditions that "outed," removed, and/or disrupted them. In each instance what is made clear is the ways in which geography, place-making, and marking come together and map in- and onto Black women—what Charyl Teelucksingh refers to as "environmental racialization."[25] That is, not only in the ways in which these experiences intersect, but how they are compounded by modes of racialization and are central to politics of structure and power. This is more than merely intersection, it is a strengthened interlocking, the layering and reinforcement of an all-permeating glue.

The Closed-Circuit Welfare Office

With the advent of new technologies running parallel to neoliberal priorities, the twentieth and early twenty-first centuries have seen apparatuses of surveillance become increasingly technological and biomedical.[26] Crucial to these networks of surveillance are mechanisms like closed-circuit televisions (CCTVs), which "consist of

---

24 Ingrid Waldron, "Re-thinking waste: mapping racial geographies of violence on the colonial landscape," *Environmental Sociology* 4, 1 (2018): 37.

25 Cheryl Teelucksingh, "Environmental Racialization: Linking Racialization to the Environment in Canada," *Local Environment* 12, 6 (2007): 649.

26 See Ruha Benjamin, "The Emperor's New Genes: Science, Public Policy, and the Allure of Objectivity," *The Annals of the American Academy of Political and Social Science* 661 (2015): 130–142, and *Race After Technology* and *Captivating Technology*.

a camera coupled by a cable to a display monitor."[27] CCTV or camera surveillance is the archetype of contemporary surveillance technology's process; historically, CCTVs were found in private spaces and were often used in commercial sites like malls and convenience stores.[28] Early models of CCTVs were propagated as an invaluable tool to protect business owners from theft, and more importantly to protect the property of owners and institutions generally.

In his study of the global growth of CCTV as a means of surveillance, Clive Norris explains the increased growth in their use since the mid-1960s.[29] CCTV units are often cheap and they have a do-it-yourself attractiveness, making them accessible; in a ubiquitously "Googleable" era, the system is often also self-contained and surveillance-ready by simple camera hookup and following basic instructions. They are accessible, "easy," and don't require any specialized skill, which is also why by the early 1990s more than ten cities in nations around the world, including Canada, had adopted the use of CCTVs. Sherbrooke, Quebec, a small, predominantly French-speaking university town known for its eight institutions of higher education, was the first Canadian site to institute a public surveillance camera in 1991.[30] A few years later in 1994, the police department in Sudbury, Ontario, a town located approximately four hours north of Toronto, installed CCTV cameras in the downtown core.[31] Sherbrooke and Sudbury shared the philosophy that the

27   Clive Norris, "There's No Success Like Failure and Failure's No Success at All: Some Critical Reflections on Understanding the Global Growth of CCTV Surveillance," in *Eyes Everywhere: The Global Growth of Camera Surveillance*, edited by Aaron Doyle, Randy Lippert, David Lyon (New York: Routledge, 2013), 23-45.

28   See Aaron Doyle, Randy Lippert and David Lyon (eds). *Eyes Everywhere: The Global Growth of Camera Surveillance* (New York: Routledge, 2012).

29   Clive Norris, "There's No Success Like Failure and Failure's No Success at All," 23.

30   Gavin Smith, "What Goes up, Must Come down: On the Moribundity of Camera Networks in the UK," in *Eyes Everywhere*, 2013, 46-66; Jennifer Whitson, Aaron Doyle, Kevin Walby, et al., "A Report on Camera Surveillance in Canada Part One," Surveillance Camera Awareness Network, 2009. https://www.academia.edu/2518732/A_Report_on_Camera_Surveillance_in_Canada_Part_One.

31   Gavin Smith, "What Goes up, Must Come down."

cameras would deter, monitor, and capture undesirable people and behaviours.[32] In both Sherbrooke and Sudbury, the cameras were placed in downtown bar districts by local police to prevent alleged "delinquent behaviour."[33]

While no direct correlation can be traced, during this same period in the early 1990s there was an influx of Black Africans and Muslims into both cities, and this may have contributed to the desire for the installation of cameras. We are also aware that frequent acts of violence in public spaces often result in the advocacy and rationalization for the installation of these devices. The cameras in the downtown core have yet to deter crime in that area. In fact, while camera and CCTV usage in Canada continues to increase steadily, and many Canadians believe that CCTVs are an effective and useful tool for keeping them safe, camera technology does not actually guarantee safety, and we have no research to date in Canada to establish any connection between CCTV surveillance and safety or lower crime rates.[34]

Moreover, numerous scholars have found that while some Canadians relish the appearance of safety via CCTV, many are simply unaware of the basic functioning of these technologies of surveillance.[35] Emily Smith notes:

> Canadians indicated that camera surveillance is 'somewhat effective' in reducing crime in both community (public CCTV systems) and in-store (private systems).

32   Jennifer Whitson, et al., "A Report on Camera Surveillance in Canada Part One,"; Emily Smith, "The Piecemeal Development of Camera Surveillance in Canada" in *Eyes Everywhere: The Global Growth of Surveillance*, edited by Aaron Doyle, Randy Lippert, and David Lyon (New York: Routledge, 2013).

33   Quebec Ministére de la sécurité publique, "Partners in Crime Prevention: For a Safer Québec, Section II Crime Prevention: a Necessity, 1993. https://www.securitepublique.gouv.qc.ca/en/police-prevention/report-of-the-task-force-on-crime-prevention/en-ligne/section-ii-crime-prevention-a-necessity.html; Patricia Pickett, "Keeping a Watchful Eye on Video Surveillance," *Canadian Security*, August 12, 2009, https://www.canadiansecuritymag.com/keeping-a-watchful-eye-on-video-surveillance/.

34   Emily Smith, "The Piecemeal Development of Camera Surveillance in Canada."

35   Dawson, et al., 2009.

However, only about one-third of those polled claimed to be even 'somewhat familiar' with CCTV as a surveillance technology.[36]

This lack of knowledge regarding CCTV cameras' function, coupled with the limited evidence that they actually deter crime, suggests that Canadians are more invested in the philosophies, policies, and practices that *allude* to safety than in substantively responding to real issues of public safety, and particularly a conception of public safety that encompasses the safety of everyone.

Aaron Doyle et al. frame the camera as the epitome of modern surveillance.[37] I would argue that despite a generalized lack of understanding of the true nature and function of camera surveillance, because of its now-presumed ubiquity—if not in an always complete physical manifestation but as an assumed presence—CCTV falls under what Foucault identifies as discipline, writing that discipline:

> may be identified neither with an institution nor with an apparatus; it is a type of power, a modality for its exercise, comprising a whole set of instruments, techniques, procedures, levels of application, targets; it is a 'physics' or an 'anatomy' of power, a technology.[38]

Multiple interlocutors highlighted the use of CCTV cameras and the hyper-securitization of the physical space they had to navigate. Interlocutor 9 related the following:

> *There are cameras all over. On the outside of the building, once you get through the main door, everywhere! You have to be buzzed in and once you enter, there are cameras all over the waiting room. It's fucking bullshit because there's*

36   Emily Smith, "The Piecemeal Development of Camera Surveillance in Canada," 124.
37   Aaron Doyle et al., *Eyes Everywhere.*
38   Michel Foucault, *Discipline and Punish* (New York, Vintage, 1979), 237.

nothing to steal. Everything is bolted to the ground, the chairs, the table, everything! [chuckles].[39]

Ridiculing the nonsensical nature of the over-securitization of the interior and exterior of the building, Interlocutor 9 (through, it should be noted, her own awareness that in the absence of any potential reason for the cameras, she herself is necessarily the camera's subject) draws our attention to the layered usage of the CCTV cameras—how the camera intersects with other mechanisms of surveillance. For her, the experience of being watched was closely linked with how she and the other women experienced and interpreted the physical space—the rationalities and irrationalities of it—including experiences of social exchange at the OW office. In our conversation she zeroed in on a number of key elements: she reflected on the sound of the buzzer and the cameras on the inside of the building, coupled with the anchored furniture in the office. She went on to add, *"even the pen is on a chain,"* highlighting how something as insignificant as a pen can be a part of the metrics of surveillance and securitization, and ultimately criminalization and dehumanization as well. Another woman explicitly compared the OW office to a prison:

I remember walking into the office and it felt like a prison. I've never been in prison before [chuckles]. But I think it would be like the office setup. The whole place has cameras. On the outside, inside, at the front desk.[40]

It is shameful but not surprising that this interlocutor's experience of accessing social services is similar to, or representative to her, of a prison. It illustrates how experiences of antiBlack gendered undesirability, poverty, and unproductivity, and a general lack of societal worth, engenders a physical, social, and emotional constriction and containment, and the ways it is inseparable from one's affective or spiritual experience of space. This is consistent with what Doyle

39   Interlocutor 9, in person interview with author, Toronto, 2018.
40   Interlocutor 16, in person interview with author, Toronto, 2018.

et al. have outlined, namely how surveillance serves to place certain groups under greater "official scrutiny" in order to increase the reach of "surveillance societies and systems" on those groups.[41] Below, Interlocutors 10, 1, and 15 eloquently relate their experiences of being placed under increased "official" and unofficial scrutiny, and how those systems of scrutiny create conditions of containment and bodily limiting of Black women who are accessing services.

There is a particular way the OW clients are asked to interact in open public spaces in the office. One interlocutor described being herded like animals while seeking service. She explained:

> *You feel like sheep. It reminded me of the refugee camp and where I was held on my way here* [to Canada]. *I remember seeing my flatmate in the office and when I wanted to say "Hi," I was screamed at by the front-desk worker. Like... why can't we talk to each other?*[42]

These testimonies affirm and further what Jonathan Finn cautions when he writes that although people typically associate surveillance with "police and state monitoring" of individuals, surveillance exists today "more as a constitutive element of social life. More than a material or technical apparatus—more than a camera—surveillance has become a way of seeing."[43] All of the women in this book described how surveillance is pervasive in contemporary life and, in particular, enforced upon those deemed as "needing" to be surveilled. Surveillance, however, is not a singular technology that operates outside of human interactions, but exists alongside and embedded within interpersonal exchanges. Some women revealed that while they may not have seen cameras on the outside of the office, it is their belief that other methods were used as mechanisms of surveillance. Interlocutor 19, for instance, shared the following:

41   Aaron Doyle et. al., *Eyes Everywhere*, 3.
42   Interlocutor 15, in person interview with author, Toronto, 2018.
43   Jonathan Finn, "Surveillance as Social Practice" in *Eyes Everywhere* (Routledge, New York, 2012), 67.

I'm not sure if there are cameras on the outside of the office
but there was a security guard working inside the office
and a camera that faced the lobby. I also think that in the
smaller rooms where you go for your appointment, there are
cameras there as well.[44]

As Norris describes, the camera is used in daily exchanges as a tool
for authentication and validation.[45] Its purpose is always to provide potential evidence; it assumes and anticipates criminality, and
it inevitably communicates to recipients of social assistance how
they have been defined within this space. As such, it co-creates the
relationships within the service office. Surveillance, Finn asserts,
"has morphed from a technology to a way of seeing and a way of
being."[46] The violence of the resulting environment is reflected in
what Interlocutor 16 describes as the, "*heaviness of the air*" and "*the
taste of dirt in the air*," which made it difficult for her to breathe
with ease.[47] Without further explanation, her experience could be
misattributed to a number of physical environmental issues, but
Interlocutor 16 was clear; she explained that for her it was "*everything—the environment, everything. That place disturbs my spirit!*"[48]

The experience of these women attests to the ways in which
surveillance is not neutral, but can affect, psychically and even
spiritually, what it "sees." A national study conducted in Milan,
Italy by Chiara Fonio found that two particular social groups
were categorized and "targeted on the basis of their appearances:
young people, in particular those who were poorly dressed, and
nice looking women."[49] This suggests that CCTV does not result

44   Interlocutor 19, in person interview with author, Toronto, 2018.
45   Clive Norris, "There's No Success Like Failure and Failure's No Success at All,"
      2013.
46   Jonathan Finn, "Surveillance as Social Practice," in *Eyes Everywhere: The Global
      Growth of Surveillance*, edited by Aaron Doyle et al. (New York: Routledge,
      2012), 78.
47   Interlocutor 16, in person interview with author, Toronto, 2018.
48   Ibid.
49   Chiara Fonio, "Surveillance and Identity Towards a New Anthropology of the
      Person," Paper presented at the British Sociological Association conference,
      2007, 14.

in an impartial seeing of undifferentiated "reality"; rather, surveillance always represents a *gaze*, and therefore comes with the biases inherent in any gaze. Rather than being an objective capture, it actually functions as the opposite, distilling and enforcing bias. Another example of this can be seen in Lynsey Dubbeld's study of railway CCTV footage in the Netherlands. In this study Dubbeld revealed the selective targeting practices of railway operators who:

> had their own ways of categorizing and classifying the objects of their surveillance. Operators identified suspicious individuals as "Naffers" (short for North Africans, usually Moroccan or Turkish men) or called them "cockroaches," "crazy pancakes," "little rats," "nazis," "faggots," "annoying little men," "mongols."[50]

It is clear that CCTV does not function within a neutral, benign, or impartial framework. There is a discourse of power, protection, and property embedded in the idea of one's need to protect one's self from something or someone, thereby making it "essential to recognize that CCTV is not merely a technical system—it is a socio-technical system."[51] The very concept of surveillance is socially wielded and lineated, and surveillance systems are not simply "capturing" undesirable acts, they are (re)producing actors and images of transgressors that contribute to socio-technical systems and a culture of seeing surveillantly.[52] Thus, although the visual culture of camera surveillance has been touted as a means of curbing police violence against Black people, for example, through cell phone video and body cameras, this optimism must be examined; the whole functionality of "seeing," of using these technologies,

---

50 Lynsey Dubbeld, *The Regulation of the Observing Gaze: Privacy Implications of Camera Surveillance*, Phd diss, University of Twente (2004), 121; Lynsey Dubbeld, "The Role of Technology in Shaping CCTV Surveillance Practices." *Information, Communication & Society* 8, 1 (2005): 84–100.

51 Clive Norris, "There's No Success Like Failure and Failure's No Success at All," 24.

52 Jonathan Finn, "Seeing Surveillantly: Surveillance as Social Practice," in *Eyes Everywhere: The Global Growth of Camera Surveillance* edited by Aaron Doyle et al. (New York: Routledge, 2012), 78-79.

is embedded in the ongoing reproduction of the Black object of surveillance, which results in a seeing, sensing, and sanctioning that is already antiBlack.

My interlocutors' testimonies illuminate how gendered antiBlack poverty serves as a systemic kindling that ensures that Black women are contained within and passed between various social service systems. Beyond this, however, the gaze of surveillance, especially in the form of gendered, antiBlack surveillance and the unscripted policies that constitute less transparent modes of monitoring, reveals how Black women are subjected to the white supremacist projections of criminality and need for control that govern the social service environment.

Surveillance does not end with CCTV footage or the physical space of the welfare office; rather, once Black women enter the office their interactions in the space are also dictated by monitoring and physical directives according to rules and policies often unknown to them. Interlocutor 10:

> *There are marks on the floor…like on the highway for distance, you know? The marks tell you where to sit, how far to stand from people, and how far to stand away from the glass* [and therefore the front desk worker]. *Why would you need to stand far away from the glass, isn't the glass already to protect them? It's stupid.*[53]

Containments appear and manifest in observable and unobservable ways. Manifestations of these modes of containment or symbols of distancing and corralling are only visible to us once they limit us, or when they emerge as a limit to our individual desires. I write this in the midst of the COVID-19 pandemic that has taken the lives of over 6.3 million people globally as of June 2022, and the lives of over 3600 people in the Greater Toronto Area as of late September

---

53   Interlocutor 10. Please note that these are pre-COVID demarcations, but they, too, serve a function of governing bodily movement through spaces.

2021.[54] "Social distancing" and "physical distancing" became every-day terms, and protests in some sectors of society against what is perceived as a restriction on citizens' freedoms have increased dramatically. My research was conducted prior to the COVID-19 pandemic, but what stands out for me in our current context is the casualness with which Interlocutor 10 reminds us that particular bodies—Black bodies yes, as well as queer, crip, disabled, Deaf, and mad bodies, among others—have always been "distanced."

The women who shared their stories and time with me were all too familiar with the entrenched physical and socio-spiritual prac-tices of distancing that have dispossessed and dislocated them for years and continue to do so today.[55] Interlocutor 1:

> *There're all these rules posted on the wall: you can't talk on*
> *your phone, you have to turn off your ringer, you can't talk*

54   Government of Ontario, 2021. https://covid-19.ontario.ca/data/case-numbers-and-spread.

55   The *Toronto Fallout: Half A Year In the life of COVID-19* report confirmed what was to be expected: the individuals and families most impacted by COVID-19 are those who earned below $30,000 a year. The fact that the "most racialized parts of the city had 10 times more cases than the least racialized parts of the city" (7) illuminates several socio-political indicators fundamental to the social determinants of health. The limits of this study do not allow for an in-depth discussion of this issue; however, these realities must be noted. There remains much to be said about the roles played by health, social and public policy and their actors in the increased surveillance of predominately racialized communities, coupled with rhetoric of rewards constructed around people with precarious citizenship status who were granted status as a result of participating in the response to COVID-19. Many racialized people must enter a battleground in order to access meaningful, good-paying jobs, healthcare, and in some cases citizenship in this country, and COVID-19 made this fact particularly visible. On Tuesday April seventh, 2020, Ontario Premier Doug Ford, in one of his many COVID addresses, said, "we are calling on reinforcements [...]. If you are listening, if you have medical training, if you want to save lives, we need you. Join the fight today because we need every person in this fight" (*Ontario Asks Anyone with Medical Background to Step Forward to Fight COVID-19*, 2020). We witnessed for the second time (the first time was during SARS) the deployment of the Medicine Act (1991); we also observed the creation of the Ontario Matching Portal (OMP, 2020) to recruit, among others, internationally trained healthcare professionals for the pandemic response. All of this demonstrates that the state was never incapable of granting status and providing quicker access to quality employment, but chose not to offer these things to often-vulnerable populations until this served its own ends.

loudly, you can't argue with the worker or they'll kick you out and call the police. But yow! There are no rules for the workers. They can carry on any and any way with you, eh. Believe me![56]

Interlocutors 3, 20, and 2 described the casual nature of the intimate indignities of privacy violations within the welfare office:

They [workers] *all get privacy, but we don't.*[57]

They [workers] *yell your name out loud in the waiting room and I'm sitting beside my neighbour who is very mix-up.*[58]

They [workers] *want us to all see each other but we can never see them. We can only ever see the one person who we work with. But all the workers and everybody can always see us.*[59]

It's notable that the indignities recounted here are often offered up in these women's declarations *in direct contrast* to the markedly free discretion of OW workers over their lives, autonomy, and privacy. The concern in this context is that not only are the interactions of the women being dictated by OW workers, but because they are poor and accessing public assistance, presumptive determinations have been made about the potential threat they pose—predominantly toward public safety and the workers, but also via an assumed inherent volatility that restricts and guards their intra-personal interactions with each other as service recipients. To be clear, the conditions that create surveillance are state-informed, condoned, and are both collectively and individually (re)enforced. And while it has been well established that Black women's experiences are embedded in gendered legacies of colonialism, there remains a gap in understanding and a lack of theorization about how policy is

---

56   Interlocutor 1, in person interview with author, Toronto, 2017.
57   Interlocutor 3, in person interview with author, Toronto, 2017.
58   Interlocutor 20, in person interview with author, Toronto, 2018.
59   Interlocutor 2, in person interview with author, Toronto, 2017.

maneuvered beyond commonly exercised ideologies that ultimately seek to control behaviour(s) between Black women and the state and its agents.

Also under-examined is how the state can intervene in and regulate Black women's relationships with each other, as became clear in this study. Interlocutor 15, for example, describes the impact of not even being able to interact with her "flatmate" in the office. She gestures here toward how surveillance seeks to interrupt and disrupt the interpersonal relationships between and amongst Black women. We must move outside of our conceptualized and often abstract framings of surveillance, power, and control in order to unearth and understand how the law and both formal and informal policies are also deployed "in [an] effort to prevent rebellion."[60] Because what is a larger threat than a Black woman? Black *women*, of course—Black women who discuss, organize, and shape the autonomy of Black communities, those who sustain Black communities, and those who over and over again create and recreate the foundations of resistance and freedom.

Surveilled Containments and Transactional Sites

The women's expressions and interactions took place in what I refer to as *surveilled containments* and *transactional sites*. I define surveilled containments as complicated life-sites; for example, the welfare office building, the housing complex, the shelter. In addition to these shared sites are all the informal and consented-to normativities, such as common knowledge of a shared struggle, which produce a shared site and structure: the shared welfare waiting room, the shared housing complex, the shared day-program room, the shared hospital ward, treatment centre, and the prison range and cell. As a result, these sites and structural containments make acceptable particularized acts and practices of surveillance, which are inseparable from what I have described as the structures that produce surveillance. An example of this can be found in the expectation and anticipation of surveillance in certain (raced,

---

60   Andrea J. Ritchie, *Invisible No More: Police Violence Against Black Women and Women of Color* (Boston: Beacon Press, 2017).

classed, abled, and gendered) spaces, particularly spaces related to need, service, and discipline; these are all what I refer to as transactional sites.

The notion of transactional sites becomes particularly important given that Ontario Works functions, or seeks to function, as a short-term income-replacement program. Emphasizing and conceptualizing the transactional nature of surveilled containment offers an entry point that suggests that if a space is transactional, so too will become the bodies of those who occupy such a space. This illuminates the temporary nature of such a space. Being surveilled or willing to be surveilled becomes in fact, an element of currency in these transactions. But the fact is that the surveillance is coerced by the very nature of the recipient's status as one of need; it is in short, an unequal exchange. The temporariness of access in the context of these exchanges has its own unique consequences, producing a form of unbelonging and fixed surveillance for these Black women that lingers beyond the primary exchange. Therefore, if we take seriously what the interlocutors brought forward in their accounts, we can then think about the ways in which service for Black women is very directly tethered to our own scrutiny and surveillance, and by extension to interruptions of our rights to respect and belonging.

Take for example the stress related to both the industrial welfare office, which was farther away from the rest of an interlocutor's life, and a much closer office, which also offered, albeit differently manifested, a set of spatially oriented consequences via exposure. An understanding of surveilled containment and transactional sites centres Black women's experience, and examines surveillance through an embodied socio-spatial, spiritual, and gendered lens. My goal of expanding on prevailing and conventional analyses lies in a desire to expand the understanding and depiction of how spatial theorizing is immersed in and reproduces surveilled containments. It is crucial to make clear the urgency of considerations such as the physical architectures of social service organizations—not just specific to locale but as the extensions of broader "service" goals and provisions—in order to address overall health and wellness for not only service seekers but for volunteers and staff, who often also tend to

be women and other marginalized people who become function-
aries for these systems.

This is so important because of the disparity between often dis-
jointed scholarly disciplines and the concrete reality of human
experiences. It seems almost absurd that it needs to be stated that
things must be considered in their totality. What the women who
spoke with me about their experience show us is that architectures
have a clear impact on their experiences, and therefore we must
consider what possibilities can come to fruition when we truly
understand that *placement* of all kinds impacts place-making and
privacy, and the extension of place-making and privacy impacts
selfhood and well-being, particularly for Black women. The narratives of these women reveal that surveilled containments produce
shared expectations of surveillance, as well as popularized, universal notions of who should be surveilled, and what those notions
look like in practice. The conclusion to be drawn is that they limit
privacy and how it is or is not extended to those deemed undeserving of privacy due to precarity. Furthermore (and this is true both
within and outside of the welfare office itself), there are no clear
mechanisms to prevent service-recipient privacy violations by workers. The freedom to invade Black women's online space via internet
and social media searches for example, represent yet another type
of spatial infraction on our personhood.

Tyranny of the Unscripted

Many episodes and experiences raised by my interlocutors illustrated the ways in which *unscripted* policies were exercised on
them undeservedly, with the aim to, as they perceived it, curb
their resistance and their efforts to build community based on
shared circumstances. My interlocutors also repeatedly highlighted
how as Black women, they are asked to live out these unscripted
policy directives.

I define unscripted policies as the directions/directives, rules,
regulations, and procedures that are unwritten but nevertheless
exercised on my interlocutors. Unscripted policies tend to change
swiftly, with no explanations and no time to adjust or respond to

new infractions or requirements, and certainly no recourse when they negatively impact Black women's lives. Collectively interwoven within the interlocutors' narratives were some common experiences and themes. Examples of these refrains include being subjected to "unwritten rules," "hidden laws," and what Interlocutor 6 described as "being double-documented."[61] In her explanation of double-documentation she expresses being subjected to the forensic documentation of Ontario Works but also to the ambiguous, ongoing assessment and documentation of her personhood and behaviour, which has a direct impact on her access to benefits yet serves as an *unauthorized* measure of her eligibility.

What my interlocutors seemed to convey through their accounts is that these unscripted policies are nonetheless expectations that had to be adhered to, and that in their roles as Black women accessing assistance, they are held accountable to these expectations regardless of the fact that they are not concrete, documented policies. A central feature in both the discourse and practice of unscripted policy is the implicit and undocumented nature of these practices. The practice of undocumenting is inherently designed, both in conceptualization and in application, to disappear, to purposely undocument both the existence and practice of unscripted documenting itself. In short, these unscripted policies are designed to be invisible and untraceable. Similar to the examples of untraced acts—such as a worker making a phone call, or a worker looking out a window and drawing conclusions about a client based on personal observations—when we think about this staking-out behaviour in the online context, it can also lead to unwelcome boundary crossing, undocumented social media searches for instance, of which there is no record and no discernable limit. This kind of searching is done on and off the clock and done on or off of a worker's personal or professional devices. Yet, to use my interlocutor's term, we don't question these kinds of "double-documenting" practices. These processes are already naturalized in many other circuits, for instance within the culture of judiciary process around surveillance, and we

61   Interlocutor 6, in person interview with author, Toronto, 2017.

only understand these practices from within that legal apparatus. In other words, we don't think that it's wrong for workers to stake out their clients in the same way that, if we do some unblurring, formal policing does. Social service workers perform the same role with impunity, invisibly, and there is enormous power attached to these actions. Their resulting decisions have very serious, often carceral, outcomes.

Finally, the unscripted policies simultaneously discipline Black women who are OW recipients and continually call into question their ability to remain in "good standing" at any given time, while never having any documented evidence that would make them ineligible. Of particular interest to me was how the women not only named their experiences of unscripted policy interventions but also spoke to how their lives and comportment were influenced while interacting with the OW workers to maintain eligibility or simply evade tensions that might result in minor punishments or outright refusal. The women described the ways that they performed these unwritten expectations amongst themselves as well as in their interactions with the workers. This, of course, represents an infringement on their social autonomy under the threat of a potential restriction to or elimination of their access to social assistance. In this way we can clearly see how behavioural policing is an enormous yet unscripted part of the control structure over Black women's lives across state constructs and social sites.

Unscripted "Consent" as Mechanism Surveillance

All the women in this research fundamentally agreed in finding the necessity of providing pertinent information to OW that would best describe their financial circumstances. From many of the women's perspectives, "truthfulness" and "honesty" "just made sense."[62] In fact, ninety percent of them made correlations between notions of "truthfulness" and being forthcoming as a means of potentially maximizing their access to the benefit and gaining access to additional resources. For example, Interlocutor 2 said:

62   Interlocutors 2, 14, 11 interviewed by the author in Toronto 2017 and 2018 respectively.

Of course, I must prove to them that I have no money. That's not a problem. And anyway, I have no money to lie about because I have no money![63]

Interlocutor 14:

I-I-I think…ummm. Yeah, they should ask for some paper- work, tax return to prove like…you know, like, you need the money, you know? But at the same time, why would anyone put themselves through all of this for a couple of hundred a month? Especially if they didn't have to?[64]

There was, however, also concern over confusion regarding the con- sent process. The women expressed not "completely agreeing" with or "understanding" the depth attached to each consent form.[65] They also expressed that often it was "unclear" what was included in the consent, what the relevance of certain questions was, who exactly was seeking the information, what this would allow the workers to ask, which other agencies to respond to, and also what information could be passed on to potential third parties.[66] One thing that we need to understand in terms of third parties and access in a time when technology is changing and developing quickly, is that by virtue of the way that technology in service provision is currently being built, system developers prioritize interconnectedness. This is the case regardless of whether people are actually meaningfully connected within these systems, and it stems from the idea of cen- tralized services, where more and more the internet is used as a system platform in the name of "efficiencies." The algorithms are designed to bring people together, but we need to begin to think about the repercussions of this and how it could and currently does negatively impact people accessing service.

---

63   Interlocutor 2, in person interview with author, Toronto, 2017.
64   Interlocutor 14, in person interview with author, Toronto, 2018.
65   Interlocutors 1 and 12 respectively, interviewed by the author in Toronto 2017 and 2018 respectively.
66   Interlocutors 1 and 6, in person interviews with the author Toronto, 2017; Interlocutors 15, 16, 17, 19, 20, in person interviews with author, Toronto, 2018.

Interlocutors were angered and disturbed by presumptive and casual acts of unscripted "consent" that were placed upon them by workers. What the women describe in these interactions is an assumed right (on the workers' part) to information gathering: interactions and exchanges that they did not consent to either verbally or in writing, but that they are susceptible to simply by virtue of being recipients of Ontario Works and subject to the power investments of individual workers. Interlocutor 5 stated:

> *All this signing of paperworks and it includes everything and excludes nothing. They probably know my bra and panty size! They dig up all your business.*[67]

Interlocutor 7 described how this forced consent to information access also presumes negative social and familial relations:

> *Think about it this way…Because my worker knows what school my daughter goes to, does that mean she can call the school and ask about what she brings for lunch? If I drop her off on time? If she has winter clothes on? They don't give me enough money to take care of her! … What would make her think I wouldn't be taking care of my daughter?*[68]

Interlocutor 4 added to the story of her girlfriend facing deportation:

> *When my girlfriend was being deported, my worker, who is not her* [the partner's] *worker, was all over me. It's like… her and my girlfriend's worker would exchange information all the time. She would remind me that my girlfriend "shouldn't go underground"…and that I shouldn't help her because I could lose my status too!*[69]

It must be understood that these kinds of threats are grounded in existing law, and that the women's expressed fears of repercussions

67   Interlocutor 5, in person interview with author, Toronto, 2017.
68   Interlocutor 7, in person interview with author, Toronto, 2018.
69   Interlocutor 4, in person interview with author, Toronto, 2017.

are well-founded. The Criminal Code of Canada addresses the prosecution of individuals found guilty of unlawful acts of association like "aiding and abetting."[70] More specifically, the Ontario Works Act (1997) clearly stipulates the following:

> No person shall knowingly aid or abet another person to obtain or receive assistance to which the other person is not entitled under this Act and the regulations. Procedures for these charges are governed by the Provincial Offences Act. The maximum penalty on conviction of either provincial offence is $5,000 fine and/or jail of up to six months.[71]

Another interlocutor related an OW worker's interest in and knowledge of details about her boyfriend. Interlocutor 18:

> *Before Caribana weekend, my boyfriend was being released from prison. My worker knew that information because I was his coee [co-accused] at one point. The Thursday before, she reminded me, any income he provides me must be reported. I don't know how she knew he was being released, other than mentioning it when I first got on welfare, which was when I was released on bail. What I thought was fucked up about it the situation was that it was almost two years after the fact. How did she remember? Was there a notification on her system? Did she call the jail? I didn't know, but the point was, him being locked up had nothing to do with her or my cheque.*[72]

So in many ways, the Black women I spoke with describe how "consent," as it relates to personal information, whether obtained

---

70   *Criminal Code of Canada*, RSC 1986, s.21:s.79 (2).
71   *Ontario Works Act*, 1997, SO 1997, c 25, Sch A, (79(4)). <https://canlii.ca/t/54bkl>.
72   Interlocutor 18, in person interview with author, Toronto, 2018.

formally or informally, has direct consequences on their access to Ontario Works. Further, as shown in the above examples, the women highlighted the informal interconnectedness of workers and systems, and workers across systems, as they relate to the disclosure of personal information. Specifically, women voiced concerns about the extent to which their own involvement with OW has an impact on their family members, roommates, and community, despite those connected people not being recipients of the benefit, nor officially documented as recipients of the benefit.

THE CASE WORKER

Case workers are quite simply a covert extension of the formal long arm of the law under the Ontario Works Act. Subsection (2):

> permits eligibility review officers to enter any place that the officer believes on reasonable grounds contains evidence relevant to determining a person's eligibility for payments under an Act set out in subsection 58 (2) of the Ontario Works Act.[1]

This often results in what my interlocutors perceived as unprofessional and unethical behaviour on the part of Ontario Works employees who went beyond their role as social assistance workers in efforts to surveil them. In examining the true nature of the case worker's role, it is no revelation that they violate the rights and privacy of benefit recipients. In the unfolding of an investigation, the powers of case workers give "their activities and documentary production almost full immunity from review by recipients or their counsel under the provincial or municipal Freedom of Information (FOI) laws."[2] This substantiates the unscriptedness as well as the ready access to information about recipients' circumstances as it relates to eligibility and potential prosecution.

1   *Ontario Works Act*, 1997.
2   Simon Shields, *Welfare (Ontario Works) Legal Guide*, http://www.isthatlegal. ca/index.php?name=fraud.welfare_law_ontario.

Fourteen of the twenty women I spoke with identified Ontario Works as one of the first places they'd sought support. The women reported, for example, that it *"made sense to first secure financial support"*[3] prior to fleeing an abusive relationship or trying to find housing, or simply as a newcomer to Canada in need of general support. In various ways, these fourteen women described not understanding and not being told the difference between the role of an OW client service worker and the role of an advocate for their personal and social needs. In many respects, they interpreted this lack of clarity as purposeful with a goal of ascertaining additional information about their personal lives, unrelated to their benefits claim. In short, a central concern was the workers', and by extension the state's, role in moral deception. Specifically, the concern was with the wilful withholding—an absence of forthrightness—about the differences between working with a person engaged in the administrative duty of dispensing funds and working with a therapeutic practitioner whose role is one of client advocate. Interlocutor 4 related the following:

> When I first met my worker, it was a few days after I'd arrived in Canada. The shelter gave me the address for the local office, and I went there. She asked a lot of questions. Many things I wanted to forget about, things I wanted to forget. I don't think she could understand but she looked like she cared. I told her everything, because they tell you to tell them everything. She never stopped me or told me that she couldn't help me with all the trauma.[4]

There is legislation as well as a body of legal and best practices governing interactions with all persons seeking services, particularly vulnerable people, and ethical practices suggest disclosing the nature and limits of the service. However, these limits and distinctions were not made apparent to the women (raising a parallel problem of lack of adherence even when policies that are deemed protections do exist). Interlocutor 1:

3   Interlocutor 8, in person interview with author, Toronto, 2018.
4   Interlocutor 4 in person interview with author, Toronto, 2017.

I thought she was like a therapist—someone I could confide in.[5]

Interlocutor 18:

I told her things because I thought she could help. Or that she would help me get help. I didn't think and I was telling her things so she could use it against me later.[6]

Interlocutor 11:

CAS took me to court, and everything was in the court documents from my OW worker.[7]

Interlocutor 19:

I would have never told her all those things if I knew what she was going to do with the information. I don't think anybody would.[8]

A few of the women also highlighted what they perceived as the workers' and the overall system's active maliciousness. Interlocutor 15 expressed that she perceived an over-investment in her failure and an overall lack of regard for her successes, be they small or large:

They also only tell each other bad things about me. When I was breaking my neck volunteering at the Food Bank for seven hours a day Monday to Friday, she never told my PO that I was doing good, you know what I mean? But…every time I was late, [or] I had to cancel an appointment, she always called my PO.[9]

---

5   Interlocutor 1, in person interview with author, Toronto, 2017.
6   Interlocutor 18, in person interview with author, Toronto, 2018.
7   Interlocutor 11, in person interview with author, Toronto, 2018.
8   Interlocutor 19, in person interview with author, Toronto, 2018.
9   Interlocutor 15, in person interview with author, Toronto, 2018.

Interlocutor 3:

> *I was accepted into college. She* [my worker] *said, good for me but most single mothers don't finish school.*[10]

It is notable that discourses about morality and deception are typically only applied in reference to service recipients within legal, academic, and broad social contexts, with service providers' moral status rarely, if ever, examined. These presumptions and misalignments are also heavily gendered among service recipients, where women's morality is analyzed, discussed, and policed far more often than that of men.[11] There is little to no information about the experiences of service recipients in relation to the state's role in moral deception and the ethical bankruptcy of universal public support programs. The experiences shared above are indicative of social and political policy designs and their failings that hurt the most marginalized. The narratives of these women allow us, and also point to the necessity for us to turn our attention to the state, illuminating its immorality while parsing out the specificities of moralizing discourses as exercised and weaponized distinctively on Black women.

The concerns brought forward by my interlocutors are echoed by numerous researchers who argue that state-sanctioned criminal

---

10   Interlocutor 3, in person interview with author, Toronto, 2017.

11   Among many explorations of such moral misalignment are: Patricia Hill Collins, "Gender, Black Feminism, and Black Political Economy," *The Annals of the American Academy of Political and Social Science* 568, 1 (2000): 41–53; Patricia Hill Collins and Sirma Bilge, *Intersectionality* (Oxford: Polity Press, 2016; Angela Davis, "Rape, Racism and the Capitalist Setting," *The Black Scholar* 12, 6 (1981): 39–45; Angela Davis *Are Prisons Obsolete?* (New York: Seven Stories Press, 2003); Patricia Hamilton, "'Now That I Know What You're About': Black Feminist Reflections on Power in the Research Relationship," *Qualitative Research: QR* 20, 5 (2020): 519–33; Claire Harris et al., *Grammar of Dissent: Poetry and Prose by Claire Harris, M. Nourbese Philip and Dionne Brand* (Fredericton: Goose Lane, 1994); M. Nourbese Philip, *Blank: Essays & Interviews* (Toronto: BookThug, 2017); Andrea Ritchie, *Invisible No More: Police Violence Against Black Women and Women of Color* (Boston: Beacon Press, 2017); Isoke Zenzele, "Black Ethnography, Black(Female) Aesthetics: Thinking/Writing/Saying/Sounding Black Political Life," *Theory & Event* 21, 1 (2018): 148–68.

surveillance is intertwined with the ongoing targeting and regulation of racialized and otherwise marginalized groups.[12] In order
to understand these implications, we must make the link between
social policy on the one hand, and groups and populations who
are constructed as the "usual suspects" on the other. More specifically, we must examine how "state policies and practices ... involve
the stigmatization, surveillance, and regulation of the poor [and]
assume a latent criminality among the poor."[13] Notions of social
order, elitism, and respectability are inherently biased against these
populations; even most of "Black Canadian historiography deals
with elites while ignoring those who lived at the bottom or on the
margins of the social order."[14] We need to consider, in this case,
how that impacts Black women specifically. Here is Interlocutor
18's account:

*I'll never forget the day that I was arrested after going to
my appointment with the wellie worker* [Ontario Works
Worker]. *I borrowed my boyfriend's car. It was a rental*

12   Katherine Beckett and Bruce Western, "Governing Social Marginality:
      Welfare, Incarceration, and the Transformation of State Policy," *Punishment &
      Society* 3, 1 (2001): 43–59; Kiran Mirchandani and Wendy Chan, *The Racialized
      Impact of Welfare Fraud Control in British Columbia and Ontario* (Toronto:
      Canadian Race Relations Foundation, 2005); Wendy Chan and Dorothy E.
      Chunn, *Racialization, Crime, and Criminal Justice in Canada*, (Toronto: University
      of Toronto Press, 2014); Dorothy Chunn and Shelly Gavigan, "Welfare Law,
      Welfare Fraud, and the Moral Regulation of the 'Never Deserving' Poor";
      Kaaryn S. Gustafson, *Cheating Welfare: Public Assistance and the Criminalization
      of Poverty* (New York: New York University Press, 2011); Robyn Maynard,
      Policing Black Lives; Janet E. Mosher, *Walking on Eggshells: Abused Women's
      Experiences of Ontario's Welfare System: Final Report of Research Findings from
      the Woman and Abuse Welfare Research Project.* Toronto: The Project, 2004);
      Andrea Ritchie, *Invisible No More: Police Violence Against Black Women and
      Women of Color* (Boston: Beacon Press, 2017); Kim Varma and Ashley Ward,
      "Social assistance fraud and zero tolerance in Ontario, Canada," *Canadian
      Review of Social Policy* 70 (2014); Janet Mosher and Joe Hermer. *Welfare
      Fraud: The Constitution of Social Assistance as Crime* (Law Commission of
      Canada, 2005).
13   Kaaryn Gustafson, "Degradation Ceremonies and the Criminalization of Low-
      Income Women," *UC Irvine Law Review* 3, 2 (2013): 104.
14   Barringon Walker, *Race on Trial: Black Defendants in Ontario's Criminal Courts,
      1858-1958* (Toronto: University of Toronto Press, 2010), 7.

car. After the appointment, she [the worker] watched me through the window, ran the license plate and reported the car stolen. As I was driving down the street, when I was pulled over by the Toronto Police. I was arrested on the street until my boyfriend came. My name wasn't on the car rental agreement, but I have a valid driver's license and I've never gotten a speeding ticket or parking ticket! When I asked them why they stopped me? They told me it was because the welfare office called them because she knew that I did not have a car, it must have been a stolen car. I never told the welfare worker how I got to the appointment. She never asked me any questions, and fuck!...It's not her business! After that she restricted and suspended my funds because if I have a boyfriend who can afford rental cars, he should be supporting me financially. She told me that I lied on my application when they asked if I had a man. I didn't lie, we weren't together when I applied, he doesn't live with me or support me financially. OH! I almost forgot…she also called the car rental company! [15]

Nuanced experiences of Black women, such as the experience related by Interlocutor 18, illustrate how the law and policy are exercised and enforced differently on Black women, and as such often "fall between the existing legal categories for recognizing injury."[16] In the context of poverty, many of the women described their experiences as systemic and very often in the context of larger, ongoing issues: inaccessibility of decent employment, education, and/or familial support; forced migration; and in a few circumstances in this limited group, intergenerational poverty and histories of growing up on social assistance. Another central concern for some of the women involved experiences and histories of violence against women, which

15   Interlocutor 18, in person interview with author, Toronto, 2018.
16   Kimberlé Crenshaw, "Whose Story Is It, Anyway? Feminist and Antiracist Appropriations of Anita Hill," in Toni Morrison, ed., *Race-ing Justice, En-gendering Power: Essays on Anita Hill, Clarence Thomas, and the Construction of Social Reality* (New York: Pantheon, 1992), 404.

in many cases impacted their existing employment and housing status, leaving them with limited supports to navigate their way out of or through complex institutional violence and trauma.

Here is a kind transgression of truth, of honesty, that lands ultimately in the realm of betrayal. People come to the case worker for help, and there's a belief that when you're at your most vulnerable, that individual help will transcend the state's violence. Not having money means more than not having money. It is desperation. People come to a worker after every kind of collapse. Black women go to these places to speak with case workers, and it is one thing to expect a level of state violence and indignation that usually comes with these interactions, but the kind of susceptibility involved in approaching someone with the collapse of your life—the fact that you have to ask someone else to intervene humanely in your life— represents another layer of vulnerability that, when transgressed, is a violence through betrayal. You are in essence punished for bothering to ask for help. Betrayal contains its own escalation of intrusivity and violence, and the exertion of that punishment is complicated by Blackness when neoliberalism gives the false hope, a false concept, that antiracism or anti-oppression are part of a worker's mandate or personal view; here is where neoliberalism distills to a presumed but absent humanity.

Ability also informs access to a great extent. Two of the women I spoke with should have had ready access to the Ontario Disability Support Program, but paradoxically for both, ongoing physical and mental health issues made their eligibility unclear to them, and no worker in any program—in ODSP, OW, or outside community workers—were offering up this eligibility information. These women's Blackness compounded with their disabilities resulted in them being perceived as undeserving of disability support. The antiBlackness of these structures is built up directly against access. Any worker who knew these women should have also known they were eligible to access other types of support, but no one was trying to facilitate that access, or open those avenues. In the case of Interlocutor 3, it took her having a near-death experience for her to be taken seriously and assessed for eligibility. Interlocutor 17 ended up caught up in the penal system, and it was only then that she was ultimately able to access ODSP funds. It was only through her very criminalization that she was able to gain access. These are the opacities that need to be exposed. If we reflect on the struggles of these two women, we see a long chain of workers who would have come into contact with them and who would have observed their dire circumstances before they ended up faced with life-threatening and carceral fallout; these workers could have helped to prevent those outcomes. The fact is that they were okay with these women being in dire circumstances, because Black women living under various forms of duress, Black women hanging on for dear life, is normalized within service structures and broader social and political climes. We must think about this outside of the limitations of data. The fact that these women eventually gained access to ODSP funding, does not account for the various hells they were forced to navigate in order to eventually achieve that access. Furthermore, we mustn't forget that some never do achieve that threshold of access, and while attempting to gain it may suffer many extreme losses: the loss of children, loss of health, loss of housing, and loss of privacy and autonomy. And, after all of this, the support that each of these women were eventually able to obtain amounted to an extra few hundred dollars a month—still not enough to sustain them—and so I would add to this list of extreme losses, the loss of life.

POVERTY AND BLACKLIFE

The Accepted Unacceptable

I don't think being poor is easy for anybody. But I just know that it's different for me. People think it's acceptable for a Black woman to be poor and suffering ... Or at least that's how I feel.[1]

My interlocutors conveyed their familiarity with persecution. Some of them—those for whom English is an additional language and/or who lived with disabilities—shared how these barriers impeded their ability to understand, and at times to make judgements or assessments about what would effectively protect their rights.[2] These women also described the ways in which power (both overt and covert) is used not only toward individual coercion, but how it is wielded to unfairly interpret and misread information, with serious outcomes for Black lives. Given this, we can consider the narratives of the women in this text alongside complicated cases like *R. v. D'Amour*, in which D'Amour, a white woman, "effectively relinquished her right to have the information she provided protected from use by the state in the prosecution of fraud."[3] In

1   Interlocutor 11, in person interview with author, Toronto, 2018.
2   I am using the term "rights" here in a judicial context, but I recognize as did my interlocutors that the concept of rights becomes complicated for Black people in general and even more so for Black women.
3   *R. v. D'Amour*, 2002 CanLII 45015 (ON CA), <https://canlii.ca/t/1cskn>.

a sense, the women in this book also implicitly relinquished their "rights" simply by accessing Ontario Works and "consenting" to the antiBlack racist assumptions and structures of its inner processes and logics. That said, Black women cannot truly relinquish rights that they were never granted in the first place under state and legislative rules. Interlocutor 6 expressed the following:

> *I think there are a lot of things that I could get away with if I wasn't a Black woman and [...] if my worker didn't think I was a liar [...] and* [if I felt] *that I deserved the welfare money I'm getting.*[4]

Spanning many eras, and various commitments to political, ideological, and philosophical espousals of feminisms and women's rights, Black women were and continue to be implicitly conceptualized as property or product.[5] Any thinking on "rights" must also be juxtaposed against ideas of *humanness,* correlated to a notion of citizenship that naturalizes, re-inscribes, and makes official who qualifies as human, and therefore who is citizen and deserving of dignified treatment under systems of state-imposed deprivation.[6]

Benefiting from her identity as a white woman, which includes an assumed innocence and a socially constructed inherent deservingness such that the state would never have deemed her suspicious to begin with, D'Amour was ultimately able to assert,

4   Interlocutor 6, in person interview with author, Toronto, 2017.
5   Carole Boyse Davies, *Black Women, Writing and Identity: Migrations of the Subject* (London and New York: Routledge, 1994).
6   David Brion Davis, *Inhuman Bondage: The Rise and Fall of Slavery in the New World* (Oxford, England: Oxford University Press, 2006); Rinaldo Walcott, *The Long Emancipation* (Windsor, ON: Biblioasis, 2021); Sylvia Wynter, "'No Humans Involved': An Open Letter to My Colleagues," *Forum N.H.I. Knowledge for the 21st Century* 1, 1 (1994): 42-73; Sylvia Wynter, "The Ceremony Must Be Found: After Humanism," *Boundary 2* 12/13, 3 (1984): 19-70; Sylvia Wynter and Katherine McKittrick, "Unparalleled Catastrophe for Our Species? Or, to Give Humanness a Different Future: Conversations," In *Sylvia Wynter,* (New York: Duke University Press, 2020), 9-89; Sylvia Wynter, "Unsettling the Coloniality of Being/Power/Truth/Freedom: Towards the Human, After Man, Its Overrepresentation—An Argument," *CR (East Lansing, Mich.)* 3, 3 (2003): 257-337.

that her privacy rights pursuant to section 7 of the Charter have been violated by the disclosure of the financial information in question in that the disclosure by the agency [Ontario Works] to the prosecution was made without either the consent of the applicant [D'Amour] or the proper judicial authorization."[7]

We must consider the social constructions that would grant D'Amour the confidence to "argue that the disclosure of her financial information subjected her to an unreasonable search and seizure in violation of her rights under section 8 of the Charter."[8] Modernist normative constructions of "policy," both formal and informal, and its extensions into public and private consciousness, particularly within the non-profit industrial complex, laud and elevate the law with false reverence, and the adjacent sites of the courtroom, the review board, and the appeals committee are perceived as equitable sites that can therefore make injustices visible. Similarly and simultaneously, there is a false narrative about access to justice—a presumption that there is such a thing as equal access. So on the one hand we have the law rendering injustices invisible, on the other hand we have the falsity of access. These things need to be held within the same continuum, but they often are not; we tend to separate what happens in one site—say in the confines of a non-profit agency—from the judiciary, when in reality there is an interconnectedness, a running parallel, and considering them distinct from one another has inherent problems and contradictions.

The approbation of legal spaces is naïve, since it is precisely these structures that have also imposed a variety of calamities upon BlackLife, particularly on Black women. The Black women's accounts in this book reveal that there is no truly secure site in which they are guarded against suspicion, or circumstances in which they are granted the "benefit of the doubt." All twenty of the women expressed disillusionment in response to suggestions that they exercise their right to complain or that they challenge their worker in

7   *R. v. D'Amour*, 2000.
8   Ibid.

any formal way. The women made clear there would be little to no outcome that would make it worthwhile to engage in systems or processes that would methodically and repeatedly have them on trial while already convicted.

The fundamental lack of awareness of the difference in *de facto* rights and privileges between different groups in Canadian society, and the white supremacist systems that allow some the privilege of not being aware of this difference, make the whole discourse of "rights" grotesque. Rights-based discourses typically assume that all people have access to the same set of rights across Canadian society; they can thereby be weaponized against those who are in fact unable to exercise these rights, and who are therefore assumed to be lazy, irresponsible, or otherwise deficient as explanation for their "failures." The Black women in this text are all too familiar with these double standards and expressed an attitude of exhaustion after decades of punitive state-sanctioned violence, often produced by these very systems, that showed no awareness of their lived realities and challenges. Interlocutor 8:

> *My worker told me … I was born here, not like other people. And that I should not be on welfare because I speak English and I know how the system works. It was like she was blaming me because I was born here, but she doesn't know my life here. I was born on welfare. My mother was raised on welfare. She tried her best, but…*[9]

Interlocutor 13 commented specifically on the intersection between poverty and BlackLife in the context of trying to find housing:

> *Try finding a place to live in Toronto as a young Black mother. Asking a landlord to fill in the first and last form for welfare. You're not getting that place. Black, young, mother and on welfare—basically you are untouchable, nobody's got you. You know that! Is that research?*[10]

9   Interlocutor 8, in person interview with author, Toronto, 2018.
10   Interlocutor 13, in person interview with author, Toronto, 2018.

What Interlocutor 13 highlights in this question—"Is that research?"—is the fact that the realities for Black women, the scales and equivocations and outcomes of life, are absurd! We are sitting together, I am asking her a set of questions that we both know are absurd because we know exactly where they stem from and lead to, all in the name of research. Moreover, it's something we can laugh at, but there's also a difficulty and pain because here we are, both Black women, well aware of what's happening, what has been happening for so long, and of the lack of change. Amber Williams King writes about the way that absurdity and laughter emerge in the horrific and humanize it, that humour is itself a kind of response to ongoing antiBlack absurdities.[11] As I write, I'm reminded as well of the absurdity of what I am trying to do, of the fact that it is *still* necessary to write such a text. What does this tell us about learning, the issue of sitating learning itself? Who can learn?

In addition to the women's concerns stated above, a minority (three) of the twenty women identified as having been students and therefore having received student loans, which at some point may have overlapped with their access to welfare and, as such, had an impact on whether or not they could return to school. With a lack of access to work, these three women ended up staying on welfare instead of returning to school. The findings show that the cycle of poverty that many women endure is not new; this in itself does not distinguish my interlocutors from other people living in poverty, rather the women specifically highlighted the sense that the distinctiveness of their circumstances is derived from their Blackness. One of these women was a student while living with multiple disabilities. She had no access to disability-related supports within her educational institution. Her experience at the intersection of education, disability, race, and gender is one that deserves much more attention than it currently draws.

The education-research landscape in Canada tends to focus on outcomes for racialized students in elementary and secondary school,

---

11   Amber Williams King. *When Palm Trees Break: The Fractured Horizons of Black Carribean World-Making in the Midst of Crisis,* masters thesis, York University, 2021.

more recently with an increased focus on Black student achievement and engagement.[12] Interlocutor 15 describes this pre-existing issue in the college or university setting, where stakes are "different" and can be "much higher":

> *Before I went back to school, I needed to collect welfare for two months until my student loan came in. I had zero dollars! A little while later, I got a letter saying that I owed welfare back money. I also got a letter from the OSAP people too! It's funny because some white girl in my class was in the same situation, but she just talked to the worker and it was fine. Someone at the university also helped her, and I ended up having to drop out of school. But it wasn't the worst part; they took out what I was given during those two months from my welfare cheque every month until it was paid off. I'm still on welfare and I still didn't finish school.*[13]

This example illustrates not just precarity but the founded fear of criminalization. Black women's criminalization can be seen through comparison with cases where the criminality of a non-Black accused person is not assumed or constructed. In the case of *R. v. Maldonado* (1998),

> a criminal court considered a charge of criminal fraud against a person who received both welfare and student loans at the same time. The court dismissed the charge, finding that an element of the fraud offence, that of knowing that the government would be deprived of money, was missing—as the defendant did not know that the money was chargeable income, the non-reporting of which would give him further assistance. The court took

12 As outlined in the Province of Ontario Board Improvement and Equity Planning Tool, June 2021, and the Toronto District School Board Multi-Year Strategic Plan, 2019, Ontario Equity and Inclusive Education Strategy, 2009.

13 Interlocutor 15, in person interview with author, Toronto, 2018. OSAP stands for Ontario Student Assistance Program.

great care to distinguish this from an "ignorance of the law" defence, which is barred under the criminal code.[14]

The court's efforts in this case to distinguish the defendant's lack of knowledge from "ignorance of the law," which would have been an inadmissible defence, provides an illuminating contrast with the experience of Interlocutor 15, as well as with the broader experiences of the other Black women in this book, who typically reported a lack of charity in the law's interpretation of their various circumstances. The charitable interpretation granted in *R. v. Maldonado* helps to illustrate the racial and gendered bias inherent in how legal discretion is applied.[15]

"Wipe asses, or kiss her ass"

The women in this book identified their own individual self-worth, or their conception of "self" or "worthiness," as being entirely independent of their status of being on welfare. That said, the experiences of shame that are nevertheless inadvertently mapped onto their experiences as Black women experiencing poverty are evident and damning. Interlocutor 1 highlights this:

> *I came to this country as a dentist from Congo. I speak French, English, and Dutch fluently. I studied in the UK before returning to Congo to work and be with my family. As the political situation got worse, they killed my father and brother and I had to leave immediately. I had no intention of being here and being on welfare, living in a shelter such and such. No! I have skills, I look for work every day. But I can't take a job for minimum wage. I can't live on that! My worker always tells me I have to lower my standards here and maybe I should go get my PSW* [personal support

14   Simon Shields. *Welfare (Ontario Works) Legal Guide*, Chapter 12—Fraud and Prosecutions 2 (d) 2020. http://www.isthatlegal.ca/index.php?name=fraud. welfare_law_ontario.

15   *R. v. Maldonado*, (1998) O.J. NO. 3209 (Prov. Div.) (QL). https://www.oaith. ca/assets/files/Publications/Poverty/Welfare-Fraud-as-Crime.pdf.

workers] *certificate. This is what she wills for me: Wipe asses [...] or kiss her ass.*[16]

Interlocutor 5:

> *It's like they think being poor is familiar for Black people. Probably even more for Black women, they think that we're used to suffering and struggling. It's almost like they assume that this is okay and that we should be okay with it. No, I don't want to make it work. My worker always tells me things like, "you know how to make this work and you'll be okay." Okay? How will I be okay? Because I make choices every month about food versus TTC? This is no way to live.*[17]

While many interlocutors perceived a need to disclose financial information given that this is a means- and needs-tested program, they were troubled and deeply impacted by the evidence before them: first, that their experience of poverty would actually serve to further their precarity; and second, that being poor has direct implications on their right to privacy.[18] The experience of Interlocutor 18 is indicative of what Robyn Maynard describes as the "underlying hostility and suspicion to which Black women are subjected by law enforcement officers"—and, I would add, by state agents and their designates.[19]

Unparalleled access to so many areas of one's life generates a coextensive level of scrutiny and paternalism that in turn also invades and permeates all dimensions of these Black women's lives. This includes but is not limited to the experiences of the interlocutors' partners and children. Two women shared what they saw as calls to "fish for" information about them. Interlocutor 4 recounts:

16   Interlocutor 1.
17   Interlocutor 5.
18   See also *R. v. D'Amour*, 1990.
19   Robyn Maynard, *Policing Black Lives: State Violence in Canada from Slavery to the Present* (Winnipeg & Blackpoint, NS: Fernwood Publishing, 2017), 119.

> *My worker has called the daycare on several occasions asking*
> *how often I drop off my children to daycare? If I drop off*
> *my child on time? How my child interacts with other people*
> *and how I interact with the daycare staff? I was shocked*
> *to hear about this because I have never given my worker a*
> *reason to think anything was wrong at the daycare or with*
> *my daughter.*[20]

Fishing for information therefore must also be understood as a mechanism of intelligence-gathering that often has deleterious outcomes for the interlocutors. I use the term "intelligence-gathering" deliberately to point to the ways that, in relationship to the state, Black women, so illegal and so untrusted, are already socially criminalized outside of judicial logic; this is not about curiosity, and that distinction needs to be made. Everything is already under suspicion when it comes to the Black woman. This is not just about the worker, but the worker as a state actor. The women's stories make us aware of the consequences of existing at the intersection of gendered antiBlack state interruption. While this is "predictable [since] there is simply silence of and about black women," in many cases it is Black women who bear the burden of being the first line of defence against the state.[21] Interlocutor 10:

> *I talk loudly. I'm just like this. I'm not angry but I just*
> *talk loud. My whole family talks loud. I took my son to the*
> *appointment with me and he's running all over the place,*
> *and I tell him in the same voice I would at home to stop.*
> *The front desk worker tells me to lower my voice and that*
> *I shouldn't talk to him like that. I said okay. Once I met*
> *with my actual worker, she asked me about what happened*
> *in the waiting area. I told her, nothing—my son was run-*
> *ning around and I told him to stop. She asked me a bunch*

20   Interlocutor 4, in person interview with author, Toronto, 2017.
21   Kimberlé Crenshaw, "Whose Story Is It, Anyway? Feminist and Antiracist Appropriations of Anita Hill," in *Race-ing Justice, En-gendering Power: Essays on Anita Hill, Clarence Thomas, and the Construction of Social Reality* edited by Toni Morrison (New York: Pantheon, 1992), 405.

of questions about being a frustrated mother. I told her I wasn't frustrated but that sometimes my kid can be annoying. I didn't think anything of this. The next day I got a call from the Children's Aid Society they told me that there was an incident that happened at the welfare office and that they wanted to talk to me about it. Nobody at the office told me that they were that concerned so I was shocked when I got the call and they later showed up to my house. To this day, I'm still dealing with them now and it was over nothing. They say once your name is in the child system [child welfare] *it never actually goes away?*[22]

For many of the women, the child welfare system and those who (co-)conspired to capture their children are feared as equally, if not more than, the police. The women did not perceive these as separate roles; rather, as discussed previously, as related ones. For them, they are positioned in opposition to all of the systems collectively. This highlights a particular kind of precarity, that Interlocutor 3 shared:

You just never know what's going to happen after an appointment. You could be a bad mother. You could be a thief. You could be arrested … you could be … you just don't know. That's the point, you just don't know.[23]

Two important perspectival pieces must be raised here. The first is around the expectations about Black women that these narratives illustrate: first, an illustration of being lacking, a subservient. Once conceptually rendered to servitude, one can therefore be directed to risky and labour-intensive work. The second concentrates on how social constructions of Black womanhood such as this revolve around implications of toughness and resilience: the strong Black woman who rubs two pennies together and makes it work. We don't often see with clarity how these concepts actually play out in policy and practice, but here we do. These women

22   Interlocutor 10, in person interview with author, Toronto, 2018.
23   Interlocutor 2, in person interview with author, Toronto, 2017.

are demonstrating that these discourses have direct deleterious and deliberate impacts on their lives. What Saidiya Hartman describes as quotidian, everyday thinking about Black women, actually materializes in ways that interrupt and keep us captured and contained via a system of thought, into very concrete manifestations.[24] I am certainly not the first person to point to this, but I want to impress upon readers that Black women are not considered unspeakable simply in the abstract; these forms of thought have material effects. There are, for example, direct implications to constructing a Black woman as loud: she can be arrested, her children can be taken away, she can be killed. Again, this is not hyperbole; these are the very real costs of the social construction of Black women's being. So over and over again, we must pull out and make that connection, solidify it, and impress upon ourselves and others how important it is to understand that the things we speak about Black women are not separate from state responses, and not separate from their livabilities.

A 2017 study that sought to assess police decisions to charge individuals in cases of child maltreatment, found that in the 4808 cases they examined, police laid charges in about one-third.[25] The fears of Black women respondents in my research are underscored by the report, which indicated that not only were the majority (86.7 percent) of those charged in their study women caregivers, but the majority of the children apprehended (57.6 percent) were also girls. These researchers acknowledge that their sample size was not particularly diverse, but the results are nonetheless clear about how "child welfare and law enforcement systems work together on a sizable minority of child welfare cases."[26] They therefore entreat researchers and practitioners to consider how issues of race and racism are exacerbating factors in laying charges. Again, there is undoubtedly limited quantitative research in Ontario that speaks

24   Saidiya Hartman, *Wayward Lives, Beautiful Experiments: Intimate Histories of Social Upheaval* (New York: W.W. Norton & Company, 2019).
25   Philip Baiden et al., "Police Charging Decisions in Child Maltreatment Investigations: Findings from the 2008 Ontario Incidence Study of Reported Child Abuse and Neglect," *Journal of Public Child Welfare* 3, 11(2) (2017).
26   Ibid, 223-224.

to the realities of Black people, children, and families within the child welfare system.[27]

But calls for continued research and additional data live along-side decades of research that continue to substantiate the role of the child welfare system as another vehicle to the incarceration and capture of Black people. A study that investigated the outcomes of Black and white child welfare cases over twenty years in Ontario (1993–2013) uncovered that in the context of "Black families the incidence [of cases] increased almost fourfold during the ... period" and suggested that issues such as the 'social safety net, the thresh-old for risk of harm, and bias and racist institutional policies and practices' be considered in explaining these outcomes."[28]

The persistent willful ignorance of the dominant city culture is striking in light of the fact that various Black communities have echoed these concerns anecdotally for decades. In Ontario we have witnessed an uptake of attention on these matters on a number of fronts. Three recent reports: "One Vision One Voice: Changing the Ontario Child Welfare System to Better Serve African Canadians," "Interrupted Childhoods: Over representation of Indigenous and Black Children in Ontario Child Welfare," and "Under Suspicion: Research and Consultation Report on Racial Profiling in Ontario," are revealing in their conclusions.[29] Cumulatively, they assert the reality that the women in this book have lived and continue to live: antiBlack racism is real and pervasive. Furthermore, these

27 Kofi Antwi-Boasiako, Bryn King, Barbara Fallon, Nico Trocmé, John Fluke, Martin Chabot, and Tonino Esposito, "Differences and Disparities over Time: Black and White Families Investigated by Ontario's Child Welfare System." *Child Abuse & Neglect* 107 (September, 2020): 104618.

28 Ibid, 1.

29 Ontario Association of Childrens' Aid Societies, "One Vision One Voice: Changing the Ontario Child Welfare System to Better Serve African Canadians," (2016), https://www.oacas.org/what-we-do/onevisiononevoice/; Ontario Human Rights Commission, "Interrupted Childhoods: Over representation of Indigenous and Black Children in Ontario Child Welfare," (2018), https://www.ohrc.on.ca/en/interrupted-childhoods; Ontario Human Rights Commission, "Under Suspicion: Research and Consultation Report on Racial Profiling in Ontario," (2017), https://www.ohrc.on.ca/sites/default/files/Under%20suspicion_research%20and%20consultation%20report%20on%20racial%20profiling%20in%20Ontario_2017.pdf.

experiences of antiBlack violence are unisolated; instead, outcomes become increasingly adverse particularly for Black women, compounded by issues around over-policing.

Further forms of antiBlack racism permeate and live between multiple systems, and as such bring Black families (often led by women) into contact with the child welfare system in ways that it does not for Black men, other racialized, or white families. According to Jennifer Clarke, "the criminalization of Afro-Caribbean mothers and youths involved in the child welfare system in Toronto" is "horrific."[30] This is evinced in the over-representation of Black children in group homes and other "treatment" or residential settings; it is also mirrored in data around adoption, kinship, the (in)eligibility of Black parents to foster children, and so on.

The suspicion and inspection inflicted upon Black women's intimate lives via their connections to Ontario Works describes both the rejection of Black women's autonomy and the paternalistic nature of the state, bolstering what Angela Davis describes as the concept of the "irrevocably fallen women, with no possibility of salvation."[31] Davis states that "if male criminals were considered to be public individuals who had simply violated the social contract, female criminals were seen as having transgressed fundamental moral principles of womanhood.[32]

This is particularly the case for Black women, as prime targets of various forms of informal morality policing. Interlocutor 8:

> *A couple years ago...I was dating a real asshole. He used to abuse me, so I left and went into a shelter. I got housing in that shelter, and it was an all-women's housing. I met somebody really nice after a while and he would come visit me every once in a while. This was allowed, by the way, the person was just not allowed to live at my house. My worker called Monday and he answered the phone. She asked me who he was. I told her that he was a friend and*

30   Jennifer Clarke, "Beyond Child Protection: Afro-Caribbean Service Users of Child Welfare," *Journal of Progressive Human Services* 9, 23 (3) (2012): 248.

31   Angela Davis, *Are Prisons Obsolete?* (New York: Seven Stories Press, 2003), 70.

32   Ibid.

she reminded me that nobody should be living in that hous-
ing with me because it's housing only for women. Of course,
I knew that but also, she didn't help me get the housing; all
she knew about it was where I lived and what kind of hous-
ing it was. Maybe a few weeks or a week after that, I got a
letter from the housing worker reminding me of the rules for
living in that unit. I can't confirm for sure that it was her
[the OW worker] but by this point he'd been visiting me
for some time and it wasn't an issue. So, I have to assume
it was her, does that make sense? Anyways, after that day
everybody in the building including the super would watch
and see what I was doing and who was coming in and out
of my apartment. I felt like I should move out.[33]

Through these high levels of intrusivity, marked by surveillance and reporting of information to multiple state and non-profit organizations, women expressed feeling "watched," "targeted" and "at risk," often solely due to individual workers' subjective interpretations of a given circumstance.[34] The women also highlighted discourses surrounding information-gathering practices, which are legitimized by policy claims related to the application process or file maintenance.

In the very few cases (two of twenty) where women identified having had some level of openness with their OW workers in the context of the service relationship, these women also identified that mundane conversations were used as retaliatory evidence for their files. They identified these "conversations" as another mechanism of surveillance. Not surprisingly, all twenty of the women identified themselves as having one of the following: a) a poor relationship, b) a bad relationship, c) a dissolved relationship, or d) a non-existent relationship with their OW workers.

Poverty, "Performance" and Sexualization

As already outlined, notions of morality and immorality have always been mapped onto women's bodies while intersecting with and

33   Interlocutor 8, in person interview with author, Toronto, 2018.
34   Interlocutor 6, in person interview with author, Toronto, 2017; Interlocutor 4, in person interview with author, Toronto, 2018.

being regulated by public moral codes. These codes in turn have an impact on the ways in which women are categorized and deemed "deserving" of public support or of being believed. Historically, a Black woman's word was not taken as truth; our own legal system once drew a connection, as a matter of law, between lack of chastity and lack of veracity, with Black women never seen as chaste.[35] In Toronto, Black women represent the largest woman-identified population stopped by police and "are also more likely to report being searched by the police (3%) than white or Chinese women (1%)."[36]

Interlocutors described being caught in a conundrum in terms of the believability of their poverty. On the one hand, they described being challenged about their class status and believability regarding being poor, on the other, there was an ever-present discourse about belonging on welfare that operated simultaneously. Interlocutor 10:

> *Everybody knows you don't go to wellie* [welfare] *dressed up. But what happens if you have an appointment after? I'm supposed to go there looking like shit? I remember I had to go for a meeting with my son's school after my appointment with my worker. She asked, "Oh, why do you look so good today? Where did you get the money for this outfit?" I said, "I have a appointment with my son's school." I found out that she called my son's school to make sure.*[37]

Interlocutor 4:

> *A friend that I went to school with gave my daughter an old laptop computer. She came with me to the appointment and the worker asked, "How do you afford a laptop?" Her kids don't have laptops! I got so angry I started yelling in the room. I told her that the laptop is probably not even*

35   Kimberlé Crenshaw, "Whose Story Is It, Anyway? Feminist and Antiracist Appropriations of Anita Hill," *Race-ing Justice, En-gendering Power: Essays on Anita Hill, Clarence Thomas, and the Construction of Social Reality*, edited by Toni Morrison (New York: Pantheon, 1992), 412.

36   Scot Wortley and Akwasi Owusu-Bempah, "The usual suspects: police stop and search practices in Canada," *Policing and Society* 21, 4 (2011): 398.

37   Interlocutor 10, in person interview with author, Toronto, 2018.

worth $50. And maybe they should be helping us get our kids laptop computers because maybe then they won't be on welfare too, instead of asking us questions about how [we] get the little things that we get from wherever we get it.[38]

Interlocutor 9:

I signed a new contract for my cell phone, so I got a new phone. I had the phone on the table, and she asked me how I could afford that phone. She told me, if I can afford such a nice phone I shouldn't be on welfare. Because she has a full-time job and she doesn't have a phone like that. I thought... stupid! Of course, I didn't buy the phone. The phone costs more than I get from welfare a month. She made me send her a copy of my new contract as well as prove to her that the phone came as a part of the new contract.[39]

Here again we see racism and antiBlackness intersecting with gendered biases and moral policing to manifest myriad gendered, white supremacist, and antiBlack realities. Interlocutor 5:

She assumed I had a medical disease because back then, I was in my mid-40s and never had children. I'll always remember...she said, I was the first she met.[40]

Interlocutor 17 related her worker proclaiming:

"All you Somali women are covering your heads but you're always having children!"[41]

Interlocutor 14 described her worker passing judgement and making pressuring statements related to her love life and religion, all while weighing in gendered subsistence values:

38   Interlocutor 4, in person interview with author, Toronto, 2017.
39   Interlocutor 9, in person interview with author, Toronto, 2018.
40   Interlocutor 5, in person interview with author, Toronto, 2017.
41   Interlocutor 17, in person interview with author, Toronto, 2018.

> *Do a lot of Black men go to church? Why don't you find a*
> *good man, Christian man, to support you and your child?*[42]

Here are numerous examples of antiBlackness and white supremacy driving assumptions made by social service workers about the
women and their lives. Caseworkers may disagree, but the above
three interlocutors were explicit and unwavering in identifying the
experiences that they outlined as being directly linked to their
Blackness.

The realities of Black women continue to be distorted by and
under the attack of idealized neoliberal notions of "progress" in
the Canadian polity, informed and exacerbated by global antiBlack
discourses, as well as by complex, varied, and in many cases
"non-academic" artifacts, including cultural and literary works that
include but are not limited to policy, practice, pictures (by which I
mean any and every kind of visual rendition), and poetry. We continue to ignore, dismiss, and devalue Black women's self-expression,
as well as our expressions of resistance to authority, particularly state
authority, in our day-to-day lives. This illustrates the brutal and violent nature of living Black while being a woman. Interlocutor 19:

> *The woman at the front desk told me this is not a strip club.*
> *I was wearing shorts and a tank top, it was a hot summer*
> *day. I–I was ... Why a strip club?* [laughs] *I'll use another*
> *example* [laughs] *... a water park? My girl ... said I came*
> *to sell pussy, yeah. Basically* [laughs].[43]

Interlocutor 6:

> *There's no dress code but they act like there is. They always*
> *have something to say about what I'm wearing.*[44]

---

42   Interlocutor 14, in person interview with author, Toronto, 2018.
43   Interlocutor 19, in person interview with author, Toronto, 2018.
44   Interlocutor 6, in person interview with author, Toronto, 2017.

Interlocutor 18:

> *"You're a popular girl! I see you with a different man all the time." I don't see her that often, maybe twice a year, and she has no idea who the men that are with me are.*[45]

Interlocutor 12:

> *I take a lot of pictures of my hair…I do hair on the side anyways … I take a lot of pictures of myself, and this woman told me … I can make money from sexy pictures, post on Facebook. I was like … she's a fucking bitch.*[46]

The women repeated back to me the words, expressions, comments, and snide offhand remarks that they deemed racist and that at one point or another were used to describe them during their interactions with their OW workers. These included:

- Agitating
- Appalling
- Baby machine
- Baby money-maker
- Belligerent
- Boy crazy
- Childish
- Crazy
- Criminal
- Delinquent
- Dirty
- Dishonest
- Disorganized
- Disrespectful
- Impolite

45   Interlocutor 18, in person interview with author, Toronto, 2018.
46   Interlocutor 12, in person interview with author, Toronto, 2018.

- Inappropriate
- Irresponsible
- ISIS
- Liar
- Lazy
- Loud
- Manly
- Mommy monster
- Non-compliant
- Provoking
- Psychotic
- Rude
- Sexual
- Terrorizing
- Threatening
- Tormenting
- Unappreciative
- Uneducated
- Ungrateful
- Unrealistic
- Useless
- Vindictive
- Violent
- Wastey
- Wild

The list speaks clearly. We must understand that regardless of "advancements" in antiracism policies, as well as awareness-raising movements against antiBlack racism in Toronto, the women in this study attest to the continued racist misreading of their existence as Black women.

Somali Women

As demonstrated, some women spoke of being challenged and dis-believed regarding how they saved money and documented financial realities outside of mainstream institutional banking systems. A few women were accused of participating in informal community-based saving practices. Interlocutor 17 recalled being asked by her case-worker, *"Do you save money in the same way that the other Somali women do?"* The caseworker was referring to *Hagbad*, women-led, saving-lending circles. *"What do you do with that money? You send it back home?"*[47] For these women, engaging such a mechanism of saving money within the community and amongst other women was not the only point of contention and alleged deception that the workers would identify. In the case of two women (Interlocutors 17 and 6), OW workers also suggested that they were saving money to send it to warlords or tribal organizing in their home country.[48] This specifically negatively impacted the Black Somali Muslim women with whom I spoke. Interlocutor 17:

> [OW workers would say,] *"You Somali women dress really nicely and wear a lot of gold. Just not when you come here."*

> *She* [the OW worker] *told me they had a training, something like that...about how the Somali women save money on welfare. She said, "All you guys sending money back home, we have to make sure that you're not sending money back home to support the war."*[49]

The discourse that constructs Somalis as "terrorists" and "tribal warlords" requires critique alongside legacies of colonialism and imperialism.[50] Numerous attempts at Somali local government have failed not due to the failings of Somalis but to the forces

---

47   Interlocutor 17, in person interview with author, Toronto, 2018.
48   Jenny Burman, "Remittance; Or, Diasporic Economies of Yearning," *Small Axe: a Journal of Criticism* 6, 2 (2002): 49-71.
49   Interlocutor 17, in person interview with author, Toronto, 2018.
50   This rhetoric may appear outrageous, but in November 1991, Lyn McLeod, former Liberal Party cabinet minister (1987-1990), was quoted in the *Toronto Star* saying that Somalis are "importing refugees to systematically pillage our vulnerable and exposed social welfare systems in an attempt to raise funds to support clan interests in the struggle for power in Somalia." (Globe and Mail, "Refugees Accused of Fraud" October 28, 1993).

behind these legacies.[51] I would argue that in some respects these very legacies that sought to destroy Somalia and Somalis are what brought Somalia into the global frame of consciousness.

In *The Black Atlantic: Modernity and Double Consciousness*, Paul Gilroy warns us about the malleability of white supremacy and how narratives of antiBlackness persist; he notes that the "crude and reductive notion of culture that forms the substance of racial politics today [is] clearly associated with an older discourse of racial and ethnic difference which is everywhere entangled in the history of the idea of culture in the modern West."[52] Until the early 1990s much of the western world was not familiar with Somalia or eastern Africa more broadly.[53] Somalia really only came onto the West's public radar in January 1991, when the regime of Mohamed Siad Barre was deposed. The following political and civil unrest, itself rooted in atrocious legacies of colonialism and western imperialism, resulted in large-scale atrocities of state violence, rape, and poverty, which saw the movement of many Somalis across the continent of Africa and into countries such as Canada.

In the context of migration, it is imperative that we understand the gender representation within Somali communities. During the post-civil-war migratory period, Somalis represented the largest single ethnic group in Africa, and among them Somali women represented approximately sixty percent of the overall Somali population.[54] Given this, it should be no surprise that the migrants who came to Canada were predominantly women, which in turn resulted in a disproportionate number of women-led households. Upon arrival to Canada these women were met with gender, racial, and religious discrimination coupled with language limitations and

---

51   Cawo M. Abdi, *Elusive Jannah: The Somali Diaspora and a Borderless Muslim Identity*, (Minneapolis: University of Minnesota Press, 2015).

52   Paul Gilroy, *The Black Atlantic: Modernity and Double Consciousness* (Cambridge, Mass.: Harvard University Press, 1993), 7.

53   Cawo M. Abdi, *Elusive Jannah*.

54   Denise Spitzer, "The impact of policy on Somali refugee women in Canada," *Refuge* 47 (2006); Ladan Affi. "Domestic conflict in the diaspora: Somali women asylum seekers and refugees in Canada," in *Somalia: The Untold Story*, edited by Judith Gardner & Judy El Bushra (London: Pluto Press, 2004), 107-115.

barriers.[55] Somali women also experienced a bias of unbelievability which, rooted in antiBlackness, was compounded by a lack of official documentation after fleeing the civil war.

For many women and their children entering Canada, their journeys often found them moving through several countries and were also often marked by several stops, which included refugee camps. One of the women who spoke with me, Interlocutor 6, described having a copy of her birth certificate with her when she fled Somalia, but said that she "*lost it somewhere between walking from one country to another.*"[56] We must acknowledge that it is rare for people fleeing their homelands to have all of the paperwork and documentation that the nations that they travel through or come to, deem necessary. More importantly, there are few to no mechanisms in place to replace or apply for new documents along these journeys. Not believing refugees and displaced persons because of their lack of official documentation is not a benign practice. It is called interdiction, which Michelle Lowry describes as: "stopping people without adequate identity papers from getting to Canada. [It] is based on the assumption that those without papers either abuse the system or pose a danger because they are not who they say they are."[57] Lowry adds:

> So, in the name of a sovereignty that is informed by raced, classed, and gendered notions of who belongs here, the human security of asylum seekers is put at risk through interdiction. Those who are intercepted before they reach Canada are unable to avail themselves of the protection needed to ensure physical safety and the emotional and psychological security that comes with escaping traumas and persecution faced in the homeland.[58]

This situation became particularly concerning for three refugee women I spoke with (Interlocutors 1, 6, and 17), who described

55   Cawo M. Abdi, *Elusive Jannah*; Robyn Maynard, *Policing Black Lives*.
56   Interlocutor 16, in person interview with author, Toronto, 2017.
57   Michelle Lowry, "Creating Human Insecurity: The National Security Focus in Canada's Immigration System," *Refuge* 21, 1 (2002): 32.
58   Michelle Lowry, "Creating Human Insecurity," 34.

having to authenticate their identity prior to accessing services, precisely due to their status as refugee claimants. Two of the three women are Somali; the other is Congolese, but she also travelled across several countries to Canada as a refugee and arrived here without documentation, thus her situation was similar. It is also important to mark the difference in circumstance between those who came as Convention refugees and those who did not. Ransford Danso explains that while Somalis and Ethiopians are both "largely refugee communities in Canada, Ethiopians were mostly selected outside of Canada and arrived already as Convention refugees with permanent residence status while the vast majority of Somalis initially came to Canada as refugee claimants."[59]

While there were some attempts to ameliorate and acknowledge this reality from the Canadian government by way of Bill C-11, The Immigration and Refugee Protection Act, this did not change conditions for the women in this book, nor for the "eighty percent of refugees who did not possess identity documents [who] were women and children."[60] The Canadian government estimates "the numbers of refugees who fell into this category [in this period] to be thirteen thousand."[61]

Additionally, Bill C-86, which "required refugees without official identity documents such as a passport to wait five years until they were able to apply for permanent residency status," also had grave impacts on the ways in which the women who spoke with me were able to make a life in Canada for themselves and for their children.[62] For example, interlocutors spoke about *"not being allowed to sponsor their families, their children"* and about how, in many cases they were *"unable to attend college or university"* given that pathways to supports such as OSAP, bank or government

59   Ransford Danso, "From 'There' to 'Here': An Investigation of the Initial Settlement Experiences of Ethiopian and Somali Refugees in Toronto," *GeoJournal* 56, 1 (2002): 5. http://www.jstor.org/stable/41147662.

60   Bill C-11, *The Immigration and Refugee Protection Act: Gender-Based Analysis* (*Legislative Summary for Bill C-11*, n.d.-a; *Legislative Summary for Bill C-11*, n.d.-c, 11), 2001.

61   Denise Spitzer, "The impact of policy on Somali refugee women in Canada," 52.

62   Ibid.

loans, and bursaries are all ultimately connected to documentation, status, and citizenship.[63]

Interlocutor 6 vividly captures the unreasonableness of the expectation that refugees arrive with official documentation when she says, "*I came to Canada with my dirac* [traditional thin transparent dress], *garbasar* [traditional thin scarf sometimes but not often transparent], *a pair of slippers that were falling apart, and I had no purse, or no bag. Just me and my kids.*" How did these women get to Canada? And how did they get to Canada from war-torn Somalia and in such high numbers? I want to address this question briefly here, because the issue cannot and should not be ignored in the context of contemporary BlackLife in Toronto. Too much of the academic literature and broader cultural discourse does not address or take seriously what is at stake for Black women's lives, nor recognize the participation of the Canadian state both in producing these high migratory numbers of Somali women refugees, the ongoing subjugation of many of the women, and the ongoing subjugation more broadly of Somali and other Black people throughout so-called Canada today.

Brian Mulroney's Progressive Conservative government established multiple bureaus and offices throughout much of the East Africa region prior to and during the influx of Somali refugees to Canada. These strategic posts throughout East Africa must be interpreted and analyzed as part of Canada's bid for Black lives, and particularly Black women and children's lives. These moves were often made under the transnational neoliberal guise of humanitarianism that depicted Canada as, in the words of Interlocutor 17, "*welcoming and full of opportunity.*"[64] Interlocutor 6 says that she was told that it was a "*safe haven for people like me, walahie* [I swear]! *That's what they said.*"[65]

After having assumed that Canada's humanitarian and immigration laws would provide and sustain a safe and welcoming culture

63   Interlocutor 1, in person interview with author, Toronto, 2017; Interlocutor 17, in person interview with author, Toronto, 2018.
64   Interlocutor 17, in person interview with author, Toronto, 2018.
65   Interlocutor 6, in person interview with author, Toronto, 2017.

in Canada, the women in this book, like others before them, spoke about the racism and Islamophobia that awaited them in Canada. Interlocutors 1 and 6 explained that upon their arrival to Canada they were called "*dirty*" and "*unhealthy,*" in one case being referred to as "*beastly.*"[66] The data reflects that in the case of many Somali women, interpretations by government officials "influence how a woman's [immigration] claim is decided."[67]

Between 1988 and 1993, the Somali population in Ontario "increased by 613 percent; with 70,000 Somalis liv[ing] in Canada, 13,000 of whom live in Ottawa, most Somalis in Canada live in Toronto, with sizeable populations in Montreal and Calgary as well."[68] During that time Toronto was "Canada's primary reception centre for immigrants and refugees. Immigration accounted for 85 percent of the population growth in the Toronto Census Metropolitan Areas in the period, 1991–1997."[69] The influx of Somalis to Ontario came with several challenges unique to this group. In her chapter entitled "War Crimes Against Women and Girls," Fowzia Musse details the brutalities visited on Somali girls and women in the civil war. She writes:

> Among the worst of the atrocities were the "rape camps," particularly in Mogadishu in the early 1990s. Militiamen abducted many women, imprisoning them in villas where they were subjected to repeated rape and other forms of sexual abuse. Although all women and girls were vulnerable, rapists tended to target female members of opposing factions, or those with weak clan affiliations and therefore little clan protection.[70]

66   Interlocutors 1 and 6, in person interviews with the author, Toronto 2017.
67   Ladan Affi, "Domestic conflict in the diaspora: Somali women asylum seekers and refugees in Canada," in *Somalia: The Untold Story*, edited by Judith Gardner & Judy El Bushra (London: Pluto Press, 2004), 110.
68   Ibid, 107.
69   Bill C-11, *The Immigration and Refugee Protection Act.* Report No. 5, Clause 1, 2001. Toronto City Clerk.
70   Fowzia Musse, "War Crimes Against Women and Girls," in "War Crimes Against Women and Girls" in *Somalia-The Untold Story: The War Through the*

With this in mind, it is important to contextualize the diversity within the population demographic of women who traveled to Canada. In the early 2000s Ransford Danso surveyed 115 Somali and Ethiopians in Toronto. This data revealed both Somalis and Ethiopians were "very young [...] refugee populations in Toronto," the mean age of his respondents being approximately thirty-three years old. Couple this with the largely refugee claimant, woman-led families, many of whom fled to Canada with their children (who again, were predominantly girls) and we begin to have a clearer picture of Canada's East African refugee populations, and in particular why they are mostly women.[71]

I am not suggesting that the Canadian state is directly responsible for the abduction and rape of Somali women; however, it is important to note the context in which policy operates, and how even with the best of intentions, it functions to exclude or not seriously consider the realities, including contextual backgrounds, of Black women. Although in March of 1993 there were some significant shifts in policy regarding gender-based immigration guidelines, the extent to which it was useful was linked to one's capacity to disclose the experience of sexual abuse or violence.[72] As indicated above, many of the women in the study spoke about their perceived lack of credibility, with one woman sharing, *"I wouldn't tell them anything! They didn't believe anything I told them about how I arrived in Canada. So why tell them about being raped in a Kenyan refugee camp?"*[73] No safe environments were provided, and the need to divulge such information should never have been deemed necessary in the first place. This is what these women were faced with when they should instead have been greeted with respect and given safe and caring treatment.

Eyes of Somali Women, edited by Judith Gardner, and Judy El-Bushra (London/ Sterling, Virginia: CIIR/Pluto Press), 70.

71   Ransford Danso. "From 'There' to 'Here': An Investigation of the Initial Settlement Experiences of Ethiopian and Somali Refugees in Toronto," *GeoJournal* 56, 1 (2002): 3–14.

72   Bill C-11/86. *The Immigration and Refugee Protection Act*, 2001.

73   Interlocutor 17, in person interview with author, Toronto, 2018.

Throughout much of the late 1990s and early 2000s, policy and academic literature—including antiracist and critical race feminist literature—often argued that Somali women could have benefitted from the changes in gender-based policy, which essentially was intended to "take into account such factors as the abuses women refugee claimants suffer[ed]."[74] These accounts suggest that there were cultural reasons why Somali women often did not end up benefitting from these policy changes:

> [u]nfortunately, in Somali society the stigma of making a claim based on rape or sexual abuse is so great that Somali women are unlikely to mention the rape or assault in the context of their claim or hearing. Without this information, their claim may be rejected. Under such circumstances women are forced to reveal the violations or remain silent for fear of being ostracised or blamed in their community.[75]

We must reject such neoliberal discourses that focus on the specificity of a particular ethnicity or culture and shift instead to understanding the ways in which antiBlackness and perceived lack of credibility are correlated, irrespective of ethnicity, culture, or tradition. The women in this book identified that it was their experience of racism, unbelievability, and gendered antiBlackness that led them to withhold their traumatic experiences; the idea that disclosure might lead to shame in their communities was not a primary factor. What their experiences indicate is that Blackness and a gendered experience of otherness is what led them to silence. For this reason, we must highlight Blackness as an entry point to understanding this phenomenon, along with a recognition of the ways in which the intersected identity of Blackness can have additional effects; we see this in the distinct dehumanization of Black

---

74   Ladan Affi, "Domestic conflict in the diaspora: Somali women asylum seekers and refugees in Canada." *Somalia: The Untold Story-The war through the eyes of Somali women*, edited by Judith Gardner and Judy L. Bushra (London: Pluto Press, 2004), 109.

75   Ibid.

women, and more specifically of Black Muslim women, Black queer women, and Black trans women, among others.

Women's unbelievability also translated into public and national discourse across the country. Somalis, and more specifically Somali women, became the embodiment of the welfare cheat within the Canadian discourse.[76] In her book *Policing Black Lives: State Violence in Canada From Slavery to Present*, Robyn Maynard states: "In Ontario [...], the racist and sexist focus on Black female welfare recipients took a particularly xenophobic turn, and though all Black women were impacted, Somali women bore the brunt of popular hostility and experienced significant state repression."[77]

The following article by John Clarke, reproduced here in its entirety, describes at a minute level, how Somali women in Toronto have organized in order to advocate for themselves and work collectively to increase their access to support. It also intimately demonstrates how the very mechanisms of state intervention that claim to offer such support enact clear obstructions to the same— through policy-rewriting, obfuscation, and targeted restrictions. Only through collective action were these women able to effectively fight back against the maneuvers of the state.

---

76   See Denise Spitzer, "The impact of policy on Somali refugee women in Canada"; Judith Gardner and Judy El Bushra, eds,. *Somalia—The Untold Story*; Robyn Maynard, *Policing Black Lives*; Anna Pratt and Mariana Valverde "From Deserving Victims to 'Masters of Confusion': Redefining Refugees in the 1990s," *Canadian Journal of Sociology* 27, 2 (2002): 135-61.

77   Robyn Maynard, *Policing Black Lives*, 132.

Relay · September/October 2006

Organizing Against Hunger and Poverty in the Somali Community

John Clarke

On the last day of March, an office opened in North Etobicoke that represented, for the Ontario Coalition Against Poverty (OCAP), a major advance. The location will be operated by a group calling itself OCAP Women of Etobicoke. They are all members of the Somali community who have been drawn into our organization by way of some very practical organizing that has touched their lives.

Toronto's Somali community gives the lie to Canadian 'multiculturalism.' Over 90% of its members live in poverty. Any professional qualifications they bring with them are disregarded. They take low paying, precarious jobs or turn to a welfare system that feels it has a right to humiliate them in return for the sub-poverty pittance it provides. The community's young people can't leave their homes without walking the gauntlet of harassment by cops and private security agencies. Those who have not yet secured their right to live here as citizens deal with an immigration system that has a strange way of 'celebrating diversity'. The Somalis of Toronto experience daily the poverty and racism that awaits 'New Canadians.'

OCAP has had a foothold in the Somali Community for a number of years and we have mobilized on a range of issue it confronts. In the last year, that working relationship reached a new level by way of a struggle around an element of the Welfare System known as the Special Diet Policy.

The Liberal Party in Ontario has, since it came to power, worked to consolidate rather than reverse the Harris Common Sense Revolution. It junked any promises it had made to address the needs of those on welfare and has given begrudged increases of less than the rate of inflation. People on assistance have seen the spending power of their cheques reduced by 40% in ten years and McGuinty has maintained this situation. Hungry people work for lower wages and he is not about to interfere with the 'competitive edge' by raising welfare rates if he can avoid it.

After McGuinty took over, OCAP began to explore ways to effectively press for him to 'Raise the Rates.' Our discussions began to focus on the notion that many things people are supposed to be able to get when they are on welfare are kept from them by the system's bureaucracy. We came across the

Special Diet Policy under which those receiving assistance could get up to $250 a month per person in food allowance if a medical provider deemed it necessary. Of course, this policy was little known and often refused to those who applied for it but we asked ourselves what would happen if we organized community-based clinics to enable people to obtain the food supplement. We also asked what would be the effect of ensuring that welfare officialdom had to deal with applicants who were organized to act collectively. Finally, we considered what would be the result if knowledge of the benefit were communicated through every available channel to poor communities.

The balance of 2005 was an exercise in finding out the answers to these three questions. We made contact with some dozens of health providers ready to work with us on clinics. In Toronto, over

8,000 people were diagnosed as being in need of the Supplement by this method and clinics were held in range of cities in the rest of the Province. From the start, it was clear that the Somali community, with its extraordinary internal communication and sense of mutual aid, would be at the backbone of organizing to access the Special Diet.

Once the Campaign was underway, the City of Toronto's welfare bureaucracy began a frantic round of initiatives to block access to the allowance. Local policies were written and rewritten almost weekly. Families accessing the Supplement were targeted for denial as suspect 'multiple entitlements'. Nurse practitioners, dieticians and midwifes were suddenly told they could no longer diagnose the need for nutritional adequacy. A round of attempts were made to force people to reapply on new Special Diet forms, even if they had recently been approved to receive the benefit.

OCAP defeated these attacks with an ongoing round of collective action. The Mayor's office was occupied, the head offices of Social Services were taken over, and local welfare offices received mass delegations of people demanding their right to the food supplement. Many communities that face poverty in Toronto responded. A clinic was held in Spanish. A Chinese language radio station requested an interview with one of our Cantonese-speaking members because they were being flooded with inquiries. Vietnamese people developed their own informal network to co-operate in securing and defending the Supplement. But I don't believe we ever had an action in this Campaign where the Somali Community was not the main force involved.

The OCAP organized drive to access the Special Diet reached a peak in October of last year when forty medical providers diagnosed 1,100 people, at a clinic on the lawns of Queen's Park, as being in need of the benefit. As large an impact as we were able to directly organize, however, the informal network in poor communities across Ontario had many times the effect. In 2005, total benefits paid out for Special Diet items doubled in size to $80 million.

After ten years of trying to reverse the destruction of income-support systems in Ontario, we finally had found a means win back some ground. We realized that Queen's Park would move against us but the transformation of the Supplement from an obscure provision to a well known entitlement was a potential change in the balance of forces and not something that the Liberals would be able to take away without a fight. The drastic cuts to the Policy that came in November did, indeed, spark a wave of indignation and a fight back that is still ongoing. Still, the recent Provincial Budget, with its miserable 2% increase in social assistance rates, shows that that fight will not be an easy one. The strength that was shown by the Somali community and by many other poor people in different parts of Ontario forms the basis for winning it.

The cut to the Special Diet Supplement has not stopped the organizing momentum in Etobicoke. Delegations from the community to local welfare offices to win benefits for families are ongoing. People have organized actions to force the property management company at a major public housing project to carry out maintenance work

that was being neglected. A recent picket of the 23 Division, to challenge police harassment of Somali youth, has emboldened people to the point where cops are being challenged when they come into areas to carry out their intimidation of the community. One mother recently told a couple of cops who were harassing her son: "Our community is safe, apart from when you show up. You're not welcome here." People are starting to stand up and fight back as the situation demands.

The OCAP Women of Etobicoke are a glimpse of the potential for organizing communities under attack. In order to support such initiatives, however, you have to stand on the appropriate side of the line. Union leaderships seeking new, collaborative relations with the Liberal Party, can't be part of this fight. Those who refuse to challenge an NDP Mayor who boasts of the number of cops he has put on the streets are, similarly, out of the running. To work with working class and poor communities under attack, you must be ready to fight their enemies. **R**

John Clarke is a longtime activist with OCAP.

This article by John Clarke, was originally printed in The Socialist Project's September/October 2006 issue of *Relay*, (issue 13), and is reproduced with permission.

While it is important to acknowledge the particularities across different populations and circumstances, it is equally important to understand the longstanding pattern of marking Black women and their children as burdensome and even criminal. For as long as many of us can remember, the Canadian state has not been welcoming of Black people; we have read rhetoric about not being able to manage the cold, about ideas of lack of productivity, and about an inability to assimilate based on language differences. In fact, many of the arguments that were made specifically about Somali women can also be seen paralleled in the ways Caribbean women who were coming to Canada in the late 1950s and '60s were also read as particularly unsafe, at times too religious and backwards, and only considered a sort of servant class of domestic help.[78] It is important to not only address and take up these differences across Blackness, but also to highlight the ways in which Blackness surfaces repeatedly, at varying intersections, as a specific target for the state. Considering the ways in which other Black women migrating to Canada have been treated gives us a site of analysis and comparison from which we can work against and move toward dismantling these false narratives that continue to emerge anew with each subsequent wave of migration.

I therefore invite Canadian feminist scholars and those in policy studies and social science research, as well as policy- and lawmakers, to consider, discuss, dissect, and expose the complexities of white supremacy that lie at the centre of the fact that the state and its individual actors are always too ready to simply cast a new representative of Blackness into the fire. Regardless of ethnic differences amongst our Black communities, it is still Black women who are the highest growing federal prison population; it is still Black youth who are over-represented within the youth penal system; and it is Black men who are over-represented within the provincial and

---

78   Makeda Silvera, *Her Head a Village: & other stories* (Vancouver: Press Gang Publishers, 1994); Makeda Silvera, ed., *The Other Woman: Women of Colour in Contemporary Canadian Literature* (Toronto: Sister Vision Press, 1995); Makeda Silvera, *The Heart Does Not Bend* (Toronto: Vintage Canada, 2003); Makeda Silvera, *Silenced Caribbean Domestic Workers Talk With Makeda Silvera* (Toronto: Sister Vision, 1983).

federal prison systems. What becomes apparent for many Black women is that irrespective of their specific presentation, it is their Blackness that consistently acts as a marker that either excludes them or makes them hyper-visible within this set of interlocking systems. In *Experiences of Black Muslims In Canada*, Abdi Osman writes:

> the "brown" Muslim tends to be the foremost image inhabiting post-9/11 non-Islamic western imaginations, while African and black diasporic Muslims are only fleetingly or ephemerally present. Appearing and disappearing within the popular imagination, yet and embodying a post-9/11 black Islamic presence, black Muslims have come to represent and articulate complicated political questions about the racialization of Islam, about surveillance in black diaspora, about the links between religious practices and nation-state discourses, and about the shifting definitions and interpretations of Muslim bodies.[79]

These are some of the meanings projected onto Somali women in Canada, including the women in this study: hyper-visible and distrusted on the one hand, not truly seen on the other. The combination of their race and their religion, along with their poverty and refugee status, leads to a very particular, and I would argue dehumanized, way of being "seen" by the Canadian state. The narrative that these women are both oppressed within their community and dishonest does not reflect their reality. In fact, girls and women have not only been valued as central to the functioning of Somali cultures and traditions, but women have been meaningful breadwinners within the familial and kinship network. Canada sees itself as having bestowed gendered freedoms to Somali women by virtue of allowing migration to Canada, but the reality is that these women were met with racialized and religious othering and have too often been silenced and exploited as a result.

79   Abdi Osman, *Post-9/11 Experiences of Black Muslims in Canada* (Toronto: Blurb, 2011), 1.

SEARCHING AND RESEARCHING

Here we need to detour to the academy, as any discussion relevant to research that will reach the eyes of academics must address the context of academically-established ways of knowing that include and exclude Black personhood. I do this less as a way of tracing a methodology than of establishing my own relationship to research and theory, and the difficulties and struggle within that relationship to work in ways that will honour the lives and realities of the Black women who have exchanged and shared their thoughts and time with me. When the words of my interlocutors converge in this text alongside thematic data and theoretical context, they are brought together in this way in order to foreground the fact that their experience, their lives, and the conditions and overall outcomes for Black women more broadly are inseparable from, and inextricably linked to, all dimensions of social and political life from its inception. This includes the academy.

Although based in a coalescence, my approach here strives for something independent of institutionally affirmed collective knowledge. I follow Charles Mills' assertion that we should refuse the outright lies of Eurocentrism; Mills states that one must instead:

> learn to trust one's own cognitive power, to develop one's own concepts, insights, modes of explanation, overarching theories, and to oppose the episteme hegemony of conceptual frameworks designed in part to thwart and

suppress the exploration of such matters; one has to think *against the grain*.[1]

I am aware of a certain irony that is built into critically taking on academic structures while relying, to whatever extent, on the power relation of citational practices, but I am also aware that how, when, and who I choose to write into this text can also work constructively away from these hegemonic concepts of authenticity. The experiences of these Toronto Black women must be animated alongside and in conversation with existing research, theory, and practice in order to broaden space to uncover direct links within their essences, even in their most quotidian materializations, and in order to demonstrate the shared, longstanding, and ongoing historicity of interconnectedness of the lives of Black women regionally and globally.

When I stated that allowing for the continuance of systems manifests as violent facilitation, it is with an understanding that exposing this functioning is one of the necessary steps of interruption and disruption. Alongside social service and legal frameworks, the epistemic frameworks that describe them must also be disrupted. Following what Saidiya Hartman describes as a "mode of close narration, a style which places the voices of narrator and character in inseparable relation, so that the vision, language, and rhythms of the wayward shape and arrange the text," I deliberately, and I hope subversively Blacken method and its concomitants of discipline, its insistence on the "scientific" terrain that is counterpart and co-conspirator to white supremacist, antiBlack, and racial-capitalist actualities.[2] Here is an effort to expose the insistence on traditional method and research as antithetical to BlackLife. I move outside of the frame of "researcher" and "researched," of "insider and outsider," or what Patricia Hill Collins describes as an "outsider within," in order to restage the research in the context of the "inseparable"

1   Charles Mills, *The Racial Contract* (Ithaca: Cornell University Press, 1997) 119.
2   Saidiya Hartman, *Wayward Lives, Beautiful Experiments: Intimate Histories of Riotous Black Girls, Troublesome Women, and Queer Radicals* (New York: W. W. Norton & Company, 2019), xi-xiv.

relation between researcher and subject, bringing into a central position the "vision, language, and rhythms" of Black people.[3] It is within this light that I want to think about the word "interlocutor" as well; the interlocutor who is equally locked within the role of subject and attendant subjectivities that we are trying to share and uncover through exchange.

As an interlocutor I position my own presence as a Black woman living in Toronto in a place of relevance as opposed to one of observational distance, that distance which too often has been in and of itself not only a form of erasure, but from a theoretical perspective, a historically problematic practice in which the often white researcher's self-erasure is a kind of ubiquity that presumes universally white objectivity, and by extension access to truth in relation to the "subject." I challenge that colonial state violence and white supremacy that remain inherent in qualitative research, specifically in "policy studies" and "method" in the Black Canadian studies context, that continues to result in a non-human status for Black women, and in the overall absenting, de-gendering, and disembodiment of Black women's lives in Toronto.

In the context of social science research, there has been a long and complicated history of so-called truth-seeking and meaning-making dictated by positivism and white supremacy. It is therefore important to always delineate how the academic world approaches its subjects of study, and to situate my own approach as an academic researcher within and against that context. Readers and researchers alike tend to look upon qualitative research as kinder or gentler, but we must always keep in our minds the fact that it emerges from and is entrenched within the persistently extractive research industrial context. Much of how the modern world and contemporary life has justified and continues to justify its ways of knowing are

---

3   Patricia Hill Collins, *Black Feminist Thought: Knowledge, Consciousness, and the Politics of Empowerment* (New York: Routledge, 2000), 11; Saidiya Hartman, *Wayward Lives, Beautiful Experiments*, xiii. Also see David Marriott, *Haunted Life: Visual Culture and Black Modernity* (New Brunswick, N.J.: Rutgers University Press, 2007); Christina Sharpe, *Monstrous Intimacies: Making Post-Slavery Subjects* (Durham, NC: Duke University Press, 2010); Christina Sharpe, *In the Wake: On Blackness and Being* (Durham: Duke University Press, 2016).

directly linked to positivism, Judeo-Christian values, and notions of cause and effect. Consider the social notions of laziness, hard work, charity, and gluttony; similar social biases are reflected in western truth-seeking and are maintained through the critiques of modernity in the 1500s–1900s.

In fact, "western cultures share a great confidence and respect for science as the way to truth," creating a social and political terrain damning of the sciences as they reproduce hierarchies "where society is organized according to scientific observations and experiments."[4] As part of this process, the value judgements that generate social hierarchies, which are in themselves extraneous to "scientific" process, appear at the same time under the guise of science in the form of, among other things, the "social sciences." These particular kinds of interventions align with histories of subjugation by way of study that have impacted groups in the social world that are "other" and "othered," including the Black women who are my focus. The relationships between Black women in particular and the social sciences as a "subject" have reverberating and ongoing impacts. The sciences are seen as a powerful tool that can help solve social problems; however, questions remain about who or what the "problem" is, and what tools and methodological interventions are used to describe such problems. The fact remains that inherent in methodological processes are raced and gendered discourses of the studied, and also of the knower/researcher.[5] This is where a committed approach of intersectionality can become useful. Though Critical Race Theory (CRT)—described by Dolores Delgado Bernal describes as an "epistemology [that] can acknowledge black people as holders and legitimate sources of knowledge where Eurocentric epistemologies consistently fail"—can provide an entry into an analysis of race more broadly, when the limited

4   Winston Jackson and Noreen Verberg, *Methods: Doing Social Research, 4th ed.* (Toronto: Pearson Prentice Hall, 2007), 5.
5   See Patricia Hamilton, "Now That I Know What You're About"; Zenzele Isoke, "Black Ethnography, Black(Female)Aesthetics: Thinking/Writing/Saying/Sounding Black Political Life," *Theory & Event* 21, 1 (2018): 148–68.

inclusion of Black women's voices is a problem in its articulation.[6] Black feminist thought, which centers specifically on the intersectional experiences of Black women, can often address what is missing. As Patricia Hill Collins states, "by taking the core themes of a Black women's standpoint and infusing them with new meaning, Black feminist thought can stimulate a new consciousness that utilizes Black women's every day, taken-for-granted knowledge."[7] An intersectional approach (though alone not unproblematic, as I discuss later in this chapter), that brings in these various pieces, alongside another, somewhat ineffable piece—personal and unspoken dialoguing—is more than simply corrective, it is clarifying. As I wrote alongside Rinaldo Walcott in 2019, "when one sees more clearly one begins to witness the ways in which discourse and practices of democracy, diversity, inclusion, and a range of ideas meant to interrupt inequality and supposedly produce a different society does not work for Black people."[8]

In illuminating, for example, the formations of Blackness and surveillance, it is useful to look to Fanon's idea "that modernity can be characterized by the 'mise en fiches de l'homme.' These are the records, files, time sheets, and identity documents that together form a biography, and sometimes an unauthorized one, of the modern subject."[9] Indeed, while critiques exist about Fanon's capacity to engender philosophies of Black women's subjectivities, and also, their encounters with surveillance and surveilled transgressions, the works of many scholars since help to complement and fill out the limitations of Fanon's work, opening up new ways

6 Dolores Delgado Bernal, as quoted in Kevin Hylton, "Talk the talk, walk the walk: Defining Critical Race Theory in research," *Race Ethnicity and Education* 15, 1 (2012): 25. Also see Patricia Hill Collins's texts, *Black Feminist Thought* and *Black Sexual Politics: African Americans, Gender, and the New Racism* (New York: Routledge, 2004); Kimberlé Crenshaw, "Mapping the Margins: Intersectionality, Identity Politics, and Violence Against Women of Color," *Stanford Law Review* 43, 6 (1991): 1241–1299; bell hooks, *Yearning: Race, Gender, And Cultural Politics* (Toronto: Between the Lines, 1990).
7 Patricia Hill Collins, *Black Feminist Thought*, 32.
8 Idil Abdillahi and Rinaldo Walcott, *BlackLife* (Winnipeg: ARP Books, 2019), 87.
9 Simone Browne, *Dark Matters: On the Surveillance of Blackness* (Durham, NC: Duke University Press, 2015), 5; Franz Fanon, *The Wretched of the Earth*, trans. Richard Philcox (New York: Grove Press, 2004).

SEARCHING AND RESEARCHING

to conceptualize surveillance and its outcomes specific to Black women's lives.[10] Many Black feminists, including Angela Davis, bell hooks, Toni Cade Bambara, and June Jordan, have noted a connection between Fanon's "analysis of the racialized disciplinary society" on the one hand and the possible movement "away from his emphasis on masculinity to imagine new modes of postrevolutionary gender identity."[11] This provides some reason for "optimism," as Browne puts it, that bringing together Fanon and Black feminist thought can lead to "another mode of reading surveillance."[12]

Over the last forty years, critical theory and critical researchers have worked toward challenging the assumption that there is one correct way of conducting human research. Rather, critical research can be best understood as "an ever-evolving criticality, a reconceptualized critical theory that was critiqued and overhauled by 'post-discourses' of the last quarter of the 20th century and has been further extended in the first years of the 21st century."[13] It is often not just counterintuitive, but damaging, to provide a singular definition for a set of complex ideas that are shifting and changing within ever-evolving social and political terrain; this is the very issue with disciplinarity. Joe Kincheloe and Peter McLaren argue that "critical theory should not be treated as a universal grammar of revolutionary thought objectified and reduced to discrete formulaic pronouncements or strategies."[14]

Within critical research in the Canadian context, there has been a notable emphasis on and in many cases an attempt to move toward decolonization, running alongside several shifts within the academy

---

10   Including and not limited to John Alexander, Toni Cade Bambara, Ruha Benjamin, Simone Browne, Carole Boyce Davies, Angela Davis, Ruth Wilson Gilmore, Saidiya Hartman, Mariame Kaba, Katherine McKittrick, Délice Mugabo, Safiya Umoja Noble, Andrea Ritchie, Dolores Jones-Brown, Julia Chinyere Oparah (formerly Julia Sudbury), and Sylvia Wynter.

11   Nicholas Mirzoeff, quoted in Simone Browne, *Dark Matters: On the Surveillance of Blackness* (Durham: Duke University Press, 2015), 6.

12   Ibid.

13   Joe L. Kincheloe and Peter McLaren, "Rethinking Critical Theory and Qualitative Research," in *The SAGE Handbook of Qualitative Research, 3rd ed.,* Norman K. Denzin and Yvonna S. Lincoln, eds. (London: Sage Publications, 2005), 303.

14   Ibid, 304.

concerning the boundaries between disciplines. Specifically, there have been increasing, yet still often resisted and rejected, notions of fixed disciplines, while simultaneous shifts occur toward "interdisciplinary" scholarship and research. There is, in other words, both a demand and a reluctance of critical research to ground itself in the rigour of multiple realities in real time. For example, the rigid notions of the sciences have been challenged by a recognition of the academic worthiness of particular types of scholarly production and research training happening within and between the arts, humanities, sciences, and social sciences.

Although I don't wish to dwell too much in methodological tracing, one concept that is useful in reflection of my work here is Lévi-Strauss's idea of the knower as *bricoleur*, essentially a metaphor used to integrate ways of knowing based on what one may have access to in order to bring about new meanings and understandings, to socially and textually animate an issue, and/or to make meaning.

> [Straus] employed the bricolage metaphor in his search for underlying structures that govern human meaning-making. More specifically, however, he used the metaphor in the context of his challenge to the, then-dominant, thinking within anthropology which bifurcated mythical and scientific rationality.[15]

Decades later, other scholars built on Levi-Strauss's theorizing by referring to the researcher as a *bricoleur* or maker of quilts, bringing together and amalgamating worldviews, theories, interpretations, tools, tasks, accounts, and a myriad of skills within the qualitative research process.[16] In this multi-form approach that not only

---

15   Matt Rogers, "Contextualizing Theories and Practices of Bricolage Research," *The Qualitative Report* 17, 48 (2012): 2.

16   See Clifford Geertz, *Works and Lives: The Anthropologist as Author* (Stanford: Stanford University Press, 1988); Joe Kincheloe, "Describing the Bricolage: Conceptualizing a New Rigor in Qualitative Research," *Qualitative Inquiry* 7(6), 679–692; Yvonna S. Lincoln, "An Emerging New Bricoleur: Promises and Possibilities—A Reaction to Joe Kincheloe's 'Describing the Bricoleur,'"

legitimizes but I would argue de-hierarchizes various knowledge fragments, is a system of knowing and life engagement that I find useful to a discussion of the lives of Black women, for it can make room for knowledge that dominant social-science structures, even those well-intentioned, would necessarily miss.

In her 2001 article entitled "An Emerging New *Bricoleur*: Promises and Possibilities—A Reaction to Joe Kincheloe's 'Describing the Bricoleur,'" Yvonna Lincoln identifies the *bricoleur* as a researcher who "looks for not yet imagined tools, fashioning them with not yet imagined connections"—like a "handyman" who searches "for the nodes, the nexuses, the linkages, the interconnections, the fragile bonds between disciplines, between bodies of knowledge, between knowing and understanding themselves."[17] Of central concern to Lincoln are the ways in which the *bricoleur* works within, between, in-between, and at the intersection of connections and disconnections, and moves through, alongside, and outside of the processes of research and knowledge. She describes this as "'boundary-work' taken to the extreme … It works the margins and liminal spaces between both formal knowledge, and what has been proposed as boundary knowledge, knitting them together, forming a new consciousness."[18] I take up this "boundary-work" not as static or fixed to a particular theoretical framework, methodology, or discipline, but as a practice that seeks to challenge, undo, and bring into the fold precisely what is occurring and what can emerge in spaces of convergence, disjuncture, and possibility. That kind of space can also be used as its own tool, as a way, from the vantage of a furthest possible boundary, to locate other, cloaked boundaries and thereby work to undo prescribed discipline. Norman Denzin and Yvonna Lincoln remind us:

> There are many kinds of *bricoleurs*—interpretive, narrative, theoretical, political, Methodological. The

Qualitative Inquiry 7, 6 (2001): 693–696; bell hooks, Yearning: Race, Gender, And Cultural Politics (Toronto: Between the Lines, 1990).

17   Yvonna Lincoln, "An Emerging New Bricoleur: Promises and Possibilities, 693–694.

18   Ibid, 694.

interpretive *bricoleur* produces a bricolage—that is, a pieced-together set of representations that is fitted to the specifics of a complex situation … The qualitative researcher as *bricoleur*, or maker of quilts, uses the aesthetics and material tools of his or her craft, deploying whatever strategies, methods, and empirical materials are at hand (Baker, 1998, p. 2). If the researcher needs to invent, or piece together, new tools or techniques, he or she will do so."[19]

This is a promising vision. However, with the ongoing commitment to disciplinary rigidity, absolutism, and academic purity, the conceptualization of researchers as *bricoleurs* has yet to come to full fruition. I am not suggesting that there has been no shift toward an interdisciplinary approach to knowledge production over the last decade, but I am noting that within the social sciences specifically there remains fracture and disjuncture in the processes of collaborative and meaningful cross-disciplinary knowledge creation, particularly within research, that make the kind of anti-disciplinary practice that I embrace difficult. In 2012 Lincoln also voiced this concern about interdisciplinary border-crossing, saying, "I believe its realization is a long way off. We have few models to show us how such interdisciplinary collaboration might work. Such collaboration is neither well understood, nor is it well rewarded in the academy."[20] In fact, she goes as far as to point researchers to the "best forms" of this work, by adding that it is "feminists and race-ethnic theorists" who are leading and should be a source of reference for researchers; she states that, "if critical race and critical race feminist work furnishes the models for such interdisciplinary border-crossing, then we have at least a place to begin."[21]

While the critical approach to research can be understood as encompassing feminist theories, approaches, and methodologies,

19   Norman Denzin and Yvonna Lincoln, *The Landscape of Qualitative Research: Theories and Issues* (London: Sage Publications, 1998), 4.
20   Yvonna Lincoln, "An Emerging New Bricoleur," 694.
21   Ibid.

feminist research is in fact aligned paradigmatically with an interpretive approach. These distinctions are important to note given the imperative for feminist researchers to unearth the social and political causes and conditions of the oppression of all women and to center the acute experiences of women in the broader context of patriarchy, sexism, and their associated logics. In their text, *Experience, Research, Social Change: Methods from the Margins*, Sandra Kirby and Kate McKenna differentiate critical and traditional interventions to research and argue that "research from the margins is not research on people from the margins, but research by, for, and with them."[22] Therefore, a point of crucial deliberation for researchers should be that research must aim not simply to study to report, but must aim to address, influence, and remedy policy-making concerns at the micro, mezzo, and macro levels of institutions and the social world.

Feminist methodology is an approach to research that both identifies women's oppression and seeks to change it, as well as advancing an epistemological and methodological critique of "malestream" research traditions.[23] Feminist thought brings to central focus the experiences of women that have been dropped from and sidelined in perspectives such as critical theory, critical race theory, postmodernism, structuralism, and Marxism, demanding a different ontological gaze that brings into focus possibilities for women, while simultaneously recognizing women's actual placement within broader social structures that seek to dehumanize and disenfranchise us. However, like feminism itself, feminist research has been severely lacking when it comes to taking seriously the lives of racialized women. As Sandra Kirby writes, "western feminist models were inappropriate for thinking of research with women in the postcolonial sites."[24] A central component of feminist research is the notion of emancipation, deployed by many researchers seeking to

22 Sandra Kirby and Kate McKenna, *Experience Research Social Change: Methods from the Margins* (Toronto: Garamond Press, 1989), 1.
23 Joan Acker et al., as cited in Patricia Hamilton, "'Now That I Know What You're About': Black Feminist Reflections on Power in the Research Relationship," *Qualitative Research: QR* 20, 5 (2020): 519.
24 Sandra Kirby, *Experience Research Social Change*, 242.

define the context of emancipatory research as it relates specifically to feminism. Historically and within the current context, the notion and political stance that "the personal is the political" centers the lives of women first and foremost outside the academy and within the social world, locally and globally. This is informed by social movements led and produced by women that "provided the necessary social basis for legitimation and political support that allowed women researchers to start publicly asking some of the questions they had long been asking privately."[25]

George Ritzer succinctly describes the aims of feminist research with the basic question: "And what about the women?" This question can have many variations depending on context: "Where are the women in any situation being investigated? Why are they not present in many situations? How do they experience a situation? What do they contribute to it? What does it mean for them?"[26] Based on my theorizing and research, I would add a subset of questions, recognizing the intersectionality of women's experiences: What are the nuanced experiences of women at the intersection of race, particularly Blackness and the experiences of antiBlackness, both in the context of research and in broader feminist discourses and scholarly works? How can Black feminism be brought into the fold as an entry point into discourses of feminism, and not as an adjunct or add-on theoretical perspective? In what ways are Black women the *absented presence* in many traditional and conventional research methods and interventions? In what ways has traditional mainstream feminist research "bracketed out" or not discursively engaged with the realities of Black women in the production of research paradigmatic interventions?

Ultimately, feminists and feminist researchers need to take seriously that Black feminism has much to offer social science research beyond having Black-identified research participants. Prior to explicitly Black feminist theorizing and research interventions, Black women were impelled to conduct research using mainstream

25   Joan Acker et. al, "Objectivity and Truth: Problems in doing feminist research," *Women's Studies International Forum* 6, 4 (1983): 424.

26   George Ritzer, *Sociological Theory, 2nd ed.* (New York: Alfred A. Knopf, 1988), 12.

white feminism while simultaneously critiquing and speaking to the gaps of these white feminist perspectives. In the same way, Black feminisms—which, put very loosely, asks us to consider the myriad of intersections that impact the lives of women—surely must not only be relevant to Black women. It is important to note, however, that Black feminist studies and Black feminist research has also given rise to multiple other feminisms, for example Chicana feminism and Afro-Latinx feminisms. As Collins reminds us, "Black feminist thought constitutes one part of a much larger social justice project that goes far beyond the experiences of African-American women."[27]

In the context of policy research and research in general, Black Canadian women often appear as a group for comparison rather than as an isolated and distinct group that requires exploration and specific engagement. It is particularly important to point out that within this kind of policy and research discussion, Black women's experience should never be entered into here from a framework that positions white women and white women's experience as a universalizing barometer, a schema that is inherently antiBlack. When considering notions of poverty, imposed disenfranchisement, lack of state responses, intervention or visibility within academe, Black Canadian women and girls tend to serve as a juxtaposition for white women but also for Black men and boys. Deborah K. King asserts quite rightly that,

the experience of black women is apparently assumed, though never explicitly stated, to be synonymous with that of either black males or white women; and since the experiences of both are equivalent, a discussion of black women in particular is superfluous. It is mistakenly granted that [...] there is no difference in being black and female from being generically black (i.e., male) or generically female (i.e., white).[28]

27　Patricia Hill Collins, *Black Feminist Thought*, 19.
28　Deborah K. King, *Multiple Jeopardy, Multiple Consciousness*: The Context of a Black Feminist Ideology," *Signs* 14, 1 (1988), 45.

This often leaves significant gaps in the literature, the data, and the complex gendered and raced matrix of "representation," offering in its wake a profound inability to conceptualize the lives of Black women more broadly within the so-called Canadian public sphere.

In *Black Feminist Thought: Knowledge, Consciousness, and the Politics of Empowerment*, Patricia Hill Collins expounds the fundamental tenets guiding her interpretation of Black feminist research. She writes that we must attend to and grapple with a) the concrete experience as a criterion of meaning, b) the use of dialogue in assessing knowledge claims, c) an ethic of care, and d) an ethic of responsibility.[29] In each of these methodological considerations lies a site for analytical assessment (socially and structurally), while demanding that we engage with the intimate daily lives of Black women in a meaningful way. This not only speaks to the centring of Black women's experiences but also challenges us to reimagine, rearticulate, and undo male-centred, white supremacist episteme.

Often, Black feminist contributions to research design and methods become taken-for-granted knowledge under the broad rubric of critical, social justice approaches or "feminist" research interventions. Take for example Deborah K. King's lamenting of "multiple consciousness in Black women's politics."[30] While many may correlate her theorizing with Kimberlé Crenshaw's intersectionality, what King is actually offering is an even broader encompassing of both theory and method, a form of bricolage. She writes that multiple consciousness "refers not only to several, simultaneous oppressions but to the multiplicative relationships among them as well."[31] King asks researchers not only to look for the inter-

29   Patricia Hill Collins, "The Social Construction of Black Feminist Thought," *Signs* 14, 4 (1989): 745–773. See also LaShawnda Lindsay-Dennis, "Black Feminist-Womanist Research Paradigm: Toward a Culturally Relevant Research Model Focused on African American Girls," *Journal of Black Studies* 46, 5 (2015): 506–520; Patricia Hamilton, "'Now That I Know What You're About': Black Feminist Reflections on Power in the Research Relationship," *Qualitative Research : QR* 20, 5 (2020): 519–33.

30   Deborah K. King, "Multiple Jeopardy, Multiple Consciousness."

31   Ibid, 45; Kimberlé Crenshaw, "Race, Reform, and Retrenchment: Transformation and Legitimation in Antidiscrimination Law," *Harvard Law Review* 101, 7 (1988): 1331–1387.

sections of oppression, but to consider the ways in which each specified oppression coalesces and enters into figurative "conversation" with others, bringing together the cumulative experiences of the oppressions Black women face in order to create a new or overlooked domain or "consciousness" that requires that analysis and interpretation be done differently, using both societal and intrapersonal perspectives.

King builds on earlier interventions by Bonnie Thornton Dill, who offers us the "dialectics of Black womanhood."[32] Dill reminds us that the "new knowledge claims" of Black women "are rarely worked out in isolation from other individuals and are usually developed through dialogues with other members of a community. A primary epistemological assumption underlying the use of dialogue in assessing knowledge claims is that connectedness rather than separation is an essential component of the knowledge-validation."[33] Dill reckons many of the epistemic and methodological concerns in today's social science struggles come from a gap in "historical data and/or the misinterpretation of that data," including "erroneous or partially conceived assumptions about the relationship of black [people] to white society." Additional problems then flow from this: "The third problem is a direct result of the second and arises because of the differences between the values of the researcher and those of the subject. Fourth is the general confusion of class and culture."[34]

Central to Collins's, King's, and Dill's arguments are the abandoned daily experiences of Black women as our livabilities are redacted in the context of research and everyday life. Collectively, these Black women scholars ask us to consider the mundanity of Black women's lives, not simply as ordinary, but as impinged upon but an ordinariness of subjugation that manifests across multiple contexts. These range from the absence of Black women's voices and perspectives in research to the upholding of and dependence

32 Bonnie Thornton Dill, "The Dialectics of Black Womanhood," *Signs* 4, 3
     (1979): 543–555.
33 Ibid, 545.
34 Ibid.

on the subjugation of Black women for the nation-building project; and they are reflected both in relationships between Black and
non-Black women. All of this brings us back to the fundamental
issue that when we remove, ignore, dematerialize, and vanish the
experiences of Black women within any disciplinary context and
within our social consciousness, we are not only failing to fulfill
the presumed "truth-seeking" goals of academic research, but we
are entrenching a world view, an entire reality, that hinges on Black
women's subjugation and erasure.

In her critique of gender studies, Sabine Broeck discusses the ways
that it should move away from the "difference" ie, "non-homo-
geneity" of women, towards what she calls "a realization of the
anti-Blackness inherent in the very category of gender, for which
women and men as humans have been the default reference, and
which thus cannot see, as it were, Black life."[35] White gender
studies, by her characterization, has enacted an "evasion of the
authority of Black theoretical interventions."[36] It is an issue that
brings serious questions to intersectionality discourse, where, outside of "white studies" there is no analysis of the white privilege that
forms the groundings of gender theory, that is, she argues "in the
very fiber of its programmatic intent," even though "Black feminism has been pushing for this epistemic break in most explicit, but
insistently unnoticed, terms."[37]

   Is it unavoidable then, that white researchers, thinkers, etcetera,
can only ever be dangers? Broeck, a white researcher, uses the concept of the "addressee" to address the question:

> I speak here as a white scholar who considers herself an
> *addressee*, a spoken-to, of the epistemic challenge which
> Black feminism has posed to any critical theory of trans-
> atlantic modernity—in my case, white gender studies.
> To read Black feminist contributions epistemically is to

---

35   Sabine Broeck, *Gender and the Abjection of Blackness* (Albany: State University
     of New York Press, 2018), 14.
36   Ibid, 1.
37   Ibid, 2.

acknowledge an intervention, which goes straight to the core of transatlantic modernity: the issue of property and its consequences.... . What would it entail for a radical critique of modern subjectivity, including modern and postmodern gender relations, to hear a position that has consistently spoken from the location, the materiality, and the inherited memory of having been literal property?[38]

One way to address the racist geneology of gender studies may be for white researchers to develop an understanding that the embodiment of research and the whiteness of postmodernity is a tool, a vehicle of epistemic violence which they must mitigate and halt. Why must we continually wield violent theoretical tools to proclaimed non-violent ends? Looking at this epistemic framework, we can envision a work process by reverse, where our interventions are opposite and opposed, going back to undo the naming and marking, we are addressing that violence and its everlasting mark on us. That in itself is enough work for every individual academic for the rest of our lives!

Broeck's recognition of what she sees in Black feminist scholarship as "a will to be done with abjection, a rage for change, and a wild longing for unownedness," as "altogether a stunning recombination of social sentiment," is an entire reinvention of subjectivity and desire.[39] When this comes to the question of Black women's bodies and being, a critique of gender studies white Enlightenment lineage becomes all the more salient. Broeck's analysis becomes very useful:

As a prototypical modern emancipatory discourse, gender carries a baggage of propertization and abjection of Blackness, which needs to be addressed from within white gender studies. If enslavement is the vantage point from which to read modernity, it follows that property needs to be that reading's counterpoint. But property with a double difference: first, in a sense that

38 Ibid, 11-12.
39 Ibid, 12.

goes beyond a post-Marxist critique. That is, property needs to be seen not just as means of production and as ownership of natural and man-made resources, but as property of Black life in its actuality, as property of Black reproductive capacity, of Black capacity to generate a future. Thus, property becomes a term that signifies not the metaphorical slavery of white post-Enlightenment theories of subjection, but the literal accumulation and fungibility, as Saidiya Hartman has called it in *Scenes of Subjection*, of Black being.[40]

What then, does intersection mean, when each line of the intersection cannot be addressed as socially equal? When some of these routes and discourses, that have been largely understood as emancipatory tools, are the regular appendages of white supremacist logics? BlackLife, Black women's lives, remain propertized. Intersectionaltiy, then, must be problematized. As Broekner agues,

> "difference is a category of lateral comparison, which avoids acknowledgment of a fundamental structural opposition, borne by white enslavist power, and thus cannot address white power—male and female—over, and use of, Black being."[41]

Insofar as intersectionality in this context forces its analysis to impose the label of "difference" upon the Black woman subject, it reaches its limit, and even its failing. Though rather than discarding intersectionality, which usage provides some undeniable fruit, I would argue for the cautious, the critical, or to borrow from Broekner, the "hesitant" intersection, the meeting with historical awareness that looks toward theory not as a set of discreet tools, but as historically formulated gestures, ones that become useful when weighed and layered carefully, rather than flattened by way of mapping a set of blank characteristics. Caution can be exercised

40   Ibid. 14.
41   Ibid, 14.

in what we take and leave; it needn't be all or nothing, and in light of all that we know of the academy, the formal completeness of a theory's embrace must always be under suspicion.

Broekner emphasizes the need to address the "multiple power sources" of "white abjectorship" instead of what I see as a continuous abstraction that is wielded through the language of "oppression," "race," and "difference"—ultimate tools of evasion from the white power relation.[42] She rightly credits Sylvia Wynter, for having thus "raised the bar to the epistemic level, which keeps one from avoiding repetitions of the additive argument that in order to produce state-of-the-art gender studies we have to incorporate racial oppression into the analysis "as well.""[43]

In light of all of these exposures, we must consider the question: What should Black feminist researchers do? As per Collins's thinking, our work must:

> be validated by ordinary [Black] women who grow to womanhood. [It must] be credible in the eyes of this group, scholars must be personal advocates for their material, be accountable for the consequences of their work, have lived or experienced their material in some fashion, and be willing to engage in dialogues about their findings with ordinary, everyday people. Second, if it is to establish its legitimacy, Black feminist thought also must be accepted by the community of Black women scholars. These scholars place varying amounts of importance on rearticulating a Black women's standpoint using an Afrocentric feminist epistemology. Third, Black feminist thought within academia must be prepared to confront Eurocentric masculinist political and epistemological requirements.[44]

---

42   Ibid, 15.
43   Ibid, 16.
44   Patricia Hill Collins, "The Social Construction of Black Feminist Thought" *Signs* 14, 4 (1989): 771-772.

I see these concepts as functional methodological tools that I found useful application for in my process of unearthing and thinking-sharing along with the women who were my interlocutors in this project. I borrow, I patch together, I stitch together, I voice, and I quote from Black locations of numerous kinds. I do this in order to historicize, complicate, and proceed within a necessary ethic of care. I am very much aware that the narratives that appear in this text are narratives that have been entrusted to me. Overall, my goal has been to engage and make heard not only these women's voices, but what Collins refers to as the "conflicts of silences" that seek to erode, bankrupt, and ultimately make unintelligible and inhuman Black women in all spaces.[45]

In the context of phenomenological research and analysis too, the question of "humanity," and by implication inhumanity, become complicated by notions of race, and in particular Blackness.[46] Traditionally, the assumption within phenomenological approaches is that all individuals are "human beings," but the conditions of BlackLife tend to not be deliberated on in this location of thought that simultaneously constantly marks Black people as non-humans.[47] Sylvia Wynter describes the fact and refusal of Black people as being constructed and understood as "non-humans"; more specifically, she describes how cases of violence against Black people have been labelled in public and legal discourse as conditions in which "no humans [are] involved."[48] Wynter's analysis of decoloniality

45   Ibid.

46   Cecil Foster, *Blackness and Modernity: the Colour of Humanity and the Quest for Freedom* (Montreal: McGill-Queen's University Press, 2007); Fred Moten, *The Universal Machine* (Durham: Duke University Press, 2018).

47   See Angela Davis, *Abolition Democracy: Beyond Empire, Prisons, and Torture* (New York: Seven Stories Press, 2005); John M. Lamola, "Biko, Hegel and the End of Black Consciousness: A Historico-Philosophical Discourse on South African Racism," *Journal of Southern African Studies* 42, 2 (2016): 183–94; John M.Lamola, "Blackhood as a Category in Contemporary Discourses on Black Studies: an Existentialist Philosophical Defence," *Transformation in Higher Education* 3, 1 (2018): 1–9; John M. Lamola, "An Ontic–ontological Theory for Ethics of Designing Social Robots: a Case of Black African Women and Humanoids," *Ethics and Information Technology* 23, 2 (2020): 119–26; Rinaldo Walcott and Idil Abdillahi, *BlackLife* (Winnipeg: ARP Books, 2019).

48   Sylvia Wynter, "'No Humans Involved': An Open Letter to my Colleagues," *Forum N.H.I.: Knowledge for the 21st Century* 1, 1 (Fall 1994): 1.

disrupts the concept of the human, its ideological and epistemic groundings. Walter Mignolo, in his articulation of Wynter's 1994 work, writes:

> Wynter suggests that if we accept that epistemology gives us the principles and rules of knowing through which the Human and Humanity are understood, we are trapped in a knowledge system that fails to notice that the stories of what it means to be Human—specifically origin stories that explain who/what we are—are, in fact, narratively constructed."[49]

In *BlackLife*, Rinaldo Walcott and I were building on the works of Wynter but putting this thought into conversation in our own lives, acknowledging that it cannot be separated from Black people's existence. We write, "we have made BlackLife one word because we believe that living Black makes BlackLife inextricable from the mark of its flesh, both historically and in our current time."[50] BlackLife is not extended to Black people as a result of the discourses concerning BlackLife, but rather "the mark of Black flesh is the foundation from which BlackLife in all of its multiplicities, varieties, potentialities and possibilities proceed from and is therefore intimately entangled."[51]

As a Black Canadian feminist researcher looking at the Eurocentric roots of theory, I am overtly aware of the shortcomings of phenomenology. However, if one is aware of the limitations coming from the potential elision of Black identity and experience within the phenomenological emphasis on "humanity," some pieces of a phenomenological approach can be useful. Firstly, because a major goal of this work is to amplify the subjective realities of a population whose perspective is underrepresented, and secondly because, as Patricia Hill Collins states, the "ties between what one does and

49   Walter Mignolo, "Sylvia Wynter: What Does It Mean to Be Human?," in *Sylvia Wynter: On Being Human As Praxis*, edited by Katherine McKittrick (Durham, NC: Duke University Press, 2015), 107.
50   Rinaldo Walcott and Idil Abdillahi, *BlackLife*, 9.
51   Ibid.

what one thinks [as] illustrated by individual Black women can also characterize Black women's experiences and ideas as a group."[52] A phenomenological design contributes power to Black women by foregrounding their own voice, alerting researchers, in David Theo Goldberg's words, to notions that "power is exercised epistemologic- ally in the dual practices of naming and evaluating."[53] Similarly, Dolores Delgado Bernal and Kevin Hylton suggest that when using CRT, Black feminist approaches or studies of BlackLife either as a method or theoretical framework, we must consider adopting research methods that privilege Black people as sites of knowledge and knowledge producers.[54] A phenomenological approach can only be wielded to do this when exercised alongside CRT and Black fem- inist thought and, I would argue, forms of interpersonal subjective knowledge that academic theory cannot address.

Always we must keep fast in our minds the unpassable reality that our Blackness as understood by the Eurocentric "postcolonial" public consciousness in which academe resides, usurps our human- ity de facto. As Rinaldo Walcott describes:

> As commodities of the colonial project, Black people have remained outside modernity's various progressive and/or libertarian re-inventions of the Human (in terms of gender, sexuality, disability, or trans-practices) and have always remained overdetermined by racist epistem- ology. I must point out that I am not attempting to produce some kind of competitive oppression exception- alism. Rather, my aim is to point to the profound ways in which Black being is directly implicated by negation and devaluation, as a negative foil, that is, in the ongoing

52   Patricia Hill Collins, *Black Feminist Thought*, 24.
53   David Theo Goldberg, *Racist Culture: Philosophy and the Politics of Meaning* (Malden, Mass.: Blackwell Publishers Inc., 1993), 150.
54   Dolores Delgado Bernal, "Critical Race Theory, Latino Critical Theory, and Critical Raced-Gendered Epistemologies"; Kevin Hylton, "Talk the talk, walk the walk: Defining Critical Race Theory in research," *Race Ethnicity and Education* 15, 1 (2012): 23–41.

production of diversity of what Wynter calls the "genres of being human."[55]

In light of this produced negation, we cannot go forward with an open embrace of any pre-existing and academically accepted methodological practices. But ultimately, when pulled apart, segmented, brought together with other fragments, and driven to particular purpose, various practices of theory and method can form a kind of anti-disciplinarity. Anti-disciplinaritity is its own power, a power that I see derived from the stitching together of these individual corners of knowledge, not because I subscribe to any single one, but specifically because I know that standing alone, they represent partial or full failures to liberatory realities for Black women and Black people. We must necessarily be against discipline, and if we are against discipline—against, for example, the idea that between the nurse and the doctor only one is the expert and the final word—we refuse the very idea of the expert narrative. People can and will continue to do the work that conforms to specific methodologies from their own social–political vantage. But to betray discipline means to betray that we are the expert holder of that knowledge or vantage, because we know that knowledge to be dispatched by Euro-western episteme. If we are anti-discipline, we have to deal with how we come to the processes of understanding this fact. We know we can't know everything, and we can't do any of this stitching, gathering, any of this anti-disciplinary work of placing knowledge into practice, in isolation. We must believe in what we do know, and have a desire and drive toward how we want to know that is based in rejecting the parts of existing knowledge systems that deny us; in other words, we must have belief in how we want to seek our own movement through knowledge.

55 Rinaldo Walcott, "The Problem of the Human: Black Ontologies and "the Coloniality of Our Being" in *Postcoloniality—Decoloniality—Black Critique: Joints and Fissures*, edited by Sabine Broeck and Carsten Junker (Frankfurt/New York: Campus Verlag, 2014), 96. Quoting Sylvia Wynter, "Unsettling the Coloniality of Being/Power/Truth/Freedom: Towards the Human, After Man, Its Over-representation—An Argument," *CR: The New Centennial Review* 3, 3 (2003): 331.

STRIPPING, VIBES, FREQUENCIES, "STRANGE SENTENCES"

Critical feminist and antiracist approaches ask researchers to look inward before, during, and after pursuing their desired projects and in their exchanges with real and potential participants and places. This would include considering realities that are born out of and consistently relegated to the margins; an example of this can include considering whose voice is present, or present-but-absent, and how a researcher produces, understands, "owns," and shares knowledge. Approaches to qualitative research methodologies and methods also place emphasis on the recognition of the researcher's positionality throughout the research process, and in relation to participants, communities, and the engagement of various archival materials. I don't actually believe that there exists a research methodology that can be—at the risk of using essentializing language—ethical, because methodologies are always in some sense rooted in and prescribed by the academic context from which they emerge. But I acknowledge that the self-recognition of qualitative processes can be useful. Understanding one's positionality is contending with how positionality is more than an individual "check-yourself-checkbox" or a lonely sentence in a research paper. What happens when, despite our best efforts, we are simply unable to "understand"—comprehend, interpret, or translate what we hear to "from "subjects" or "participants"—by no fault of our own?

As scholars and researchers, we often appear at this intersection where we paradoxically stand in the way of our own knowledge-seeking via the privilege of being able to exercise the assumed right to engage with, and (re)produce knowledge(s); this relates to the way that we handle the knowledge that is gifted us. Those who feel the right to treat the lived realities of others without gentleness and respect reproduce the same academic violence that violates our "subjects" under the guise of newer, more "wholistic," "progressive," or "ethical" frameworks that, although labeled differently, fall within the same conceptual rubric as all of the traditional forms of academic violence. If we take seriously that "conquest and domination are so fundamentally linked to naming," then what is to be made of a researcher's ability to name or to analyze?[1] We must acknowledge that there exists a domain of codification and analysis that demands we make room for what M. Jacqui Alexander calls the "unromanticized dimensions of human experience," which at the intersection of modernity and BlackLife still remain fractured. Here I am not assessing the merit of any individual's "technical process or training," or the academic knowledge and expertise of any researcher.[2] Instead, I offer some reflections that demand we conceptualize the inherent power attached to the tasks of asking questions and interpreting responses.

Reflecting on this, I consider the ways in which I have falsely replicated institutional notions of "participatory research" and "grassroots research." If most critical approaches to research suggest that participants are often involved from the onset of the research project, then what we must also acknowledge is that by virtue of the way that such projects are developed, and by the nature of institutional constraints—for example, research ethics boards—a "participant" can in fact never be involved in the research project

1   Carole Boyce Davies, *Black Women, Writing and Identity: Migrations of the Subject* (London and New York: Routledge, 1994), 7.
2   M. Jacqui Alexander, *Pedagogies of Crossing: Meditations on Feminism, Sexual Politics, Memory, and the Sacred* (Durham NC: Duke University Press, 2005), 17.

from its inception. And if, in fact, a person is involved in the process from inception, then are we actually being intellectually honest about our research processes? Whose "ethics" and "honesty" are we privileging: those of the institution, which suggests that we must operate within frameworks that mitigate and manage risk, or those within the critical and radical frameworks, that suggest that "subjects" can and should be involved in the framing of the project, and that they have the autonomy to do so? At what point do we step outside "ethics" frames to do critical research in the way that it is intended? What do we have to struggle toward, and against, as the academy becomes increasingly antiBlack, neoliberal, and intertwined with legal and market-driven goals?

By returning to the transcripts and audio interviews with my interlocutors after I completed my initial data analysis, I found myself inadvertently reflecting on another set of questions. I therefore went back to speak with eight of the twenty women and shared with them that I found it curious that I did not ask particular questions at certain points. I wondered how I had understood what the women "meant," and how I knew *how* to respond, or not respond. I wondered how my interlocutors had understood what I meant, without needing to ask. M. Jacqui Alexander refers to this as "stripping": "a methodology in the most literal, perhaps mundane sense, of constituting the practices through which we come to know what we believe we know."[3] I extended and applied Alexander's notion of stripping by deploying it as an analytic tool in my post-analysis conversations. Stripping, taken up as method, was used to reckon with and "confront the limits of the methodology I had devised to know"—in this case, the subtle social complexities of interaction between myself and my interlocutors, and resultant mutual understanding.[4] Stripping in this sense also meant stripping the text, the transcript, as a site devoid of temporality, and insisting on the (il)legibility—depending on the reader—of the unspoken and unexpressed within it.

3   Ibid.
4   Ibid, 294.

I engaged in this process by revisiting and studying our silences, laughter, and all the things that I am unable to document with any conventional markers of truth or accuracy here.[5] These were the unspoken exchanges—glances, eye contact, head nods, and side-eyes. These were expressions—the lip pout, which meant many things, like pointing me to the direction of the camera at Ryerson library or the staff member outside the shelter door. At times, the lip pout meant agreement or disagreement. After I completed my analysis, I wondered: why did I not notice all of this earlier in my research process?

Interlocutor 5 put it best when she said this is because, "it was a vibe." When I asked her to say more about what a vibe meant, her response was, "Stop being dumb, you know what I mean, Idil." She added, "It was fine. Chill, that's it."[6] She was right! I knew exactly what she meant. What I didn't know was how to capture what she meant or how to account for what she meant in the context of my research. And maybe I'm not meant to. Should I use this moment to interpret, uninterpret, and resist by endarkening feminist epistemology, recognizing that the "vibe" remains an active ingredient in this research process and outcome and requires some tending to and reflection?[7] This is where I attempt that reflection.

Regarding the generative conversation and my individual and, with these women, collective re-analysis and interpretation of the data, the eight women whom I spoke with again made very clear that it was a shared language, vibe, understanding, or mood that led both to their understanding of our exchanges and to their comfort. Essentially what they gesture toward, similar to what Interlocutor 5 had noted, was the notion of what another woman, Interlocutor 19, explicitly referred to as a "*vibration*" or what I've come to call a *frequency*, that operated between us.[8] Acknowledging this led me to consider that what is, to borrow Alexander's words,

5   Claire M. Harris, Dionne Brand, and M. Nourbese Philip, *Grammar of Dissent*.
6   Interlocutor 5, in person interview with author, Toronto, 2017.
7   J. L. Dillard, "A Sketch of the History of Black English," *The Southern Quarterly* 45, 2 (2008): 53.
8   Interlocutor 19, in person interview with author, Toronto, 2018.

"at stake [here] is not only whether emotion is made to count in the knowledge process, but *how* [I] made [it] count."[9] My twenty interlocutors explained, gestured toward, or emoted on a frequency that allowed us to engage in communicative interactions and explanations that often did not require probing questions, clarifications, or translations.

J.L. Dillard provocatively asserts that "in order to transform [a] reality, the very language we use to define and describe phenomena must possess instrumentality: It must be able to do something toward transforming particular ways of knowing and producing knowledge."[10] If we know there is an inherent inability—especially by non-Black people—to analyze, and/or interpret some BlackLife processes, plights, and lived experiences, then we need to understand and name the insistence of white, off-white, and non-Black researchers who continue to insert themselves into BlackLife as akin to, and an instance of, the continued conquest and active domination of Black people. Without minimizing or diluting this point, I also need to recognize that my own positionality—the location, experience, or syntax that allowed me to understand these Black women—is not static, and the fact that I understand these women today does not guarantee that this will remain the case in the future.[11] My time, place, language, and access to certain communities will at times make me more or less able to understand and to relate.

Defined as "the rate at which a vibration occurs that constitutes a wave, either in a material (as in sound waves), or in an electromagnetic field (as in radio waves and light), usually measured per second," the detectability of frequency requires a temporal alignment, and I embrace the thought of a metaphorical and

9   M. Jacqui Alexander, *Pedagogies of Crossing*, 17.
10   J. L. Dillard, "A Sketch of the History of Black English," 4.
11   Some of the texts that make me think through syntax include: Claire Harris, M. Nourbese Philip, Dionne Brand, and Carol Morrell, *Grammar of Dissent*; June Jordan, "Nobody Mean More to Me than You and the Future Life of Willie Jordan," *Harvard Educational Review*, Aug 58, 3 (1988): 363; Rinaldo Walcott, *Black Like Who?: Writing Black Canada*. 2nd rev. ed. (Toronto: Insomniac Press, 2003).

social frequency as having emerged as a mode of thinking in this research.[12] Interlocutors revealed what I identify here as frequency, which for them also meant a general feeling, mood, or unspoken and often (but not always) unacknowledged shared expression in space, text, and presence. Therefore, I think through this framing of frequency within epistemic challenges brought forward by Alexander, who writes:

> Documents gave me proximate access to daily life, [but] they were unable to convey the interior of lived experiences, the very category I needed to inhabit in order to understand how cosmological systems are grounded and expressed. Reading against the grain to fill in the spaces of an absent biography was simply not sufficient. I couldn't rely on the knowledge derived from books, not even on the analytic compass that I myself had drawn.[13]

Alexander's theorizing allowed me to move outside of the text and the norm of overwhelmingly linear research and analysis processes. For example, after my initial analysis, I created a post-analysis subspace that centered co-reflectivity and conversations with my interlocutors. This unrushed space, years after learning to *be* and *think* differently, allowed the women and I to describe and discuss our exchanges and interactions, separate from but connected to the initial research questions. We unearthed modes of thinking and analysis parallel to but not so apparent in my original findings; of central importance in this was the way they expressed a deep sense of intuitiveness in the process, which was indicative of a sense of connectivity. Of particular significance to the women was the inexplicability of the rapport or connection; something that is not tangible, cannot be named, and in many cases cannot even be built over time. It is either there or it is not at the time of speaking.

12   University of Minnesota website. *Physics Force.* "Vocabulary: Frequency". Retrieved from https://physicsforce.umn.edu/antinode#:~:text= Frequency%3A%20the%20rate%20at%20which,)%2C%20usually% 20measured%20per%20second.
13   M. Jacqui Alexander, *Pedagogies of Crossing*, 294.

It is also not singular, does not reflect one particular experience; for example, it could be only a feeling, or only a mood—but it could be multiple things at one time, or one thing at a time. It is a strange, but also not strange, way to account for the atmospheric or climactic connection that cannot, and maybe should not—a larger question—be analyzed.[14] What does it mean for a qualitative researcher to try to take up the fact that there are and will always be a mode of analysis that simply cannot be tapped into regardless of their efforts? There is something to be celebrated here. In whatever you choose to call it—an affinity, a resonance, a frequency, a silent knowledge—there is something to be celebrated in that thing that resists analysis, that thing that denies the assumption built into each end every form of academic methodology: that it need be scrutinized outside of its moment.

"Strange Sentences": A Black Diasporic Canadian Syntax

In an effort to further think through frequency, I also came to consider language and language exchanges as they are constitutive of the frequencies on which interlocutors made those exchanges clear and clarified their explanations, or silences; I came essentially to consider the position of language and syntax in shedding light on their Black livabilities, and to think of this as one other form of frequency that may be unmeasurable.

The creation and collective communicative meaning and expression in the words below do not require a full grasp of the English language as we formally understand it in its colonial expression. As a conceptual mode of analysis I offer that the notion of frequency also emerges from everyday dialectical exchanges and from engaging across Black languages, or what I refer to as Black Diaspora Canadian Syntax.[15] I include the word "Canadian" here

14   Christina Sharpe, In the Wake, 117-119.
15   I am drawing here on Stuart Hall's formulation of diasporization (H. Adlai Murdoch, "Stuart Hall: diasporic Caribbeanness and discourses of ethnocultural belonging," African and Black Diaspora: An International Journal 11, 3 (2018): 232-246); Kobena Mercer's idea that diaspora is a set of logics of "culture and the dialogic imagination": Kobena Mercer, Welcome to the Jungle: New Positions in Black Cultural Studies (New York: Routledge, 1994), and June

not just to situate these exchanges geographically, but as an acknowledgement of contestation; (as the word gains its well-earned stain, we continue to operate, willingly or unwillingly, under a fictional state's fictional moniker). When speaking, thinking, and questioning alongside the women in this book, I came to realize that, as the introduction to June Jordan's essay "Nobody Mean More to Me than You and the Future Life of Willie Jordan," describes, "every sentence assume[d] the living and active participation of at least two human beings, the speaker and the listener."[16] Therefore, our interactions, within which speaker-listener roles were held by both conversants, brought to the surface a humanity that was present in making each other visible. Acknowledging this is not an effort to transplant one geopolitically and contextually specific Black English into an entirely different context. Rather, it is to use it as a jumping-off point to further illustrate the ways in which certain kinds of communicative interactions and interventions continue to be inaccessible and untranslatable for non-Black people.[17] It may seem obvious, but within a culture of invisibility matched with negative hyper-visibility, it is also important to reiterate the ingredient of visibility: the fact that these conversations made both conversants visible, not just one. My own presence alongside each woman was part and parcel of the process of mutuality that leads to understanding and is therefore not extricable from it.

So I use Jordon's framing of Black English to express how my interlocutors made meanings of words, and how trust and relationships were built based on these often-shared meanings. It is the relationships built, the understanding or knowledge of a broader social, political, cultural, and religious value, that gives meaning to not only the word but the weight of the word in the context of Black community identity. It is the intelligibility and responsibility that recognizes that "language has historically served and continues

Jordan's framing of "Black English" in "Nobody Mean More to Me than You and the Future Life of Willie Jordan."

16   June Jordan, "Nobody Mean More to Me than You and the Future Life of Willie Jordan," 363.

17   Claire Harris, M.Nourbese Philip, Dionne Brand, and Carol Morrell, *Grammar of Dissent*; Rinaldo Walcott, *Black Like Who?*

to serve as a powerful tool in the mental, spiritual, and intellectual colonization of African and other marginalized peoples."[18] What is central here is not the mere linguistic fluency in Black languages and cultures, but the ontological imperatives grounded in temporal context, which are simply unattainable to some. ⸳

In my exchanges with interlocutors, they would make references such as: *"these things been happening," "just so,"* or *"from long-time";* or, as the researcher, I would ask, *"how did your worker explain that policy to you? How was your worker able to think doing that was ok?"* and one woman responded, *"I don't know! Duppy* [a ghost] *must have whispered in her ears."* Or they might state, in the context of finding hidden information about the policies, *"it's in God's back!"* Jordan's depiction of the "language of Black English [as] adher[ing] to a distinctive Black syntax [...] postulat[es] a profound difference between white and Black people, per se."[19] I see embedded within my framing of *frequency* the idea that Black syntax makes room for the *vibe* the women I spoke with describe. I also think about the texture and complications that Carole Boyce Davies delineates in her description of the Black woman's embodiment in space, place, time, and movement when she writes: "She lives in the United States; she lives in America. She also lives in that in-between space that is neither here nor there, locating herself in the communities where her children, grandchildren, family and friends reside."[20] This also points us to what Rinaldo Walcott refers to as the "in-between," as another complex site of unique frequency and interpretation, that solidifies the importance of an ontological location of understanding within a politics of dislocation. I kept that in-between in my mind as I navigated efforts to locate or at least localize my *own* understanding of my interlocutors.[21]

In the so-called Canadian context these Black syntaxes are infused with diasporic Black cultures and languages. For instance, in

18   J.L. Dillard, "A Sketch of the History of Black English," 4.
19   June Jordan, "Nobody Mean More to Me Than You And the Future Life of Willie Jordan," 367.
20   Carole Boyce Davies, *Black Women, Writing, and Identity: Migrations of the Subject* (London and New York: Routledge, 1994), 2.
21   Rinaldo Walcott, *Black Like Who?*

Toronto we notice the mélange of Caribbean languages co-mingled with what we commonly understand as Somali and words from other East African languages, to create a new and distinctive dialogic that is neither solely Caribbean nor East African. We have witnessed phrases such as "walahie," imbued in Islamism and originating from an Arabic word, become Blackened and popularized by Black Muslim East Africans in Canadian arts, culture, and policing discourses. In the context of my research, this term emerged as a signifier of "truth-telling" and interestingly was expressed more by non-Muslim than by Muslim women in the study. "Walahie" became an unspoken, assumed, shared experience and measurement of trustworthiness for these women. It functioned as an intended guarantor of the believability of their narrative—however, it is important to note that I never assumed or expressed that they were being dishonest. I came to fully understand a twofold significance of this term. Firstly, it was to validate their truth claims. Secondly, rightly or wrongly, it also functioned to honour a truth claim about me as the researcher whom they had come to frame like they have other East-Africans. When I asked my interlocutors what made them think "walahie" would have had a specific or unique meaning to me, they shared that it was less about me and served as a cross-Black diaspora *lingua franca* in order to assert connection across difference, based on the interactions they'd had with others—East African and otherwise—who understood the term. So, while the word has no religious or cultural significance for the non-East-African, non-Muslim, it has a social, spatial, and linguistic strength and significance that has been co-created locally. I recognize this as organic osmosis of new languages that are brought about by diasporic Black people by way of being, living, and needing to communicate with others. Christina Sharpe writes of a shared Black experience that, "we are not only known to ourselves and to each other by that force"; rather, these distinctive local but diasporic Black vernaculars also serve as languages of Black resistance, and even as means to protect communities from white supremacist surveillance in some cases.[22] Hence, in the context of analysis

22   Christina Sharpe, *In the Wake.*

and method, it became important for me to consider what was "expected and accepted," and what was interpreted and understood in the absence of explanation.

In trying to make sense of the above example for myself, I also considered the use of the term "ase," "ashe," or "àṣẹ," taken from the West African Yoruba language in Nigeria, a collective symbolism of agreement, praise, or the "power to make things happen and produce change."[23] In my experience, the term is often (though not always) used as an affirmative in the Toronto Black diaspora. To be clear, I am not asserting that collectively as Black we all ascribe to terms like "walahie" or "àṣẹ," but we do have some cross-community Black exchanges that allow us to meet across the Atlantic and affirm and engage in taxonomies that hold different meaning here. I return to Rinaldo Walcott, who reminds us, "the writing of Blackness in Canada, then might begin with a belief that something important happens here," and in fact something uniquely Black "Canadian" and diasporic happens here.[24] In *Black Like Who? Writing Black Canada*, Walcott introduces us to the intimacies and nationalistically absented presences of Black personhood in so-called Canada, including, among other things, the linguistic (dis)be-longing. He describes and theoretically marks the materiality of belonging, mapped onto/into/over cartographies of white nationalism, transnationality, neoliberalism, and the "dominant discourses of race and [Blackness] structured by North American white supremacy."[25] In the trans-local Black life-making scripts, Walcott colloquializes Black Canadianness to Black diasporic people, while simultaneously reanimating, re-intervening, and disrupting ontological and epistemic formations of BlackLife in Canada. He captures taxonomies of futurity and historicizes un-*sea*-ds BlackLife as not of land and not of sea.

In studying space, be it structurally or seductively, Walcott brings forward the "strange sentences" in Black existence and survival.[26]

---

23   Ashe Leadership Fellows. *About.* Retrieved from https://www.ashefellows.org/.
24   Rinaldo Walcott, *Black Like Who?*, 27.
25   Ibid, 44.
26   Ibid, 47.

These strange sentences he locates within the state fabric, somewhere in-between, here, there, nowhere, and somewhere. Drawing on the works of Dionne Brand, Walcott traverses across disciplines, marking the scholarly artist experience in so-called Canada as a "tough geography" and an "uneasy place."[27] It is in the tough and uneasy places where frequency emerges as well. Brand and Walcott insist that Black people do not understand their identities as belonging to or tied to a limited space and place. In Walcott's words: "The political identification of Black peoples are crucial and essential to resistance. Making outer-national identifications with other Black people is important to the kinds of struggles that might be waged within national boundaries."[28] These expositions and theoretical orientations are also foundational to a Black feminist standpoint on research.[29]

When brought together, adapting and extending Bonnie Thornton Dill's 1979 *Dialectics of Black Womanhood* and Deborah King's theorizing about "multiple consciousness in Black women's politics," we can see how conscious exchanges and processes of inquiry that situate frequency extend Black women's unique, material, and epistemic standpoints.[30] The white supremacist contention might be, does the application of frequency, as I have proffered, "make the process of intelligibility into a spiritual undertaking"?[31] Does it create a space of outright exclusion, which would suggest that frequency as a method of analysis is also a resistive mode of analysis? What does it mean to create a resistive mode of analysis? How much of this study is in fact reactive to the academic prescription that

27 Ibid, 67.
28 Ibid, 66. Also see Dionne Brand, *No Language is Neutral*.
29 See Patricia Hill Collins, "The Social Construction of Black Feminist Thought"; Patricia Hill Collins, "Gender, Black Feminism, and Black Political Economy"; and Patricia Hill Collins and Sirma Bilge, *Intersectionality* (Oxford: Polity Press, 2016).
30 Deborah King, "Multiple Jeopardy, Multiple Consciousness"; Bonnie Thornton Dill, "The Dialectics of Black Womanhood."
31 M. Jacqui Alexander, *Pedagogies of Crossing: Meditations on Feminism, Sexual Politics, Memory, and the Sacred* (Durham: Duke University Press, 2005), 295; Deborah K. King, "Multiple Jeopardy, Multiple Consciousness: The Context of a Black Feminist Ideology," *Signs: Journal of Women in Culture and Society* 14, 1 (1988): 42-72.

demands Black women's lives be categorized and contained? How much of it is complicit in the same? How far can we go within structures of inquiry that claim to be ethical, humanistic, and non-dogmatic, while repeating a set of dehumanizing values in which extraction—of stories, time, emotion, *life*—are an unavoidable part of inquiry? While I do not claim to have those answers, I borrow from M. Jacqui Alexander's articulation of dispossession and betrayal; at this stage I've come to the conclusion that research and interpretation are, as Alexander articulates, "not sufficiently expansive to the task of becoming more fully human," and never will be.[32] The academy is not and never will be our home. At best, when we are at our best, the academy is a tool to wield back on itself, to pry open and expose the contradictions that saturate our existence.

32   M. Jacqui Alexander, *Pedagogies of Crossing*, 17.

THE GLASS FRAME

I hope that my effort here will do some good work toward carving out small, meaningful, and useful enclaves in which Black women's accounts of their experiences can be not just chronicled but counted and consulted as crucial contributions toward action. I want these contributions to become apparent not only within Black Canadian feminist scholarship, social policy, surveillance studies, and emerging scholarship confronting the social, political, and material manifestations of antiBlack racism, but within cultural and policy spaces beyond the academy. This is crucial because of the fact that "we have been unable to unsee the ways in which liberal, conservative and left discourses continue to fail Black people, constantly endangering our lives not only in Canada but globally as well."[1] In striving beyond academe, my work also opens dialogues with Black women that have the potential to directly influence and challenge antiBlack policy and praxis. In this sense, it aims to disrupt the existing praxis of white supremacy and neoliberalism.

I have referred, throughout this book, to the twenty Black women who spoke with me as interlocutors rather than "participants" for a reason. Although I have linked my research findings to broader discourses and analyses that are in my own estimation important, I want to openly state that these women's stories are their own, and as such are more important than any study; by which I mean to say: people over "data," always. Lives over data. Black women's lives

1   Rinaldo Walcott and Idil Abdillahi, *BlackLife*, 87.

over data. If I felt this articulation were actually broadly understood and accepted, undertaking the writing of this book would not have been necessary. The goal of the original work at its root, as part of a PhD dissertation, was to explore the experiences of twenty Black women in Toronto accessing social assistance. But the academy's prescription of objective ethics would dictate that my approach to this inquiry be through a mode of presumed objectivity, one that, despite the existence of many progressive theoretical modes, haunts the social-scientific. I do regard this work as legitimate research; I presented thematic data and short vignettes, and the themes that emerge are clear: around the interviews again and again swirls the concept of Black women's surveillance, of Black women's poverty, and of our questioned morality. As we navigate the academy, we must imbue our work with our own structures and approaches, and we must continuously reject the knowledge standards of an academic structure that, every day, participates in and props up racial violence in the same manner that the state does.

I have deep gratitude for the spiritual, emotional, cognitive, and physical energy each woman shared with me in this research process; each interaction was meaningful, and each word was valid. Every breath, pause, gasp, and laugh; every nod, head tilt, and hand gesture contributed to my cognition, a mutual understanding, and a temporal embodiment of my theorizing. The ongoing lamentations, analysis, and reflections of these twenty women, put forward here, was at the most the fundamental level a personal engagement. That said, the scope of the research from which this book evolved, along with many external factors and competing Black realities that manifested during its writing, did not allow for every moment of each woman's living reality to be shared in its fullness. Some of my work through early stages, and some of my writing, felt to be merely a synthesis and an academic obligation, informed by a myriad of constraints, with the end goal of delivering history as a headline. I acknowledge this—my awareness of it is acute—and here I have attempted something different, something that doesn't fear the personal. The findings and discussion here demand a longitudinal, contextual, and immediate emotional relationship to the data. For that reason, it also now demands my representation of not just the data but my whole relationship with it, as this relationship changed over time based on my own incremental process of meaning-making and knowledge production.

For many of the Black women I interviewed, the process of "participating" in these conversations was about talking back to or challenging Ontario Works, even if indirectly. Some of the women were apprehensive initially because their livelihoods, no matter how meagre, are sustained by these systems, and speaking up about their experiences could come with very tangible risks, including potential consequences for their material well-being. However, they were at the same time attracted to the subject because they spoke about a need to directly resist and work against what they have been exposed to during their time in the OW system; they felt drawn to the opportunity to, as Interlocutor 6 expressed it, "talk the truth about what really goes on behind the glass frame."[2]

I am with her. From my position of relative privilege, I have my own glass frame. This process was, for these women, work. The rough work of living through life, the rough work of storying and of storing (physically!) the toil. It is rough as in difficult, and it is rough as in unrefined; it is incomplete, it lacks clarity, and yet, it is always firm. We are questioned, and our work is in question. Whether we will ever get to a place where not everything is rough work is in question. It is also what keeps me willing and able to realize.

Rough doesn't only mean painful; rough work allows you to take some risks, to laugh about the work itself, to even play, in ways that wouldn't be possible if I wasn't able to name it as rough. Hard living, breathing, operating. It's a rugged thing. It's hard to live. To be rid of that would also mean we'd have to relate to so much of this world differently: how we reproduce, replicate, and honour ideas, memories, and more. A lot of rumination, and a lot of toil. There's been a running from the rough work that needs to get done, and that kind of running produces its own unnecessary roughness on the heart and mind. Run up, and do rough work. It's an acknowledgement of life, of movement toward a future life where we won't

2   Interlocutor 6.

have to. Please accept my invitation to sit with and think about the obvious. No grand claims have been made in this book—it is, in fact, all restated, resaid, reframed. It is, after everything, an invitation, and if you want to think about these obvious realities in an obvious way, this book is an invitation to read society. What we actually do with what we receive is always and invariably up to us.

Index

References

Abdi, Cawo M.. *Elusive Jannah: The Somali Diaspora and a Borderless Muslim Identity*. Minneapolis: University of Minnesota Press, 2015.

Abdillahi, Idil. *Blackened Madness: Medicalization, and Black Everyday Life in Canada* (forthcoming, 2024).

Abramovitz, Mimi. "The Largely Untold Story of Welfare Reform and the Human Services," *Social Work* 50, 2 (2005): 175–186. https://doi.org/10.1093/sw/50.2.175

Acker, Joan, Kate Barry, and Joke Esseveld. "Objectivity and Truth: Problems in doing feminist research." *Women's Studies International Forum* 6, 4 (1983): 423-435.

Acker, Sandra. "Women, the other academics." *Women's Studies International Forum* 6, 2 (1983): 191-201.

Affi, Ladan. "Domestic conflict in the diaspora: Somali women asylum seekers and refugees in Canada." *Somalia: The untold story–The war through the eyes of Somali women*, edited by Judith Gardner and Judy L. Bushra. London: Pluto Press, 2004. 107-115.

Ajandi, Jennifer. "'Single Mothers by Choice': Disrupting Dominant Discourses of the Family Through Social Justice Alternatives." *International Journal of Child, Youth and Family Studies* 3, 4 (2011): 410-431. https://doi.org/10.18357/ijcyfs23/420117757.

Alexander, M. Jacqui. *Pedagogies of Crossing: Meditations on Feminism, Sexual Politics, Memory, and the Sacred*. Durham NC: Duke University Press, 2005.

Andrew, Caroline. "Women and the Welfare State," *Canadian Journal of Political Science / Revue Canadienne de Science Politique* 17,4 (1984): 667–683. http://www.jstor.org/stable/3227962.

Antwi-Boasiako, Kofi, Bryn King, Barbara Fallon, Nico Trocmé, John Fluke, Martin Chabot, and Tonino Esposito. "Differences and Disparities over Time: Black and White Families Investigated by Ontario's Child Welfare System." *Child Abuse & Neglect* 107 (September, 2020): 104618. https://pubmed.ncbi.nlm.nih.gov/32653746/.

Applebaum, Lauren D. "The Influence of Perceived Deservingness on Policy Decisions Regarding Aid to the Poor." *Political Psychology* 22, 3 (2001): 419–442. https://doi.org/10.1111/0162-895X.00248.

Arat-Koç, Sedef. "Invisibilized, Individualized, and Culturalized: Paradoxical Invisibility and Hyper-Visibility of Gender in Policy Making and Policy Discourse in Neoliberal Canada." *Canadian Woman Studies* 29, 3 (2012): 6–17.

Ashe Leadership Fellows. *About.* Retrieved from https://www.ashefellows.org/.

Baiden, Philip, Fallon, Barbara, den Dunnen, Wendy, Black, Tara. "Police Charging Decisions in Child Maltreatment Investigations: Findings from the 2008 Ontario Incidence Study of Reported Child Abuse and Neglect." *Journal of Public Child Welfare* 3, 11(2) (2017).

Bain, Beverly. "Uncovering Conceptual Practices: Bringing into 'Lived Consciousness' Feminists' Activities on the Toronto Police Sexual Assault Audit and the Follow-up Sexual Assault Audit Steering Committee." *Canadian Woman Studies* 28, 1 (2009).

Bain, Beverly, Amanda Dale, and Jane Doe. "A New Chapter in Feminist Organizing: The Sexual Assault Audit Steering Committee." *Canadian Woman Studies* 28, 1 (2009).

Baines, Carol T., Patricia M. Evans, and Sheila M. Neysmith, Eds.. *Women's Caring: Feminist Perspectives on Social Welfare 2nd ed.* Oxford: Oxford University Press, 1998.

Baines, Carol T., Patricia M. Evans, and Sheila M. Neysmith. "Confronting Women's Caring: Challenges for Practice and Policy." *Affilia* 7, 1 (1992): 21–44. https://doi.org/10.1177/088610999200700103.

Baines, Donna. *Doing Anti-Oppressive Practice: Social Justice Social Work.* Winnipeg: Fernwood Pub., 2011.

Ball, Kirstie, Kevin Haggerty, and David Lyon, eds.. *Routledge Handbook of Surveillance Studies*, Hoboken: Taylor & Francis Group, 2012.

Bannerji, Himani. "The Paradox of Diversity." *Women's Studies International Forum* 23, 5 (2000): 537–60.

Bannerji, Himani. *The Dark Side of the Nation: Essays on Multiculturalism, Nationalism and Gender.* Toronto: Canadian Scholars' Press. 2000.

Barnoff, Lisa. "New Directions for Anti-oppression Practice in Feminist Social Service Agencies." PhD diss., University of Toronto, 2002.

Barnoff, Lisa, and Ken Moffatt. "Contradictory Tensions in Anti-Oppression Practice in Feminist Social Services," *Affilia*, 22, 1 (2007): 56–70. https://doi.org/10.1177/0886109906295772.

Beckett, Katherine, and Bruce Western. "Governing Social Marginality: Welfare, Incarceration, and the Transformation of State Policy." *Punishment & Society*, 3, 1 (2001): 43–59. https://journalssagepub-com.ezproxy.lib.ryerson.ca/doi/10.1177/14624740122228249.

Benjamin, Ruha. "The Emperor's New Genes: Science, Public Policy, and the Allure of Objectivity." *The Annals of the American Academy of Political and Social Science* 661 (2015): 130–142.

Benjamin, Ruha. "Cultura Obscura: Race, Power, and "Culture Talk" in the Health Sciences." *American Journal of Law & Medicine* 43, 2–3 (2017): 225–238. https://doi.org/10.1177/0098858817723661.

Benjamin, Ruha, ed. *Captivating Technology: Race, Carceral Technoscience, and Liberatory Imagination in Everyday Life.* Durham, NC: Duke University Press 2019. http://ebookcentral.proquest.com/lib/ryerson/detail.action?docID=5779780.

Benjamin, Ruha. *Race after Technology: Abolitionist Tools for the New Jim Code.* Oxford, England: Polity, 2019. Press. http://ebookcentral.proquest.com/lib/ryerson/detail.action?docID=5820427.

Bernal, Dolores Delgado. "Critical Race Theory, Latino Critical Theory, and Critical Raced-Gendered Epistemologies: Recognizing Students of Color as Holders and Creators of Knowledge." *Qualitative Inquiry* 8, 1 (2002): 105–126. https://doi.org/10.1177/107780040200800107.

Block, Sheila, and Grace-Edward Galabuzi. "Canada's Colour Coded Labour Market: The gap for racialized workers." Canadian Centre for Policy Alternatives and Wellesley Institute, 2011. https://www.policyalternatives.ca/sites/default/files/uploads/publications/National%20Office/2011/03/Colour%20Coded%20Labour%20Market.pdf.

Boyce Davies, Carole. *Black Women, Writing, and Identity: Migrations of the Subject*. London and New York: Routledge, 1994.

Brand, Dionne. *No Language is Neutral*. Toronto: Coach House Press, 1990.

Brand, Dionne. *Bread Out of Stone: Recollections, Sex, Recognitions, Race, Dreaming, Politics*. Toronto, Coach House Press, 1994.

Brand, Dionne. *In Another Place, Not Here* (1st ed). Toronto: A.A. Knopf Canada, 1996.

Brand, Dionne. *In Another Place, Not Here* (1st Vintage Canada ed). Toronto: Vintage Canada, 1997.

Brand, Dionne. *A Map to the Door of No Return*. Toronto: Doubleday Canada, 2001.

Brand, Dionne. *Thirsty*. Toronto: McClelland & Stewart, 2002.

Brand, Dionne. *Inventory*. Toronto: McClelland & Stewart, 2006.

Brand, Dionne, and Lois De Shield. *No Burden to Carry*. Toronto: Women's Press, 1991.

Brand, Dionne, Rabindranath Maharaj, and Tessa McWatt, Eds. *Luminous Ink: Writers on Writing in Canada*. Toronto: Books, 2018.

Bringer, Joy, Lynne Johnston, and Celia Brackenridge. "Maximizing Transparency in a Doctoral Thesis: The Complexities of Writing About the Use of QSR*NVIVO Within a Grounded Theory Study." *Qualitative Research* 4, 2 (2004). https://doi.org/10.1177/1468794104044434.

Bristow, Peggy, Dionne Brand, Linda Carty, Afua P. Cooper, Sylvia Hamilton, and Adrienne Shadd. *We're Rooted Here and They Can't Pull Us Up: Essays in African Canadian Women's History*. Toronto: University of Toronto Press, 1994. https://books-scholarsportal-

Brodie, Janine, Ed. *Critical Concepts: An Introduction to Politics 2nd Ed*. Toronto: Prentice Hall, 2002.

Broeck, Sabine. *Gender and the Abjection of Blackness*. Albany: State University of New York Press, 2018.

Burman, Jenny. "Remittance; Or, Diasporic Economies of Yearning." *Small Axe: a Journal of Criticism* 6, 2 (2002): 49–71.

Burman, Patrick W.. *Poverty's Bonds: Power and Agency in the Social Relations of Welfare.* Toronto: Thompson Educational Publishing, 1996.

Brown, Leslie, and Susan Strega Eds.. *Research As Resistance: Critical, Indigenous, & Anti-opressive Approaches.* Toronto: Canadian Scholars' Press, 2015.

Browne, Simone. *Dark Matters: On the Surveillance of Blackness.* Durham, NC: Duke University Press, 2015.

Burman, Patrick. *Poverty's Bonds: Power and Agency in the Social Relations of Welfare.* Toronto: Thompson Educational Publishing, 1996.

Calliste, A. "Race, Gender and Canadian Immigration Policy: Blacks from the Caribbean, 1900-1932." *Journal of Canadian Studies* 28, 4 (1994), 131–148. https://doi.org/10.3138/jcs.28.4.131

Caragata, Lea. "Neoconservative Realities: The Social and Economic Marginalization of Canadian Women." *International Sociology* 18, 3 (2003): 559–580. https://doi.org/10.1177/02685809030183006.

Carruthers, Errlee. "Prosecuting Women for Welfare Fraud in Ontario: Implication for Equality." *Journal of Law and Social Policy* 11, 10 (1995): 241-262. https://digitalcommons.osgoode.yorku.ca/jlsp/vol11/iss1/10.

Chakrabarty, Bidyut. *Social and Political Thought of Mahatma Gandhi.* London: Routledge, 2005.

Chan, Wendy, and Dorothy E. Chunn. *Racialization, Crime, and Criminal Justice in Canada.* Toronto: University of Toronto Press, 2014.

Cherlin, Andrew, Karen Bogen, James M. Quane, and Linda Burton. "Operating within the Rules: Welfare Recipients' Experiences with Sanctions and Case Closings." *Social Service Review* 76, (2002): 387–405. https://doi.org/10.1086/341181.

Chunn, Dorothy E., and Shelly Gavigan. "Welfare Law, Welfare Fraud, and the Moral Regulation of the 'Never Deserving' Poor." *Social & Legal Studies* 13, 2 (2004): 219-243. https://digitalcommons.osgoode.yorku.ca/scholarly_works/1216/.

City of Toronto. "Assistance Through Ontario Works." (Toronto, Ontario, Canada, 2017, November 15). https://www.toronto.ca/community105people/employment-social-support/support-for-people-in-financial-need/assistancethrough-ontario-works/.

City of Toronto Commissioner of Community and Neighbourhood Services, "Ontario Works Service Delivery Model" 2000, 2-3. https://docplayer.net/52085196-Ontario-works-service-delivery-model.html.

Clarke, Jennifer. "Beyond Child Protection: Afro-Caribbean Service Users of Child Welfare." *Journal of Progressive Human Services* 9, 23, 3 (2012).

Cole, Desmond. *The Skin We're In: A Year of Black Resistance and Power.* Toronto: Penguin Random House, 2020.

Collins, Patricia Hill. "The Social Construction of Black Feminist Thought." *Signs* 14, 4 (1989): 745–773. http://www.jstor.org/stable/3174683.

Collins, Patricia Hill. "Gender, Black Feminism, and Black Political Economy." *The Annals of the American Academy of Political and Social Science* 568, 1 (2000): 41–53. https://journals-sagepubcom.ezproxy.lib.ryerson.ca/doi/10.1177/000271620056800105.

Collins, Patricia Hill. *Black Feminist Thought: Knowledge, Consciousness, and the Politics of Empowerment.* New York: Routledge, 2002.

Collins, Patricia Hill. *Black Sexual Politics: African Americans, Gender, and the New Racism.* New York: Routledge, 2004.

Collins, Patricia Hill, and Sirma Bilge. *Intersectionality.* Oxford: Polity Press, 2016. http://ebookcentral.proquest.com/lib/ryerson/detail.action?docID=4698012.

Cooper, Afua. *The Hanging of Angélique: The Untold Story of Canadian Slavery and the Burning of Old Montréal.* Toronto: Harper Collins, 2006.

Creese, Gillian, and Daiva Stasiulis. "Introduction: Intersections of Gender, Race, Class, and Sexuality." *Studies in Political Economy* 51, 1 (1996): 5–14. https://doi.org/10.1080/19187033.1996.11675327.

Crenshaw, Kimberlé. "Race, Reform, and Retrenchment: Transformation and Legitimation in Antidiscrimination Law." *Harvard Law Review* 101, 7 (1988): 1331–1387. https://doi.org/10.2307/1341398.

Crenshaw, Kimberlé. "Mapping the Margins: Intersectionality, Identity Politics, and Violence Against Women of Color," *Stanford Law Review* 43, 6 (1991): 1241–1299. https://doi.org/10.2307/1229039.

Crenshaw, Kimberlé. "Whose Story Is It, Anyway? Feminist and Antiracist Appropriations of Anita Hill," in *Race-ing Justice, En-gendering Power: Essays on Anita Hill, Clarence Thomas, and the Construction of Social Reality*, edited by Toni Morrison. New York: Pantheon, 1992.

Creswell, J. W. *Qualitative Inquiry and Research Design: Choosing Among Five Approaches*. London: SAGE Publications, 2013.

Daenzer, Patricia M. "Social welfare in global context. James Midgley. London, Sage, 1997," *Scandinavian Journal of Social Welfare* 7, 1 (1998): 65–67. https://doi.org/10.1111/j.1468-2397.1998.tb00276.x

Danso, Ransford. "From 'There' to 'Here': An Investigation of the Initial Settlement Experiences of Ethiopian and Somali Refugees in Toronto." *GeoJournal* 56, 1 (2002): 3–14. http://www.jstor.org/stable/41147662.

Da Silva, Michelle. "Toronto police sell out sanctuary city." NOW Magazine. February 11, 2016. https://nowtoronto.com/toronto-police-sell-out-sanctuary-city.

Davis, Angela Y. "Rape, Racism and the Capitalist Setting." *The Black Scholar* 12, 6 (1981): 39–45. https://doi.org/10.1080/00064246.1981.11414219.

Davis, Angela Y.. *Women, Race, & Class*. New York: Random House, 1981.

Davis, Angela Y. *Are Prisons Obsolete?* New York: Seven Stories Press, 2003.

Davis, Angela Y. *Abolition Democracy: Beyond Empire, Prisons, and Torture*. New York: Seven Stories Press, 2005.

Davis, David Brion. *Inhuman Bondage: The Rise and Fall of Slavery in the New World*. Oxford: Oxford University Press, 2006.

Dei, George J. Sefa. Anti-racism Education: Theory and Practice. Winnipeg: Fernwood Pub. 1996.

Denzin, Norman K., and Yvonna. S. Lincoln, Eds.. *The Landscape of Qualitative Research: Theories and Issues*. London: Sage Publications, 1998.

Dillard, J. L.. "A Sketch of the History of Black English." *The Southern Quarterly* 45, 2 (2008).

Dominelli, Lena. "Deprofessionalizing Social Work: Anti-Oppressive Practice, Competencies and Postmodernism." *British Journal of Social Work* 26, 2 (1996):153–175. https://doi.org/10.1093/oxfordjournals.bjsw.a011077.

Dornan, Paul, and John Hudson. "Welfare Governance in the Surveillance Society: A Positive-Realistic Cybercriticalist View." *Social Policy & Administration* 37, 5 (2003): 468–482. https://doi.org/10.1111/1467-9515.00352

Doyle, Aaron, Randy Lippert and David Lyon Eds. *Eyes Everywhere: The Global Growth of Camera Surveillance.* (New York: Routledge, 2012).

Dua, Enakshi, and Angela Robertson. *Scratching the Surface: Canadian, Anti-Racist, Feminist Thought.* Toronto: Women's Press, 1999.

Dubbeld, Lynsey. "The Regulation of the Observing Gaze: Privacy Implications of Camera Surveillance" Maastricht: Netherlands Graduate Research School of Social Science, Technology and Modern Culture, University of Maastricht. 2004.

Du Bois, W. E. B.. *The Souls of Black Folk: Essays and Sketches.* Chicago: A.C. McClurg & co., 1903.

Fanon, Franz. *Toward the African Revolution: Political Essays.* New York: Grove Press, 1967.

Fanon, Franz. *The Wretched of the Earth,* translated by Constance Farrington. Harmondsworth, England: Penguin, 1967.

Fanon, Franz. *The Wretched of the Earth,* translated by Richard Philcox. New York: Grove Press, 2004.

Fanon, Franz. *Alienation and Freedom.* Edited by Jean Khalfa and Robert J. C. Young. Translated by Steven Corcoran. Bloomsbury Publishing, 2018.

Finn, Jonathan. "Surveillance as Social Practice" in in *Eyes Everywhere: The Global Growth of Surveillance.* Edited by Aaron Doyle, Randy Lippert, and David Lyon. New York: Routledge, 2012.

Fonio, Chiara. "Surveillance and Identity Towards a New Anthropology of the Person." Paper presented at the British Sociological Association conference, 2007. 12-14.

Foster, Cecil. *Blackness and Modernity: the Colour of Humanity and the Quest for Freedom.* Montreal: McGill-Queen's University Press, 2007.

Foucault, Michel. *Discipline and Punish.* New York: Vintage Books, 1979.

Fraser, Nancy and Linda Gordon. "A Genealogy of Dependency: Tracing a Keyword of the U.S. Welfare State." *Signs* 19, 2 (1994): 309–336. http://www.jstor.org/stable/3174801.

Frenette, Marc, David Green, and Garnett Picot, "Rising Income Inequality in the 1990s: An Exploration of Three Data Sources." Ottawa: Business and Labour Market Analysis Division, 2004.

Frenette, Marc, and Garnett Picot. "Life After Welfare: The Economic Well-being of Welfare Leavers in Canada During the 1990s." Statistics Canada, Analytical Studies Branch Research Paper Series, 2003.

Gabel, Todd, Jason Clemens, and Sylvia LeRoy. "Welfare Reform in Ontario: A Report Card." Fraser Institute Digital Publication, September, 2004. https://www.fraserinstitute.org/sites/default/files/WelfareReformInOntario.pdf.

Galabuzi, Grace-Edward. "Re -locating mineral -dependant communities in the era of globalization, 1979–1999: A comparative study of the Zambian Copperbelt and Timmins, Ontario." Phd diss., York University, 2006. http://search.proquest.com/pqdtglobal/docview/304979826/abstract/A77A578D2BED46B7PQ/1.

Gardner, Judith & Judy El Bushra, eds. *Somalia—The Untold Story: The War Through the Eyes of Somali Women*. London: Pluto Press. 2004.

Gates, Henry Lewis, Jr., and Cornel West. *The Future of the Race*. New York: A.A. Knopf, 1996.

Gazso, Amber. "Balancing Expectations for Employability and Family Responsibilities While on Social Assistance: Low-Income Mothers' Experiences in Three Canadian Provinces." *Family Relations Interdisciplincary Journal of Applied Family Science* 56, 5 (2007): 454–466. https://doi.org/10.1111/j.1741-3729.2007.00473.x.

Geertz, Clifford. *Works and Lives: The Anthropologist as Author*. Stanford: Stanford University Press, 1988.

Gilens, Martin. *Why Americans Hate Welfare: Race, Media, and the Politics of Antipoverty Policy*. Chicago: University of Chicago Press, 1999.

Gilliom, John. *Overseers of the Poor: Surveillance, Resistance, and the Limits of Privacy*. Chicago: University of Chicago Press, 2001.

Gilroy, Paul. *The Black Atlantic: Modernity and Double Consciousness*. Cambridge, Mass.: Harvard University Press, 1993.

Goldberg, David Theo, *Racist Culture: Philosophy and the Politics of Meaning.* Malden, Mass.: Blackwell Publishers Inc., 1993.

Gustafson, Kaaryn. *Cheating Welfare: Public Assistance and the Criminalization of Poverty.* New York: New York University Press, 2011.

Gustafson, Kaaryn. "Degradation Ceremonies and the Criminalization of Low-Income Women." *UC Irvine Law Review Volume 3 Issue 2: Critical Race Theory and Empirical Methods,* (UC Irvine School of Law, 2013): 297-358.

Haas, Jack, and William Shaffir, Eds.. *Decency and Deviance: Studies of Deviant Behaviour.* Toronto: McClelland & Stewart, 1974.

Hamilton, Patricia. "'Now That I Know What You're About': Black Feminist Reflections on Power in the Research Relationship." *Qualitative Research: QR* 20, 5 (2020): 519–33.

Hamilton, Patricia. *Black Mothers and Attachment Parenting: A Black Feminist Analysis of Intensive Mothering in Britain and Canada.* Bristol: Bristol University Press, 2021.

Hamilton, Sylvia. *And I Alone Escaped To Tell You.* Kentville, NS: Gaspereau Press, 2014.

Harell, Allison, Stuart Soroka, and Kiera Ladner. "Public opinion, prejudice and the racialization of welfare in Canada." *Ethnic and Racial Studies* 37, 14 (2014): 2580–2597. https://doi.org/10.1080/01419870.2013.851396.

Harris, Claire. M. Nourbese Philip, Dionne Brand, and Carol Morrell. *Grammar of Dissent: Poetry and Prose by Claire Harris, M. Nourbese Philip and Dionne Brand.* Fredericton: Goose Lane, 1994.

Hartman, Saidiya. *Scenes of Subjection: Terror, Slavery, and Self-making in Nineteenth-century America.* New York: Oxford University Press, 1997.

Hartman, Saidiya. *Wayward Lives, Beautiful Experiments: Intimate Histories of Riotous Black Girls, Troublesome Women, and Queer Radicals,* New York: W. W. Norton & Company, 2019.

Henman, Paul, and Greg Marston. "The Social Division of Welfare Surveillance." *Journal of Social Policy* 37, 2 (2008): 187–205. https://doi.org/10.1017/S0047279407001705.

Henson, Kenneth T. *Curriculum Planning: Integrating Multiculturalism, Constructivism, and Education Reform, Fifth Edition.* Long Grove, IL: Waveland Press. 2015.

Herd, Pamela. "Do Functional Health Inequalities Decrease in Old Age? Educational Status and Functional Decline Among the 1931-1941 Birth Cohort" *Research on Aging* 28, 3 (2006): 375–392.

hooks, bell. *Yearning: Race, Gender, And Cultural Politics*. Toronto: Between the Lines, 1990.

Hylton, Kevin. "Talk the talk, walk the walk: Defining Critical Race Theory in research." *Race Ethnicity and Education* 15, 1 (2012): 23–41. https://doi.org/10.1080/13613324.2012.638862.

Isoke, Zenzele. "Black Ethnography, Black(Female)Aesthetics: Thinking/Writing/Saying/Sounding Black Political Life." *Theory & Event* 21, 1 (2018): 148–68.

Jackson, Winston, and Noreen Verberg. *Methods: Doing Social Research 4th ed.*. Toronto: Pearson Prentice Hall, 2007.

Jordan, June. "Nobody Mean More to Me than You and the Future Life of Willie Jordan." *Harvard Educational Review* 58, 3 (August 1988): 363–75.

Katshunga, Jen, Notisha Massaquoi, "Confronting Anti-Black Racism Unit, City of Toronto, Ontario Council of Agencies Serving Immigrants (OCASI), and Justine Wallace," "Black Women in Canada, Behind the Numbers." 2020. http://behindthenumbers.ca/shorthand/black-women-in-canada/.

Kelly, Maura. "African Americans Are Overrepresented in the News Stories About Poverty and Public." *Journal of Poverty* 1, 14 (2010).

Keung, Nicholas. "Toronto police urged to stop immigration 'status checks'." *The Toronto Star*. November 24, 2015. https://getintheknow.ca/news/toronto-police-urged-to-stop-immigration-status-checks/.

Khosla, Punam, and Community Social Planning Council of Toronto. "If Low Income Women of Colour Counted in Toronto: Final Report of the Action-Research Project Breaking Isolation, Getting Involved." Community Social Planning Council of Toronto, 2003. http://www.oaith.ca/assets/files/Publications/Low_Income_Women_of_Colour.pdf.

Kincheloe, Joe L. "Describing the Bricolage: Conceptualizing a New Rigor in Qualitative Research." *Qualitative Inquiry* 7,6 (2001): 679–692. https://doi.org/10.1177/107780040100700601.

Kincheloe, Joe L., and Peter McLaren. "Rethinking Critical Theory and Qualitative Research." In *SAGE Handbook of Qualitative Research, 3rd ed.*. Edited by Norman K. Denzin and Yvonna S. Lincoln. London: Sage Publications, 2005.

King, Amber Williams. *When Palm Trees Break: The Fractured Horizons of Black Carribean World-Making in the Midst of Crisis.* Masters thesis, York University, 2021.

King, Deborah K.. "Multiple Jeopardy, Multiple Consciousness: The Context of a Black Feminist Ideology." *Signs* 14, 1 (1988): 42–72. http://www.jstor.org/stable/3174661.

Kirby, Sandra L., and Kate McKenna. *Experience Research Social Change: Methods from the Margins.* Toronto: Garamond Press, 1989.

Kneebone, Ronald D., and Katherine White. "The Rise and Fall of Social Assistance Use in Canada, 1969-2012." *The School of Public Policy Publications* 7, 5 (2014). Canadian Business & Current Affairs Database; International Bibliography of the Social Sciences (IBSS); https://doi.org/10.11575/sppp.v7i0.42457110

Kohler-Hausmann, Julilly. "'The Crime of Survival': Fraud Prosecutions, Community Surveillance, and the Original 'Welfare Queen.'" *Journal of Social History* 41, 2 (2007): 329–354. http://www.jstor.org/stable/25096482.

Lamola, John M. "Biko, Hegel and the End of Black Consciousness: A Historico-Philosophical Discourse on South African Racism." *Journal of Southern African Studies* 42, 2 (2016): 183–94.

Lamola, John M. "Blackhood as a Category in Contemporary Discourses on Black Studies: an Existentialist Philosophical Defence." *Transformation in Higher Education* 3, 1 (2018): 1–9.

Lamola, John M. "An Ontic–ontological Theory for Ethics of Designing Social Robots: a Case of Black African Women and Humanoids." *Ethics and Information Technology* 23, 2 (2020): 119–26.

Lankin, Francis, and Munir A. Sheikh. *Brighter Prospects: Transforming Social Assistance in Ontario* (Government of Ontario, 2012).

Lawson, Erica. "Single Mothers, Absentee Fathers, and Gun Violence in Toronto: A Contextual Interpretation." *Women's Studies* 41, 7 (2012): 805–28.

Lawson, Erica. "The Gendered Working Lives of Seven Jamaican Women in Canada: A Story About 'Here' and 'There' in a Transnational Economy." *NWSA Journal* 25, 1 (2013): 138.

Lawson, Erica. "Bereaved Black Mothers and Maternal Activism in the Racial State." *Feminist Studies* 44, (2018): 713–35.

Lévi-Strauss, Claude. *The Savage Mind.* Chicago: University of Chicago Press, 1966.

Lightman, Ernie S. and Graham Riches. "From Modest Rights to Commodification in Canada's Welfare State." *European Journal of Social Work* 3, 2 (2000): 179–190. https://doi.org/10.1080/714052823.

Lightman, Ernie, Andrew Mitchell, and Dean Herd. "Welfare to What? After Workfare in Toronto." *International Social Security Review* 58, 4 (2005): 95–106. https://doi.org/10.1111/j.1468-246X.2005.00227.x.

Lightman, Ernie, Andrew Mitchell, and Dean Herd. "Cycling Off and On Welfare in Canada." *Journal of Social Policy* 39, 4 (2010): 523-542.

Lincoln, Yvonna S. "An Emerging New Bricoleur: Promises and Possibilities—A Reaction to Joe Kincheloe's 'Describing the Bricoleur.'" *Qualitative Inquiry* 7, 6 (2001): 693–696. https://doi.org/10.1177/107780040100700602.

Lincoln, Yvonna S.. "The Political Economy of Publication: Marketing, Commodification, and Qualitative Scholarly Work." *Qualitative Health Research* 22, 11 (2012): 1451–1459.

Lindsay-Dennis, LaShawnda. "Black Feminist-Womanist Research Paradigm: Toward a Culturally Relevant Research Model Focused on African American Girls." *Journal of Black Studies* 46, 5 (2015): 506–520. https://journals.sagepub.com/doi/10.1177/0021934715583664.

Little, Margaret Hillyard. "Manhunts and Bingo Blabs": The Moral Regulation of Ontario Single Mothers." *The Canadian Journal of Sociology / Cahiers Canadiens de Sociologie* 19, 2 (1994). 233–247. https://doi.org/10.2307/3341346.

Little, Margaret Hillyard. *No Car, No Radio, No Liquor Permit: The Moral Regulation of Single Mothers in Ontario, 1920-1997.* Oxford: Oxford University Press, 1998.

Little, Margaret Hillyard. "A Litmus Test for Democracy: The Impact of Ontario Welfare Changes on Single Mothers," *Studies in Political Economy* 66, 1 (2001): 9–36. https://doi.org/10.1080/19187033.2001.11675209.

Little, Margaret Hillyard, and Ian Morrison. "'The Pecker Detectors are Back': Regulation of the Family Form in Ontario Welfare Policy." *Journal of Canadian Studies* 34, 2 (1999): 110–136. https://doi.org/10.3138/jcs.34.2.110.

Lorde, Audre. *Sister Outsider: Essays and Speeches*. Trumansberg, NY: Crossing Press, 1984.

Lowry, Michelle. "Creating Human Insecurity: The National Security Focus in Canada's Immigration System." *Refuge* 21, 1 (2002).

Lyon, David. *Surveillance Society: Monitoring Everyday Life*. Maidenhead, Berkshire: Open University Press, 2001.

Lyon, David. *Surveillance as Social Sorting: Privacy, Risk and Automated Discrimination*. London and New York: Routledge, 2003.

Maki, Krystle. "Neoliberal Deviants and Surveillance: Welfare Recipients Under the Watchful Eye of Ontario Works." *Surveillance & Society* 9, 1/2 (2011): 47–63. https://doi.org/10.24908/ss.v9i1/2.4098

Marriott, David. *Haunted Life: Visual Culture and Black Modernity*. New York: Rutgers University Press, 2007.

Martin, Dianne L. "Passing the Buck: Prosecution of Welfare Fraud; Preservation of Stereotypes." *The Windsor Yearbook of Access to Justice* 12 (1992): 52.

Maynard, Robyn. *Policing Black Lives: State Violence in Canada from Slavery to the Present*. Black Point NS & Winnipeg: Fernwood Publishing, 2017.

McKittrick, Katherine. *Demonic Grounds*. Minneapolis: University of Minnesota Press, 2006.

McKittrick, Katherine. "Reclaiming Difference: Caribbean Women Rewrite Postcolonialism." *Resources for Feminist Research* 31, 3/4, (2006): 146-148.http://search.proquest.com/docview/194882698/abstract/4F2FCD77143E4610PQ/1.

McKittrick, Katherine, and Rinaldo Walcott "Of Dionne Brand's Difficult Pleasures." *Topia* 34, (2016): 6–11. https://doi.org/10.3138/topia.34.6.

Mercer, Kobena. *Welcome to the Jungle: New Positions in Black Cultural Studies*. New York: Routledge, 1994.

Midgley, James. *Social Welfare in Global Context*, London: SAGE Publications, 1997.

Mignolo, Walter. "Sylvia Wynter: What Does It Mean to Be Human?," in *Sylvia Wynter: On Being Human As Praxis*. Edited by Katherine McKittrick. Durham, NC: Duke University Press, 2015.

Mills, Charles W.. *Blackness Visible: Essays on Philosophy and Race*. Ithaca and London: Cornell University Press, 1998.

Mills, Charles W.. *The Racial Contract.* Ithaca: Cornell University Press, 1997.

Ministry of Community and Social Services, "Ontario Works Program" annual report, 1998. https://www.auditor.on.ca/en/content/annualreports/arreports/en98/302en98.pdf

Ministry of Community and Social Services, and Commissioner of Community and Neighbourhood Services Report, 2000, 1. https://docplayer.net/52085196-Ontario-works-service- delivery-model.html.

Mirchandani, Kiran and Wendy Chan. *The Racialized Impact of Welfare Fraud Control in British Columbia and Ontario.* Toronto: Canadian Race Relations Foundation, 2005.

Moffatt, Ken. "Surveillance and Government of the Welfare Recipient" in *Reading Foucault for Social Work,* edited by Chambon, Adrienne S., Allan Irving, and Laura Epstein, 219-246. New York: Columbia University Press, 1999.

Moffatt, Ken. *Postmodern Social Work: Reflective Practice and Education.* New York: Columbia University Press, 2019.

Moffatt, Ken, Usha George, Bill Lee, and Susan McGrath. "Advancing citizenship: A study of social planning," *Community Development Journal* 34, 4 (1999): 308–317. https://doi.org/10.1093/cdj/34.4.308

Mofette, David, and Karl Gardner. "Often Asking, Always Telling: The Toronto Police Service and the Sanctuary City Policy," (No One is Illegal—Toronto, 2015). http://surl.li/cefbw.

Morrison, Ian. "Ontario Works: A Preliminary Assessment." *Journal of Law and Social Policy* 13 (1998): 1-46.

Mosher, Janet E., "Walking on Eggshells: Abused Women's Experiences of Ontario's Welfare System." *Commissioned Reports, Studies and Public Policy Documents.* Paper 160 (2004). https://digitalcommons.osgoode.yorku.ca/reports/160.

Mosher, Janet and Joe Hermer. *Welfare Fraud: The Constitution of Social Assistance as Crime* (Law Commission of Canada, 2005).

Moten, Fred. *The Universal Machine.* Durham, NC: Duke University Press, 2018.

Moustakas, Clark. *Phenomenological Research Methods* (1st edition). Newbury Park, CA: SAGE Publications, 1994.

Mugabo, Délice. "Black in the City: On the Ruse of Ethnicity and Language in an AntiBlack Landscape." *Identities* 26, 6 (2019): 631–648. https://doi.org/10.1080/1070289X.2018.1545816.

Murdoch, H. Adlai. "Stuart Hall: diasporic Caribbeanness and discourses of ethnocultural belonging." *African and Black Diaspora: An International Journal* 11, 3 (2018): 232-246. 10.1080/17528631.2018.1452528.

Naples, Nancy. *Feminism and Method: Ethnography, Discourse Analysis, and Activist Research*. New York and London: Routledge, 2003.

Nyberg, Gail, Pedro Barata, Pat Capponi, Grace-Edward Galabuzi, Kira Heineck, Mary Marrone, Michael Mendelson, Valerie Monague, Colette Murphy, Michael Oliphant, and John Stapleton. "Recommendations for an Ontario Income Security Review, Report of The Social Assistance Review Advisory Council." 2010.

Philip, M. Nourbese. *Blank: Essays & Interviews* (Toronto: BookThug, 2017).

Prince, Althea. *Being Black: Essays*. Toronto: Insomniac Press, 2001.

O'Connell, Anne. "Deserving and Non-deserving Races: Colonial Intersections of Socail Welfare History in Ontario," *Intersectionalities: A Global Journal of Social Work Analysis, Research, Polity, and Practice* 2 (2013). http://surl.li/ccxqe.

O'Connor, Julia S., Ann Shola Orloff, and Sheila Shaver. *States, Markets, Families: Gender, Liberalism, and Social Policy in Australia, Canada, Great Britain, and the United States*. Cambridge: Cambridge University Press, 1999.

Ontario asks anyone with medical background to step forward to fight COVID-19. (2020, April 7). Toronto. https://toronto.ctvnews.ca/ontario-asks-anyone-with-medical-background-tostep-forward-to-fight-covid-19-1.4885936.

Ontario Association of Childrens' Aid Societies, "One Vision One Voice: Changing the Ontario Child Welfare System to Better Serve African Canadians," (September, 2016). https://www.oacas.org/what-we-do/onevisiononevoice/.

Ontario Human Rights Commission. *Paying the Price: The Human Cost of Racial Profiling*. 2003, 6.

Ontario Human Rights Commission, "Toronto Police Service racial profiling and carding: deputation to Toronto Police Services Board" (April 8, 2014), https://www.ohrc.on.ca/en/news_centre/toronto-police-service-racial-profiling-and-carding-deputation-toronto-police-services-board.

Ontario Human Rights Commission, "Under Suspicion: Research and Consultation Report on Racial Profiling in Ontario," (2017). https://www.ohrc.on.ca/sites/default/files/Under%20suspicion_research%20and%20consultation%20report%20on%20racial%20profiling%20in%20Ontario_2017.pdf.

Ontario Human Rights Commission, "Interrupted Childhoods: Over representation of Indigenous and Black Children in Ontario Child Welfare," (2018). https://www.ohrc.on.ca/en/interrupted-childhoods.

Ornstein, Michael. "Ethno-Racial Inequality in the City of Toronto: An Analysis of the 1996 Census," City of Toronto Access and Equity Unit, 2000. https://povertyandhumanrights.org/docs/ornstein_fullreport.pdf

Osman, Abdi. *Post-9/11 Experiences of Black Muslims in Canada.* Toronto: Blurb: 2011.

Pierson, Christopher. *Beyond the Welfare State? The New Political Economy of Welfare.* University Park, Pennsylvania: Pennsylvania State University Press, 1991.

Pierson, Christopher, and Francis G. Castles, Eds.. *The Welfare State: A Reader.* Malden, Mass.: Polity Press with Blackwell Publishers Ltd., 2000.

Pollack, Shoshana. "Labelling Clients 'Risky': Social Work and the Neo-liberal Welfare State." *The British Journal of Social Work* 40, 4 (2010): 1263–1278. https://doi.org/10.1093/bjsw/bcn079.

Pratt, Anna and Mariana Valverde. "From Deserving Victims to 'Masters of Confusion': Redefining Refugees in the 1990s." *Canadian Journal of Sociology* 27, 2 (2002): 135–61.

Province of Ontario, "Eligibility for Ontario Works financia assistance." accessed July 2022. https://www.ontario.ca/page/eligibility-ontario-works-financial-assistance.

Razack, Narda. Transforming the field: Critical Antiracist and Anti-oppressive Perspectives for the Human Service Practicum. Halifax: Fernwood Publishing, 2002.

Razack, Sherene, Melinda Smith, and Sunera Thobani, Eds.. *Race, Space, and the Law: Unmapping a White Settler Society.* Toronto: Between the Lines, 2002.

Rice, James J., & Prince, Michael J. *Changing Politics of Canadian Social Policy,* 2nd Ed.. Toronto: University of Toronto Press, 2000.

Ritchie, Andrea J. *Invisible No More: Police Violence Against Black Women and Women of Color.* Boston: Beacon Press, 2017.

Ritchie, Andrea J., and Delores Jones-Brown. "Policing Race, Gender, and Sex: A Review of Law Enforcement Policies." *Women & Criminal Justice* 27, 1 (2017): 21–50.

Ritzer, George. *Sociological Theory, 2nd ed..* New York: Alfred A. Knopf, 1988.

Rogers, Matt. "Contextualizing Theories and Practices of Bricolage Research." *The Qualitative Report* 17, 48 (2012): 1-17.

Rossiter, Amy. "Innocence Lost and Suspicion Found: Do We Educate for or Against Social Work." *Critical Social Work* 2, 1 (2001).

Saloojee, Anver. "Social Inclusion, Anti-racism and Cemocratic Citizenship," *Joint Centre for Excellence for Research on Immigration and Settlement* 14 (2005). 1–5.

Schissel, Bernard. And Linda Mahood, Eds.. *Social Control in Canada: A Reader on the Social Construction of Deviance.* Oxford: Oxford University Press, 1996.

Sexton, Jared. Amalgamation Schemes: Antiblackness and the Critique of Multiracialism. Minneapolis: University of Minnesota Press, 2008.

Sharpe, Christina. "Black Studies: In the Wake." *The Black Scholar* 44, 2 (2014): 59–69. https://doi.org/10.1080/00064246.2014.11413688

Sharpe, Christina. *In the Wake: On Blackness and Being.* Durham, NC: Duke University Press, 2016.

Shields, John. "Review of Service in the Field: The World of Front-Line Public Servants by B. W. Carroll & D. Siegel." *Canadian Public Policy / Analyse de Politiques* 26, 1 (2000): 134–135. https://doi.org/10.2307/3552264.

Shields, Simon. *Welfare (Ontario Works) Legal Guide*, Chapter 12— Fraud and Prosecutions 2 (d) 2020. http://www.isthatlegal.ca/index.php?name=fraud.welfare_law_ontario.

Silvera, Makeda. *Silenced Caribbean Domestic Workers Talk With Makeda Silvera.* Toronto: Sister Vision, 1983.

Silvera, Makeda. *Silenced: Makeda Silvera Talks with Working Class West Indian Women About Their Lives and Struggles as Domestic Workers in Canada.* Toronto: Williams-Wallace, 1984.

Silvera, Makeda. *Her Head a Village: & other stories.* Vancouver: Press Gang Publishers, 1994.

Silvera, Makeda, ed.. *The Other Woman: Women of Colour in Contemporary Canadian Literature.* Toronto: Sister Vision Press, 1995.

Silvera, Makeda. *The Heart Does Not Bend.* Toronto: Vintage Canada, 2003.

Smith, Emily. "The Piecemeal Development of Camera Surveillance in Canada." In *Eyes Everywhere: The Global Growth of Surveillance.* Edited by Aaron Doyle, Randy Lippert, and David Lyon. New York: Routledge, 2012.

Spitzer, Denise L. "The impact of policy on Somali refugee women in Canada." *Refuge* (Summer, 2006). https://link.gale.com/apps/doc/A148367816/AONE?u=anon-b2f19b8c&sid=googleScholar&xid=2f0fc5ea.

Sudbury, Julia, Ed.. *Global Lockdown: Race, Gender, and the Prison-Industrial Complex.* Milton Park, Oxfordshire: Routledge, 2005.

Teelucksingh, Cheryl. "Environmental Racialization: Linking Racialization to the Environment in Canada." *Local Environment* 12, 6 (2007): 645–661. https://doi.org/10.1080/13549830701657455

Thobani, Sunera. *Exalted Subjects: Studies in the Making of Race and Nation in Canada.* Toronto: University of Toronto Press, 2007. http://ebookcentral.proquest.com/lib/ryerson/detail.action?docID=4634696.

Thobani, Sunera. "White Wars: Western Feminisms and the 'War on Terror.'" *Feminist Theory* 8, 2 (2007): 169–85.

Thornton Dill, Bonnie. "The Dialectics of Black Womanhood," *Signs* 4, 3 (1979): 543–555. http://www.jstor.org/stable/3173400

Toronto Police Services Board meeting, April 24, 2014.

Valverde, Mariana, Ed.. *Studies in Moral Regulation.* Toronto: Centre of Criminology, University of Toronto, 1994.

Vosko, Leah F., ed.. *Precarious Employment: Understanding Labour Market Insecurity in Canada.* Montreal: McGill-Queen's University Press, 2006.

Wacquant, Loïc. "Deadly Symbiosis: When Ghetto and Prison Meet and Mesh." *Punishment & Society* 3, 1 (2001): 95–133. https://doi.org/10.1177/14624740122228276.

Wacquant, Loïc. "The Penalization of Poverty and the Rise of Neo-liberalism." *European Journal on Criminal Policy and Research* 9 (2003): 401–412.

Walcott, Rinaldo. *Black Like Who? Writing Black Canada*. London ON: Insomniac Press, 1997.

Walcott, Rinaldo. "'A Tough Geography:' Towards a Poetics of Black Space(s) in Canada." In *Un-homely States: Theorizing English-Canadian Postcolonialism*. Edited by Cynthia Sugars. Peterborough, ON: Broadview Press, 2004.

Walcott, Rinaldo. "The Problem of the Human: Black Ontologies and "the Coloniality of Our Being." in *Postcoloniality—Decoloniality—Black Critique: Joints and Fissures*, edited by Sabine Broeck and Carsten Junker. Frankfurt/New York: Campus Verlag, 2014.

Walcott, Rinaldo, and Idil Abdillahi. *BlackLife: Post-BLM and the Struggle for Freedom*. Winnipeg: ARP Books, 2019.

Walcott, Rinaldo. *On Property*. Windsor, ON: Biblioasis, 2021.

Walcott, Rinaldo. *The Long Emancipation: Moving Toward Black Freedom*. Durham NC: Duke University Press, 2021.

Walker, Barrington. *Race on Trial: Black Defendants in Ontario's Criminal Courts, 1858-1958*. Toronto: University of Toronto Press, 2010.

Weight, Jill. "Compromises to Carework: The Social Organization of Mothers' Experiences in the Low-Wage Labor Market after Welfare Reform." *Social Problems* 53, 3 (2006): 332–51.

Winks, Robin W. *The Blacks In Canada: A History 2nd ed*. McGill-Queens University Press, 1997.

Wortley, Scot, and Akwasi Owusu-Bempah. "The usual suspects: police stop and search practices in Canada." *Policing and Society* 21, 4 (2011).

Wynter, Sylvia. "'No Humans Involved': An Open Letter to my Colleagues." *Forum N.H.I.: Knowledge for the 21st Century* 1, 1 (Fall 1994): 1-16. https://people.ucsc.edu/~nmitchel/sylvia.wynter_-_no.humans.allowed.pdf.

Wynter, Sylvia. "Unsettling the Coloniality of Being/Power/Truth/Freedom: Towards the Human, After Man, Its Overrepresentation—An Argument." *CR: The New Centennial Review* 3, 3 (2003): 257-337. https://muse.jhu.edu/article/51630.

Case Law and Legal Citations

Bill C-11, The Immigration and Refugee Protection Act. Report No. 5, Clause 1, 2001. Toronto City Clerk.

Bill C-11, *The Immigration and Refugee Protection Act: Gender-Based Analysis* (*Legislative Summary for Bill C-11*, n.d.-a; *Legislative Summary for Bill C-11*, n.d.-c, 11), 2001.

Criminal Code of Canada, RSC 1985, c. C-46, s 380(1).

Criminal Code of Canada, RSC 1986, s.21:s.79 (2).

Ontario Works Act, 1997, SO 1997, c 25, Sch A, (79(4)). <https://canlii.ca/t/54bkl>.

R. v. D'Amour, (2002) CanLII 45015 (ON CA), <https://canlii.ca/t/1cskn>.

R. v. Maldonado, (1998) O.J. NO. 3209 (Prov. Div.) (QL). https://www.oaith.ca/assets/files/Publications/Poverty/Welfare-Fraud-as-Crime.pdf.

Interviews

Interlocutor 1, in person interview with author, Toronto, 2017.
Interlocutor 2, in person interview with author, Toronto, 2017.
Interlocutor 3, in person interview with author, Toronto, 2017.
Interlocutor 4, in person interview with author, Toronto, 2017.
Interlocutor 5, in person interview with author, Toronto, 2017.
Interlocutor 6, in person interview with author, Toronto, 2017.
Interlocutor 7, in person interview with author, Toronto, 2018.
Interlocutor 8, in person interview with author, Toronto, 2018.
Interlocutor 9, in person interview with author, Toronto, 2018.
Interlocutor 10, in person interview with author, Toronto, 2018.
Interlocutor 11, in person interview with author, Toronto, 2018.
Interlocutor 12, in person interview with author, Toronto, 2018.
Interlocutor 13, in person interview with author, Toronto, 2018.
Interlocutor 14, in person interview with author, Toronto, 2018.
Interlocutor 15, in person interview with author, Toronto, 2018.
Interlocutor 16, in person interview with author, Toronto, 2018.
Interlocutor 17, in person interview with author, Toronto, 2018.
Interlocutor 18, in person interview with author, Toronto, 2018.
Interlocutor 19, in person interview with author, Toronto, 2018.
Interlocutor 20, in person interview with author, Toronto, 2018.

Acknowledgements

To each of you, Interlocutors 1, 2, 3, 4, 5, 6, 7, 8, 9, 10, 11, 12, 13, 14, 15, 16, 17, 18, 19, and 20, I thank you. With love, until after freedom.

This book would have never existed without my mother, her struggles, her strength and her steadfastness, her looking out the window to make sure I get on the bus at five a.m., her consistent love-laughter, and utmost confidence in her baby girl. It's through your life, laughter, and your courage to traverse borders, that this text comes to life.

I want to acknowledge the significant contributions of my dissertation committee who guided and supported the work that evolved into this book: Dr. Lynne Lavallée, Dr. Lisa Barnoff, Dr. Pamela Robinson, Dr. Grace-Edward Galabuzi, and Dr. Eve Haque.

Often in the academic industrial complex we don't acknowledge those that do the necessary and rough work of keeping students in programs, of checking off progress reports, and making sure institutional bills are paid so that we can complete degrees; for this I sincerely thank Sonya Taccone and Mary Beth Halferty Kraay.

Thank you to those who kept me "healthy" and supported me in what was a difficult journey for the last few years: Myra Lefkowitz, and my two favourite women on Murray Street.

To my people. There are so many of you, that I can't name you individually. So I will do it by space, place, and location. To the apartment crew, I thank you for the nights of music, laughter, drama, and mess. The nights that we shared Eritrean/Ethiopain food collectively, strategized and decided to organize instead of writing, this book would not have been possible without any of you.

To all of you in the Skypad Soup Kitchen, where we shared gourmet meals and I listened to your relentless hours of encouragement to write my dissertation, to sit with it, and not be afraid of completion, I thank you. Karaoke has never sounded better than on the 7th floor.

To all my Black and my working-class students, I thank you for your confidence, your support, and your belief in my capacity to teach, live, and learn alongside you. I am thankful every day for our reciprocity.

I want to thank ARP Books for their trust and commitment to radical activist texts, not just in claim, but in practice.

Thank you to Irene Bindi, not only for the cover of this book, but for your unrelenting love, support, and friendship. For our long conversations across scenes, over zoom, and throughout life crises. I would never have chosen to publish this book with anyone but you.

Finally, to my good friends, cooks, and travel buddies, Rinaldo Walcott and Abdi Osman. There are no words to express my love and gratitude for the both of you. I first read my dissertation proposal out in your home, where I was enveloped with love and care, challenge, and the confidence to reach completion. My human and academic journey would not have been the same had we not been in community. You have shaped my thinking, living, and being, and have allowed me to navigate complex terrain in ways that only we can understand. You are real "ninjas."

Nrayo, with love, always, and in all ways. Thank you for your encouragement, your patience, and your love.

Idil Abdillahi is an Assistant professor in the School of Disability Studies at Toronto Metropolitan University (formerly Ryerson University). A critical interdisciplinary scholar, she has published on a wide array of topics, such as mental health, poverty, HiV/AIDS, organizational development, and several other key policy areas at the intersection of BlackLife and state interruption. Most notably, Abdillahi's cutting-edge research and scholarship on anti-Black Sanism has informed the current debates on fatal police shootings of Black mad-identified peoples. She co-authored *BlackLife: Post-BLM and the Struggle for Freedom* (ARP Books, 2019), and is currently working on her forthcoming book, *Blackened Madness: Medicalization, and Black Everyday Life in Canada* (ARP Books). Abdillahi is the newest addition to the editorial team of *Mad Matters: A Critical Reader In Canadian Mad Studies* (Canadian Scholars Press).